A PLAGUE

OF

EXPERTS

Intellectual Hubris and the Failure of Expertise

MICHAEL T. DEVANEY

NA

NorthAmerican
Business Press
Atlanta – Seattle – South Florida – Toronto

"Death as a Cutthroat" engraving by Alfred Rethel (1851)
inspired by an 1832 outbreak of cholera during the carnival of Paris.

To My Parents, Catherine, Maggie and Cate

North American Business Press, Inc
Atlanta, Georgia
Seattle, Washington
South Florida
Toronto, Canada

A Plague of Experts:
Intellectual Hubris and the Failure of Expertise
ISBN: 9780985394967
© 2013 All Rights Reserved.

Along with trade books for various business disciplines, the North American Business Press also publishes a variety of academic-peer reviewed journals.

Library of Congress Control Number: 2012955270
Library of Congress
Cataloging in Publication Division
101 Independence Ave., SE
Washington, DC 20540-4320
Printed in theUnited States of America
First Edition

TABLE OF CONTENTS

PREFACE

We live in the age of the expert. There are experts on real estate, witch-craft, serial killers and terrorism. Personal service experts teach us how to exercise, manage our time, organize our closets, control our dog and talk to our children. Cable television orchestrates an endless parade of talking heads willing to pontificate on any subject while Craigslist and a variety of other web sites render access to expert advice that is only a mouse click away.

The provision of expert witnesses for litigation is a burgeoning industry. If the price is right, litigants in civil trials can always find "hired guns" willing to advocate the opposite side of any argument. Despite being on the losing side half the time, expert witnesses have little trouble finding work. Some people, such as football coaches riding a winning streak, can find themselves elevated from the rank of "expert" to the lofty realms of "genius." With refreshing can-dor New York Giants coach Jim Fassel reminded the sports media: "there are no geniuses in our business, we're all PE majors coaching PE majors."

If sports commentators are prone to hyperbole, those with expertise in other realms can display a quiet certitude. Engineers for British Petroleum (BP) were able to drill deep-water oil wells but lacked the technical expertise to fore-stall environmental catastrophe when one exploded in the Gulf of Mexico. Our naïve faith in experts is so ingrained that it became a newsworthy event when former Secretary of State Colin Powell remarked that stopping the flow of oil in the gulf could be "beyond the capacity" of BP. Three decades before the BP disaster, there was a partial meltdown at the $1 billion Three Mile Island power plant all because technicians failed to replace a faulty valve costing fifty dollars. The nuclear industry has never recovered. An investigation into why the $125 million Mars Climate Orbiter disintegrated on entering the Martian atmosphere found that scientists failed to accurately convert the metric system into feet, a common test question in grade school science class.

It doesn't seem to matter whether the experts work in the private sector or for the government. Japan's nuclear regulators and the operator of the crippled Fukushima reactors were warned that a tsunami could overwhelm the plant's defenses but both failed to acknowledge the threat. The U.S. Mineral Management Service and the Department of Energy were just as ineffectual as the oil industry in identifying a solution to the Deepwater Horizon gusher. It was the second time in five years that the Gulf Region was victimized by expert ineptitude. In 2005, the network of levies and pumps constructed by the Corps of Engineers to protect New Orleans were promptly breached under the onslaught of Katrina. Other government experts fair no better. An army of over 300 Federal Reserve PhDs failed to anticipate the severity of the financial meltdown and despite repeated attempts by private investors to blow the whistle on Bernie Madoff, lawyers at the Securities and Exchange Commission remained clueless.

The proliferation of experts is thought to reflect the economic principle known as division of labor. Historically, more complex production processes have contributed to a rise in labor specialization and an increase in labor productivity. The more recent ascendancy of the expert in virtually all realms of life is more a manifestation of postmodern culture than the economic imperative of labor specialization. The gains from division of labor have been so extensive that we tend to think there are benefits from specialized expertise even when none exists. Bottom-up alternatives to top-down experts in areas such as voting, markets and informal regulation, to name three, are frequently dismissed with a shrug of indifference, if not outright ridicule. Indifference is reflected in the 48% voter turnout in federal elections while media coverage of markets is more likely to focus on "ill gotten gains" or "price fixing" than their enormous economic and social benefit. Informal regulatory mechanisms such as ostracism and moral sanction are regarded as hopelessly old fashioned and inferior compared to the vast network of formal regulatory bureaucracy perpetuated by government. Our belief in experts is further reinforced by an almost childlike faith in the power of science and technology to solve problems. One critic described government regulators as being "romanced" by the seemingly infallible deep-water drilling technology developed by the oil companies.

Who is an expert? It is anyone who by virtue of credentials, experience or self-appointment, claims knowledge sufficient to evaluate and/or prescribe a course of action for those being advised but expert advice need not be proprietary. Information on diet and exercise is readily accessible on the Internet but a personal trainer may also motivate their client to reach a higher level of performance, not to mention getting them out of bed in the morning. It is difficult to overestimate the importance of "hand holding" in the market for personal service experts, such as physical trainers and stockbrokers.

Some experts create complexity in an effort to appear more profound and/or perpetuate dependence on their expertise. Years ago, I attended a presentation where the speaker described the decomposition of a mortgage pool into multiple "tranches" many of which defied realistic estimates of risk. When someone in the audience suggested that it looked as if the securitizer was designing complexity into some tranches to purposely render them opaque, perhaps to generate future fees, his comment was dismissed as not worthy of a response. Yet, the symbiotic relationship between the experts who perpetuate complexity and those who resolve it, is impossible to ignore. Evermore, ingenious computer malware requires that we purchase perennially up-dated security systems to combat it.

Gratuitous complexity is even apparent in the arts. Fred Lerdahl argues that the hyper-complex atonal music of some modern composers contains too many "non-redundant events per unit of time" for the brain to process, and that "much contemporary music pursues complicatedness as compensation for lack of complexity." Critic Terry Teachout believes that the same gratuitous complexity can be found in modern literature. He asks whether it is worth the time to slog through James Joyce's "Finnegan Wake" or reread Marcel Proust's "Remembrance of Things Past" which Teachout describes as a "modern masterpiece that is not gratuitously complicated but rewardingly complex."

Despite nagging doubts about the competence of experts, we continue to be mesmerized by artificial complexity and pseudo scientific jargon. As part of their response to the Deepwater Horizon catastrophe, BP attempted a variety of methods to cap the well including a "top hat," "junk shot," and various applications using "drilling mud." A number of late night talk show comedians had fun with these oil field names. BP was known as one of the more public relations savvy oil companies. They should have realized that oil field

slang may be acceptable in the oil patch but public confidence in their expertise requires that they play the jargon game: a "top hat" should be referred
to as a "a sub-surface high pressure containment vessel" and the company
spokespersons appearing on CNN should have described drilling mud as "non-
aqueous drilling fluid."

There is no denying that those with intense training in specialized fields such
as trial lawyers, physicians, architects, etc., have command of knowledge not
possessed by those without similar education. But it is naïve to assume that they
will participate in the development of rules and policies that are consistent with
the best interests of the rest of us. Credential cartels claim to support improvements in the quality of the product offered to customers, but many exist simply
to protect the turf of their members. They increase prices, dampen innovation
and discriminate against young people who are just beginning their careers.

The price of healthcare continues to rise with no end in sight and the performance of U.S. school children lags behind many other developed countries.
Two ill-conceived wars have cost thousands of lives and trillions of dollars in
American treasure. A steady stream of bad advice exacerbated the financial
crisis and various environmental disasters throughout the world. Despite a
"meritocracy" that produces a bumper crop of experts, America's competitive advantage in a variety of industries continues to erode. If asked to pick
the most competent person in the room at a high powered Washington or Wall
Street confab, many taxpayers would choose the waiter serving the coffee—at
least he does his job and spends his own money.

Political discontent on the left and right is partly a revolt against failed expertise and the perception among many Americans that those calling the plays
have fumbled the ball, repeatedly. Disillusioned voters across the political
spectrum express a profound populist distaste with the paternalistic, "trust
fund capitalism" that motivates government bailouts—"Junior gets in trouble
so Daddy writes a check." Of course, Daddy doesn't have enough money to
write checks for everyone.

This book is a critique of experts.; not expert bakers, personal trainers or even
trial lawyers and physicians whose clients in their private dealings bear the
benefits and costs of their advice. Rather, it is a critique of big picture experts
who dispense expertise on behalf of the multitudes. Specifically, these are

the experts whose bad advice can have dire consequences for shareholders, employees, consumers, patients, taxpayers, students, soldiers and citizens.

Because so many experts are affiliated and/or produced by universities, higher education is subjected to particular scrutiny. I take a decidedly pro-market stance throughout the book but also advocate on behalf of other bottom-up processes. This is not a book on epistemology, the branch of philosophy concerned with the nature of human knowledge, nor is it a polemic against government, despite the fact that experts employed in the public sector number among the most dangerous practitioners of misguided expertise. The danger derives not from the public sector *per se*, but from the ability of the expert to marshal the top-down legal authority and resources of government in the practice of their specialty. "Government" is an amorphous institutional construct; I take the position that one must be a person in order to be an expert.

The origin and performance of experts in a variety of public and private arenas will be examined. Not unlike expert witnesses, much expert advice has been demonstrated to be wrong a large proportion of the time. Yet, competence as measured by performance does not necessarily disqualify the expert. Many display their failure like a badge of honor. In general, the larger the canvas on which the expert paints, the more suspect is their expertise.

Why do we persist in seeking and heeding bad advice? A confident expert skilled in the art of persuasion can be a calming influence. Their siren song is most seductive when they promise to solve complex problems with low-cost, painless remedies. It is not surprising that the most successful experts brandishing credentials from high status organizations and prestigious universities, have a touch of the snake oil salesman—we want to believe and so they help us.

How can we combat the plague? We should insist on plain language and refuse to be intimidated by artificial complexity. Bottom-up systemic knowledge is an alternative to top-down expert advice but the outcome can seem messy and disruptive causing us to yearn for a more perfect solution. The first step in weaning ourselves from the plague of experts is to recognize that life is imperfect and, although not all problems have solutions, we do have choices—some better than others. Often the best response to a problem is to identify the most tolerable trade-off and live with it like a gimpy knee or male-pattern baldness. Foremost, we should cultivate a healthy skepticism as Bertrand Russell observed: "even when the experts all agree, they may well be mistaken."

CHAPTER 1

LET'S FACE IT, PEOPLE ARE NOT THAT SMART

Experts are no smarter than the rest of us and the rest of us are not that smart. Yet, any challenge to the triumph of human intelligence flies in the face of postmodern culture and the stilted opinion that we have of ourselves. After all, man has walked on the moon, cured disease, and is even formulating a new climate science to remedy Mark Twain's observation that "everyone complains about the weather but no one does anything about it." Anyone unwilling to concede the supremacy of human intelligence must be either a religious fanatic or a Luddite, but challenging conventional notions of individual intelligence is not the same as questioning man's collective accomplishments.

The quantification of innate intelligence is a less-than precise science. Over a century before German psychologist William Stern coined the phrase "intelligent quotient," Adam Smith remarked on what he considered a curious absence of variation in the intelligence of most people. Smith based his opinion on personal observation and believed that there was greater diversity in the intelligence of dogs than there was among the human population. This does not mean that individual intelligence is unimportant. Perceptions of intelligence color human interaction. We are more solicitous in our dealings with small children whose brains are not yet fully developed, than we are with adults. The same is true of the elderly who suffer from forgetfulness or the on-set of more serious mental impairment. The mentally challenged are accorded special consideration, particularly in the performance of more complex tasks, while the courts deem mental competence a necessary condition for legal liability.

Alternatively, those who exhibit above average intelligence, as evidenced by formal testing, can qualify for enhanced social status. So-called gifted children may be placed in accelerated classes or tracked to special schools. Higher education in the U.S. is a status pyramid with SAT scores and financial wherewithal largely determining the students position in the pyramid. About thirty percent of the population earns a college degree that places them in a pool of workers who have traditionally enjoyed much higher incomes and lower unemployment rates than those without degrees. A much smaller percentage of people earn an advanced degree and very few win special prizes such as the Nobel.

Our inclination to segment and award special status based on perceived intelligence does not stop with people. Some cultures refrain from eating dogs, cats and horses based partly on the assertion that they are more "intelligent companion animals" despite evidence indicating that swine are smarter than many traditional pet species, although certainly not as aesthetically appealing. A team of scientists declared bottlenose dolphins the world's second most intelligent creatures after humans. They are so bright that some believe they should be granted special status as "non-human persons."[1] Long recognized among the most intelligent animals, dolphins have been typically relegated to third place after chimpanzees, which some studies have shown can achieve the intelligence level of a three-year-old child. When corrected for body size, dolphin brains are second only to the human brain. Researchers have used magnetic resonance scans to map the brains of dolphins and compare them with those of primates. The brain cortex of bottlenose dolphins has the same convoluted folds that are linked with human intelligence. Dolphins will look in a mirror and unlike most animals appear to understand that they are looking at their own image. This strong sense of self-awareness is combined with the ability to think about the future. For humans, the research raises the ethical question of whether or not it is acceptable to hold dolphins captive in amusement parks or slaughter them for food or sport.

More impressive than individual dolphin IQ is their ability to coordinate, learn and teach. Dolphins taught to walk on their tale and released back into the wild have been known to teach the trick to other wild dolphins within a very short period of time. They operate with near military precision to round up schools of fish and teach each other how to use sponges to protect their sensitive snouts when hunting for spiny fish. It is the ability to cooperate, teach and learn that renders dolphins most like humans. And like humans, it is collective rather than individual intelligence that is most important in the propagation of the species.

WISDOM VERSUS INTELLIGENCE

No one has polled bottlenose dolphins on whether or not they accept "non-human person" status in the fraternity of Homo sapiens. Groucho Marx said he would never join a club that would have him and dolphins may be far less impressed with human intelligence than we are. Historically speaking, the human pre-occupation with brainpower is a relatively new obsession. For much of recorded time, the multitudes believed that it was our immortal soul that defined us as human beings, rather than our intellectual acuity. Wisdom, not intelligence, was the most valued mental facility but the wisdom of the wisest was trivial when compared to the Almighty. According to St. Paul:

God chose the foolish of the world to shame the wise, the weak of the world to shame the strong, and the lowly and despised of the world, those who count for nothing, to reduce to nothing those who are something, so that mankind can do no boasting before God.

St. Paul to the Corinthians 1, 1:27-29

Early man regarded himself as a powerless bystander unable to understand, much less influence the course of events. The occurrence of good or bad things was attributed to God, Providence or luck. The mysteries of the world were beyond our comprehension; it was pointless to even try and explain the unexplainable. When Horatio expresses his bewilderment over an apparition of the late King, Hamlet tells him: "There are more things in heaven and earth, Horatio, than are dreamt of in your philosophy" (Hamlet, Act 1, Scene V). The wise man understood the limits of his intellect.

What distinguishes wisdom from intelligence? Clearly, intelligent people are frequently not very wise but, the wise are usually thought to possess a modicum of intelligence. Some regard wisdom as pertaining to human problems while intelligence is more abstract. Ancient philosophers believed virtue, happiness and wisdom were interrelated. Confucius writes that a "superior man is always happy; the small man sad." The superior or wise man is happy because he always makes the correct moral choice.

Paul Graham argues that the wise person knows what to do in most situations while an intelligent person does spectacularly well in a few. He maintains the distinction is similar to the rule that one judges talent at its best and character at its worst, "except you judge intelligence at its best and wisdom by its average." [2] Certainly, a definition of wisdom is more elusive than intelligence. It refers to a mix of qualities that might include tenacity, patience, compassion, self-discipline, etc. We tend to think of wisdom as deriving from informed experience, while intelligence is more innate.

Graham believes that in the modern era, intelligence and wisdom have diverged such that intelligence has won out over wisdom. We now admire the genius much more than the sage. There is no MacArthur Foundation "wisdom grant." He attributes the ascendancy of intelligence to the fractal increase in knowledge and the complexity that accompanies it. Time and again, a discovery or even a research error that seemed small and insignificant spawned "fractal buds that have exploded" into new sources of knowledge. In the pre-modern world, wisdom seemed most important and even today, the majority of people do work that involves selecting the best alternative from a variety of choices. However, as knowledge has grown specialized, more people are doing a greater variety of work that requires them to make up things as they go along. New knowledge opens the door to new ways of doing things that diminish the importance of experience-derived wisdom in favor of path breaking intelligence.

Graham thinks that wisdom and intelligence have diverged so much that we may have to *choose* whether we want to be an intelligent or a wise person. He believes the choice occurs because wisdom derives from largely curing childish qualities while intelligence indulges them. Ancient recipes for wisdom require that we "put aside childish things" in an attempt to empty our heads of the trivial and "obliterate our idiosyncrasies." In contrast, the cultivation of intelligence is often characterized as indulging a child-like curiosity that can border on compulsion. Like the rigorous exercise needed to grow strong muscles, intelligence is developed from working on hard problems: "instead of obliterating your idiosyncrasies in an effort to make yourself a neutral vessel of truth, you select one and try to grow it from a seedling into a tree." [3]

How many people on a daily basis actually perform the kind of work that demands the path-breaking intelligence described by Graham? Indeed, the work of many of the most highly trained experts, such as surgeons and airline pilots, includes elements that can be surprisingly rote in their successful execution. Gawande explains how a simple ninety-second checklist in a small sample of hospitals reduced deaths and complications by more than one third.[4] Checklists rely on the conventional wisdom of past experience to reduce task complexity; one wonders how many people died because the checklist was not adopted sooner. Rather than promote innovation, the over confidence and organized obstinacy of experts can also delay change.

Graham's assertion that individual intelligence has "won out" over wisdom in contemporary society, may partly explain the ascendancy of the expert but, it may also explain the rise in expert failure. In our personal dealings we attempt to defend against expert failure by getting a second opinion but when big picture experts fail, the consequences can be catastrophic. Is it the intelligence of enlightened experts or the conventional wisdom of experience that accounts for the bulk of human progress?

If intelligence in the 21st century has "won out" over wisdom, the difference first emerged as a consequence of many 18th century Enlightenment writers. Among many of these authors the word "wisdom" no longer referred to the ancient mix of qualities derived from human experience; instead, it assumed a modern connotation more akin to "intelligence." For Rousseau, the collective wisdom reflected in existing social institutions was a source of corruption that prevented man from realizing his full potential. Rousseau, like many of his contemporaries, advocated a society governed by enlightened experts: "it is the best and most natural arrangement for the wisest to govern the multitude."[5] Echoing this view was William Godwin who believed that, "the pretense of collective wisdom is the most palpable of all impostures." [6] Rather than the unspoken, widespread and fragmented knowledge of the masses, Godwin thought knowledge was concentrated in the articulated reason of the "cultivated mind."

Those who fear that enlightened rulers may be tempted to place their personal agenda above the common good received little sympathy from Godwin who was convinced that higher intelligence was accompanied by a just temperament. With proper education, even the masses could be trained to make decisions consistent with the common welfare. To Godwin, the *intention* to benefit others was "the essence of virtue" and unintended social benefits were not worthy of notice.[7] The assertion that ordinary men were capable of placing the needs of others before their own was not an observation of how people actually behaved but, a statement of what was thought to be man's underlying potential. The "perfectibility of man" was a common theme among many late 18th century writers and would reemerge in the 20th century as a fascist and communist archetype. In *Literature and Revolution,* Trotsky wrote:

"Homo sapiens will once again enter the stage of radical reconstruction and become in his own hands the object of the most complex methods of artificial selection and psychophysical training...man will make it his goal ...to create a higher sociobiological type, a *superman* if you will" [8]

The importance of Friedrich Nietzsche's *Übermensch* or Superman in the development of Hitler's personal philosophy has been widely debated but, there is little doubt that Nietzsche was used as a kind of philosopher-mascot for the Third Reich. There is evidence that Hitler distributed *Thus Spoke Zarathustra* to some of his soldiers and sent a copy to Mussolini in an attempt to stiffen the Italian dictator's spine against the Allied invasion. The Nietzsche connection was also apparent in Leni Riefenstahl's 1934 film of the Nurbemberg rally titled *The Triumph of the Will.* In his book *The Rise and Fall of the Third Reich* William Shirir writes that although Nietzsche was never anti-Semitic, the Führer selected from his philosophy that which served his purpose. To quote Shirir, "Hitler often visited the Nietzsche museum in Weimar and published his veneration for the philosopher by posing for photographs of himself staring in rapture at the bust of the great man." [9]

Nietzsche thought that man should strive to replace his old self with a new, perfected model. To Nietzsche, "man is something which ought to be overcome." He believed the new Superman would one day look on us much as we appraise apes, "a laughingstock or painful embarrassment." [10] Like Nietzsche, Hitler despised weakness and attempted to transform himself into the precursor of the *Übermensch* and become what Nietzsche called a "lord of the earth." For Hitler, a critical element of the German social transformation was the replacement of contemporary social values with a system that nurtured the aggressive instinct.

That so much evil can find affinity with ideas that are ostensibly devoted to human improvement, serves as a cautionary tale. Man as a malleable lump of clay is a metaphor that is still in use, but history reveals that the finished product is just as likely to be a demon as a saint. Many Enlightenment writers such as John Locke and Adam Smith were far less sanguine in their evaluation of human potential. In his *Theory of Moral Sentiments*, Smith probed the distasteful nature of man's egocentricity when he asked:

"how a man of humanity in Europe would respond to hearing that the great empire of China... was suddenly swallowed up by an earthquake...?" Smith wrote that "If he [this man] was to lose his little finger tomorrow, he would not sleep tonight; but, provided he never saw them [i.e, the people of China], he would snore with the most profound security over the ruin of a hundred million of his brethren, and the destruction of that immense multitude seems plainly an object less interesting to him than this paltry misfortune of his own"[11]

For those who would *choose* their little finger over the countless multitudes, Smith goes on to write that "human nature startles with horror at the thought, and the world, in its greatest depravity and corruption, never produced such a villain as could be capable of entertaining it." Of course, we do not get to choose.

Smith may have lamented the moral limitations of man, but he never regarded them as something that could be changed. Instead he believed self-interest was a fact of life, a human character trait that was shared by the most learned gentleman and the village simpleton. Fortunately, it could be exploited to serve the common good. In the *Wealth of Nations* Smith described how the economic benefits to society, that were largely unintended, occurred systematically in the marketplace by virtue of competition and the incentive for individual gain. Rather than attempt to change or perfect man's moral character so that he places the welfare of others before his own, Smith believed that systemic processes represented the best possible trade-off between social and personal benefit. Smith was not alone in his opinion regarding man's moral and intellectual limitations. In politics, his contemporary Edmund Burke spoke of a "radical infirmity in all human contrivances."[12] Burke's distrust of enlightened experts was evident when he wrote "happy if learning, not debauched by ambition, had been satisfied to continue the instructor and not aspired to be the master."[13] To Burke, those who ignored the knowledge and distilled experience of their predecessors did so at their own peril; he defined society as a contract between the dead, the living and those yet to be born.

What most distinguishes people who have faith in experts from those who distrust expertise, is a fundamental difference in the interpretation of how human knowledge is deployed in everyday life. Those who place their faith in experts believe superior individual intelligence accompanied by impressive credentials endows them with knowledge sufficient to make good decisions on behalf of others. In contrast, doubters tend to regard knowledge as more likely to derive from experience than intelligence or credentials. They believe that the most important knowledge is transmitted socially in largely inarticulate form through traditions, social relations, markets, court precedent and other processes. Competition among institutions results in the survival of cultural traits that "work" even if the winners or losers never fully understand how or why they worked. Rather than concentrated among experts, most knowledge is fragmented and widely dispersed among the population. Instead of top-down, it emanates from the bottom-up and derives from the distilled social experience of the many and not the articulated reason of a gifted few. To quote Hayek, there is "more 'intelligence' incorporated in the system of rules of conduct than in man's thoughts about his surroundings." [14]

In his book *A Conflict of Visions*, Sowell characterizes those who place their faith in experts as adhering to an *unconstrained* vision while the agnostics espouse a *constrained* vision of human nature. Enlightened experts and their advocates tend to believe that there are final solutions to "social problems" while doubters think there are only trade-offs, some better than others. In an effort to create equality in results, experts design elaborate systems that can foster unintended consequences that are often worse than the problem. Doubters place greater faith in the equality of process and are more willing to acknowledge that life is imperfect and not all wrongs can be righted. For them, experience and fidelity to duty are just as important as intelligence and credentials, if not more so. Unlike the wise man who understands the limits of his intellect, critics of expertise believe many highly intelligent people in positions of power feel no such constraint.

THE CULT OF IQ

In the Farrelly brothers comedy *Me, Myself and Irene,* Jim Carey plays a Rhode Island state trooper named Charlie who, along with his bride, is chauffeured home on his wedding day by an African-American limo driver who happens to be a dwarf. An argument ensues regarding Charlie's use of the phrase "you people" and the limo driver goes to work on Charlie with his *Nunchucks.* In the process, the driver reveals that he is really a Mensa member and Brown University professor conducting field research. Charlie's bride, also a Mensa member, is smitten. One gets the impression that Charlie was cuckolded on his wedding day since nine months later his wife gives birth to African-American triplets. His bride soon departs with her Mensa soul mate explaining to Charlie "the heart wants what the heart wants." Charlie raises the kids as a single parent in what appears to be an idyllic seaside cottage and, like their birth parents, the triplets are obviously very bright

Mensa is a non-profit organization open to people that score at or above the 98th percentile on certain standardized IQ tests. Mensa's constitution lists three objectives: "to identify and to foster human intelligence for the benefit of humanity; to encourage research into the nature, characteristics, and uses of intelligence; and to provide a stimulating intellectual and social environment for its members."[15] Like the limo driver in *Me, Myself and Irene*, Mensa members have a knack for revealing their membership at the most in-opportune times. How should one respond when a Mensa member declares his genius like a latter day Oscar Wilde? If intelligence is the result of hard work and diligence, then it is a commendable accomplishment; alternatively, if it is inherited, then it seems disingenuous to congratulate someone for something they had no part in developing. Of course, this occurs with respect to other traits. Beautiful people are frequently complimented and rewarded for a variety of desirable physical attributes that are inherited and beyond their control.

More than 90% of respondents in some surveys describe their driving skills as better than average. How much of driving skill is innate versus learned? How do we measure it and what does it mean for average drivers? Is the difference between average drivers and those more than three standard deviations above the mean, significant enough that they should be granted special status as "genius drivers" and awarded their own fast lane? Insurance companies like to define driving skill based on the number of accidents, traffic citations, etc., but most people would agree that these measures are influenced by a large variety of intervening variables such as driver education and the driving environment. Everything else equal, a driver who spends three hours a day commuting in Los Angeles traffic is going to have more fender benders and traffic citations than an occasional driver on the plains of western Nebraska. Highly skilled drivers may actually cause more accidents if they are over confident, drive faster, talk on the phone and take more risks than less skilled drivers. Safety on our highways depends more on the skills of average drivers if for no other reason that there are so many more of us. The creation of a "driver's quotient" that measures innate driving skill and corrects for intervening variables, should be an easier task than measuring an innate "intelligence quotient," but it remains a devilishly difficult problem.

Some attribute the scientific lore surrounding the Manhattan Project with giv-ing birth to post-WWII America's fascination with human intelligence, but public curiosity was also fanned by the media. Television quiz show audiences fawned over a handsome young Columbia University professor named Charles Van Doren. Mr. Van Doren displayed a breathtaking command of knowledge in a variety of fields and would eventually win over $129,000 or the equivalent of about $1 million today. In 1957, he appeared on the cover of *Time* magazine and would later admit to a Congressional Committee that the show's producer fed him the correct answers to the questions he aswered.[16] Despite the scandal, the popular press continued to feature stories on how to increase brainpower. *Dianetics* author and Scientology founder L. Ron Hubbard claimed in a 1964 article, in *The Saturday Evening Post*, that Scientology's "most spectacular feat was raising a boy from 83 IQ to 212." [17]

A high IQ score does not carry the same social cache it once did since young adults are now more likely to bandy about SAT or ACT scores. From kindergar-ten to early adulthood, society bombards those who aspire to the meritocracy with a battery of standardized tests (i.e., SATs, GREs, CPA, LSAT, MCATS, bar exam, etc.) such that IQ tests are viewed by many as just another exam rather than the Rosetta Stone of human intellect. Standard IQ tests decompose scores into several categories with some people scoring exceptionally high in one or two categories and average or below average in others. IQ tests are designed to approximate the normal distribution which have a relatively small number of extreme values compared to the "fat tails" that characterize distributions with greater diversity. The scoring of modern IQ tests such as the Wechsler Adult Intelligence Scale is based on the subject's rank order on the test with the average score set to 100 and a standard deviation of 15. IQ scores two standard deviations from the average encompass a range from 70 to 130 that includes approximately 95% of the population. Mental retardation is typically defined as an IQ score below 70. Someone with an IQ score of 145 is three standard deviations above the mean and in Mensa or "genius" territory, a modern sta-tistical contrivance. To be sure, genius does exist but it probably cannot be meaningfully reduced to the standard deviations on an IQ test.

The scores for the same person on different IQ tests can vary by as much as 20 points or one-and-one third standard deviations, although the variation across tests becomes smaller as the distance from the average increases.[18] Further complicating the interpretation of IQ is the so-called Flynn Effect which found that for a variety of populations, IQ scores since the early part of the 20th century have been rising at an average rate of about three points per decade and the increase applies across different IQ groupings. The Flynn Effect suggests we are getting smarter, perhaps as a consequence of education, or it may simply reflect deficiencies in the methodology used to design the tests. Despite these problems, when properly used, IQ tests can be a valuable diagnostic tool for psychologists, educators and mental health providers.

Problems arise when experts attempt to draw sweeping conclusions based on the statistical relationship between IQ and a variety of socio-economic measures. Arthur Jensen claimed in a 1969 article published in the *Harvard Educational Review* that much of intelligence, as measured by IQ, depends on heredity and that differences across races may be genetic. Following Jensen, Herrnstein speculated that because intelligence is largely inherited, public policies that promote equality of opportunity would lead to an increasing stratification of U.S. society as the more intelligent win out over the less bright. Charles Murray critiqued anti-poverty policies and concluded that, rather than ameliorate poverty, many programs have perverse incentives that perpetuate dependency and reduce work effort thereby contributing to the increasing social stratification identified by Herrnstein. Murray's critique was well within the mainstream of neo-conservative social scientists such as Daniel Patrick Moynihan, Nathan Glazer and others.

In 1994, Herrnstein and Murray combined their ideas in an ambitious and controversial book called *The Bell Curve*, a reference to the bell-shaped normal distribution followed by IQ scores. The authors attempt to link intelligence, which they claim is primarily a function of heredity, with race, social pathology and socioeconomic achievement. They argue that U.S. society is moving inexorably toward greater social stratification that cannot be remedied by policy. The book ignited a firestorm of controversy. Any suggestion of a link between intelligence, genetics, race and economic success conjures up menacing images of the *Übermensch*. For a society that cultivates the notion that those who work hard can get ahead, the Herrnstein and Murray (HM hereafter) thesis seems too deterministic. If they are correct, then it would appear to provide justification for Godwin and Rousseau's assertions that those of a "cultivated mind" have been endowed by nature with the intelligence to orchestrate society while the rest of us should follow directions and reconcile ourselves to lives as low-paid drones.

Early reviews of *The Bell Curve* appearing in *Time, Newsweek, The Wall Street Journal, The New Republic, Forbes, National Review* and other popular publications were highly favorable. Pre-publication publicity helped ensure commercial success but it is not clear how many of these reviewers actually read the whole book with a critical eye. *The Bell Curve* is an eight-hundred page tome much of which is devoted to the kind of numbers crunching and arcane statistical analyses that are usually subjected to peer review before finding their way to national bestseller lists. Not all early reviews in the popular press were flattering. *New York Times* columnist Bob Herbert described *The Bell Curve* as "a scabrous piece of racial pornography masquerading as serious scholarship... Mr. Murray can protest all he wants, but his book is just a genteel way of calling somebody a nigger."[19]

Herrnstein was a psychologist who died before the book's release and Murray has a PhD in political science. Anyone who tackles such a controversial topic and arrives at such far-reaching social conclusions must expect close scrutiny of the data and research methods. In such instances, the authors have a responsibility to proceed meticulously and resist the temptation to over reach. When HM's data and methods were subjected to a more rigorous scrutiny by those better schooled in statistics, the reviews were far less favorable. The problems begin with their use of a standardized test given by the military to predict potential success as a soldier rather than a more conventional IQ test. The test HM used is known as the Armed Forces Qualification Test (AFQT). They assert that the AFQT has a .80 correlation with more conventional IQ exams.

Clearly, the triplets in *Me, Myself and Irene* inherited much of their smarts from their card carrying Mensa birth parents but how much of their intelligence could be attributed to the living environment that Charlie provided in his small seaside cottage notwithstanding letting them watch too much HBO? In *The Bell Curve*, HM writes that IQ is "substantially heritable." "The genetic component of IQ is unlikely to be smaller than 40 percent or higher than 80 percent...for purposes of this discussion we will adopt a middling estimate of 60 percent of heritability, which by extension, means that IQ is about 40 percent a matter of environment." They go on to assert a "general rule, as environments become more uniform, heritability rises" and refer to "the limits that heritability puts on the ability to manipulate intelligence." [20]

Goldberger and Manski point out that a major misconception with the HM framework is that heritability is *not* a measure of parent-child resemblance in IQ or a biological parameter that sets limits on policy. Instead, "the heritability of an observable characteristic is the proportion of the variance that is associated with variance in genetic factors." HM employ what is known as a biometric model in which IQ score (I) is the sum of genotype (G) and environment (E) or $I = G + E$ and are assumed to be statistically uncorrelated. With a few calculations Goldberger and Manski demonstrate that the relative-to-relative correlation on IQ is a weighted average of their genotypic correlation and their environmental correlation: "The fact that observed parent-child IQ correlations run about .4 to .5 is consistent with heritability from 0 to 1.0." [21] In other words, based on the HM model and observed parent-child IQ correlations, we can attribute all or none of our intelligence to Mom and Dad's genes or any proportion in between.

Contrary to the HM model, genes and environment are not uncorrelated. Along with their genes, parents transmit an environment which can include both parents present in a large house in a leafy suburb, SAT tutors, vacations in Europe, books and computers in the home, a healthy breakfast and private schools with state of the art science and computer labs. Alternatively, the environment can be a household headed by an unwed teenage mother living in a drug infested housing project, no vacations or books, a hit-or-miss breakfast and a crumbling inner city school where instructors teach "keyboarding" on fifty-year-old typewriters. But all may not be well even in the pastoral suburbs of Winnetka or Scarsdale. An alcoholic or abusive parent can cancel material advantage just as a strong single parent can mitigate much of the disadvantage of being raised in the projects. High heritability in intelligence depends on a healthy environment. Research finds that when children are raised in extreme poverty or under severe stress, heritability of IQ falls and the influence attributed to the shared family environment rises.[22]

In their zeal to demonstrate that inherited IQ dominates environmental factors in predicting economic success or failure in life, HM constructed a Socioeconomic Environment Status Index (SES) from a limited assortment of parental characteristics. The crux of the HM argument that IQ is more important than environment in explaining economic success in life is based on a single graph that plots IQ and their Environmental Index against the probability of being in poverty on the y axis and the respective standard deviations of IQ and the Environmental Index on the x axis. A steeper slope for IQ relative to the Environmental Index below the mean is interpreted by HM as evidence that "cognitive ability is *more important* than parental SES [environment] in determining poverty."[23] The statistical problems associated with comparing the standard deviation of variables when they are in quantitatively different units, conjures the cliché of apples and oranges since a larger standard deviation in an infinite variety of alternative environmental indices would render them "more important" according to HM's reasoning.

Those taking the AFQT in the HM study were young adults 15-23 years of age whose scores likely reflect education experience and environmental influence, unlike say 8 year olds whose IQ results would be more representative of an innate component. HM simply dismiss the issue of education-influenced IQ and maintain that using IQ scores from younger subjects would not materially change the results. The correlation between IQ and more years of schooling is usually explained by the assumption that those with higher IQ have a *preference* for more education. However, a controlled long-term study used data on men born between 1950 and 1958 to measure change in IQ between ages 19 and 30 relative to the level of schooling by age 30. The effect of schooling on IQ is characterized as "quite large," one additional year of schooling raised IQ scores by an average of 3.7 points.[24] Education appears to have a lasting effect on cognitive skills such as those measured by IQ tests. The results of the study are also consistent with the literature on the Flynn effect showing that IQs are modifiable across as well as within generations and have been rising since the beginning of the 20th century.

It is indisputable that a significant component of cognitive ability is genetically transferred and plays an important role in life. The average IQ correlations among genetically related persons is .15 for cousins, .42 for parent-child, .60 for fraternal twins and is highest for identical twins who have an average correlation of .74. In *Born Together-Reared Apart* Nancy Segal summarizes the history of the famous University of Minnesota project that tracked 137 pairs of identical twins that were raised apart. In perhaps the most remarkable case, one twin was raised as a Nazi while the other was reared by a Jewish family.

Researchers measured traits related to almost every conceivable aspect of human life: personality, cognition, health, ambition, happiness, career, creativity, sex, religion, politics and more. What they found is that there are genetic effects associated with virtually every trait; some are stronger than others; but there is no denying that among identical twins, genes consistently dominated the limited influence of parenting.

What is much less apparent is the role that parent-child IQ resemblance plays in predicting economic success relative to environment and the heritability of other behavioral traits. Identical twins may arrive at very similar economic circumstances in life but it is by no means clear that it was caused primarily by IQ resemblance. They also share high genetic resemblance in patience, ambition, competitiveness, creativity, thrift, health and stamina not to mention unappealing traits such as greed, sloth, ruthlessness, selfishness and narcissism. It is likely that one or combination of appealing and unappealing genetically transferable traits do a better job explaining economic success in life than IQ. Anxiety, insecurity and the 'darker angels of our nature' can be powerful economic motivators.

Thomas Edison noted that invention was 1% inspiration and 99% perspiration. Intelligence influences economic success but it is also determined by hard work as evidenced by persistent effort. In one study researchers gave 10 year-old children a series of problems; the first eight problems required careful thought but none were too demanding. The last four problems were far too difficult for 10 year-old kids to solve in the allotted time. The children all reacted similarly to the first eight problems but there was a distinct difference in the response to the difficult problems. One group surrendered in the face of difficulty saying things like "I'm not smart enough" while the second group continued to labor apparently telling themselves that the problems could be solved with more effort. The psychologists labeled the first group of kids "helpless." Some intelligent kids who think of themselves as generally bright often become helpless because they fear failure will undermine their self-image as "one of the smart kids." In contrast, the second group believes that they can expand their abilities through additional effort and so they persist longer even when they have lower IQs. The researchers suggest that the "helpless" kids give up in part because parents, teachers and the culture impart the notion that intelligence as measured by IQ is fixed.[25]

HM argue that economic success derives from inherited intelligence and that, because people tend to select marital partners with similar IQ, the U.S. will be transformed into a "custodial state...resembling a caste society" within which the cognitive elite "will implement an expanded welfare state for the underclass that also keeps it out from underfoot."[26] The vision that HM formulate for the future is in many ways similar to the one some conservative writers ascribe to the social policies of liberals. It is in stark contrast to Hayek and many others who harbor a visceral distrust of elites and believe that the most important knowledge in society is dispersed across the population. In which case, people with average or below average IQ may possess knowledge of greater social value than many high IQ citizens. HM tend to conflate *high income* with *high social product* and intelligence with entry into the so-called professional meritocracy discussed in chapter 2. Because members of the professional meritocracy are especially skilled at extracting "economic rent" from the political process, the *net social product* of a high IQ Washington lobbyist with an Ivy League law degree may be less than a fast food worker earning minimum wage.

Although not necessarily correlated with low IQ, the economic importance of people who are "different" from those produced by the mainstream meritocracy has been well documented. Studies have found that people with attention deficit disorder (ADHD) are six times more likely to end up running their own business, a highly productive social activity given the current economy.[27] One survey reports that 35% of entrepreneurs suffer from dyslexia compared to 10% of the population and 1% of corporate managers.[28] Prominent dyslexics include the founders of Ford, General Electric, IBM, IKEA, as well as Charles Schwab, Richard Branson, John Chambers and Steve Jobs. It has been suggested that dyslexics may learn early to delegate tasks to others and appear to gravitate toward activities that require few formal credentials; dyslexia complicates the lives of those afflicted, but there may be intuitive advantages from interpreting the world in a less literal fashion. Many highly productive programmers and some venture capitalists, referred to as being "on the spectrum" in the language of Silicon Valley, exhibit symptoms of autism known as Asperger's Syndrome. Most employers avoid severely autistic persons but one Danish company known as Specialist People matches autistic workers with jobs that demand an excellent memory or a high tolerance for repetition. Rather than surrendering their destiny to elites, successful societies exploit human differences to their advantage.

William F. Buckley famously remarked that he would rather be governed by the "first 100 names in the phone book than the faculty of Harvard University" and while the comment is a not-so-veiled jab at liberals in higher education, there may be some scientific validity to his assertion. Studies suggest that the problem solving ability of homogeneous groups in which everyone is of equally high intelligence, is inferior to groups with greater cognitive diversity primarily because people in homogeneous groups think alike.[29] They bring a highly correlated knowledge set to any problem and tend to make the same mistakes in judgment. If the first 100 names in the phone book include a smattering of Harvard professors, then any additional number likely represents redundant knowledge. One wonders why HM were so intent on arriving at such an elitist interpretation of how knowledge is deployed in society and why so many public experts eagerly embraced their vision.

The Bell Curve is an important book because it illustrates a reoccurring problem with much expert research. The author's desire to demonstrate the futility of education or policy to ameliorate the inexorable ascendancy of the cognitive elite depends on high heritability in IQ and the theory that IQ *determines* economic success in life. The failure to establish their hypotheses did not preclude the authors from arriving at their pre-conceived conclusion. The effusive reviews immediately following publication is a reminder of the intellectual frailty that afflicts many highly visible public experts who are too easily seduced by "science" and its jargon. The Bell Curve celebrates the cult of IQ and illustrates the uneven quality of expertise that is too often propagated by the plague of experts.

COLLECTIVE VERSUS INDIVIDUAL IQ

It is our collective IQ rather than the intelligence of specific individuals that is most important in the forward march of human progress. For approximately 500,000 years man's precursors had big brains, fire, tools and language—all of the ingredients essential to the process of human development as we know it. Yet, the species failed to advance beyond a primitive level. Surely, at some point in the previous half-million years some of these prehistoric men and women had IQs equivalent to modern day Mensa members. Before they disappeared nearly 30,000 years ago, Neanderthals are known to have had brains larger than ours and possessed the same genetic mutation that facilitates speech in modern humans. Why did the prehistoric cognitive elite fail to lead mankind to the promise land?

Instead, for a half million years the species muddled along with little change; then about 50,000 years ago something happened. Man began to evolve from just another ape into a master of his environment who started to make new tools, plant crops, build cities and design new technologies. What spurred the change? Initially, scientists searching for an answer looked in the wrong place. Because of the contemporary pre-occupation with individual intelligence, they assumed that the answer could be found in the human brain. This precipitated the search to identify the neurological tipping point or genetic mutation that transformed human beings from prehistoric dullards into modern men with high IQs who think, plan and strategize; men and women who unleashed a brave new world of ever accelerating technological advance.

The notion that human progress was driven by a sudden transformation in individual intelligence about 50,000 years ago is no longer considered credible. Instead of a quantum leap in individual IQ explaining man's eventual dominance of the planet, most scientists now believe that the harnessing of collective intelligence provides the key to understanding human achievement. The forward march of human progress is a collective enterprise that depends on the fragmented knowledge that is disbursed among millions of brains rather than concentrated in the intelligence of the exceptional few. To quote Matt Ridley, the process of cumulative innovation is driven by "ideas having sex." Ideas tend to be more promiscuous in larger populations with greater cognitive diversity.[30]

Ridley argues that the notion of innovation occurring as a consequence of promiscuous ideas has a close parallel in biological evolution. He writes, "the Darwinian process by which creatures change depends crucially on sexual production which brings together mutations from different lineages. With sex, they come together and join the same team."[31] Via reproduction, evolution becomes a collective and cumulative process that allows individual members access to the gene pool of the species. Species with large gene pools do better than those with small ones, which also explains the vulnerability of small, isolated island species in competition with the continental variety.

New innovations are typically a combination of existing technologies that are brought to fruition through collaboration. When our ancestors first emerged from the primordial forest and engaged one another in trade, the collective IQ began to expand. Great cities like Alexandria, Athens, Tyre, Baghdad, etc., sprang up and prospered at key points along historical trade routes. Smaller cities connected with the larger ones to form a vast trade network that permeated the mountains and valleys of the ancient world. Civilizations that for one reason or another were cut off from the collective brain, shriveled and died like an appendage disconnected from the central nervous system. One of these atrophied civilizations was Tasmania. The population of Tasmania prospered and made tools for over 200,000 years but when rising sea levels 10,000 years ago cut the island off, the population shrank and the collective brain became too small to sustain an isolated society much less foster its technological advance. Most Neanderthal tools are found very close to their place of origin suggesting they were much less likely to engage in trade than their counterparts who evolved into modern humans. Anthropologists believe that their disappearance can be explained by their failure to perpetuate and maintain broader social networks rather than a failure in their hunting skills or the ability to innovate.

The notion of collective intelligence and its importance in everyday life has been around for quite some time. Friedrich Hayek wrote extensively on embodied social knowledge and Leonard Reed's 1958 essay titled *I, Pencil* is a classic on the subject. Reed's essay traces the genealogy of an ordinary pencil that we take for granted but is so complex that its construction is beyond the capacity of the most intelligent individual without the help of a multitude of people who contribute their knowledge to the process. Interest in collective intelligence has accelerated because of the Internet and the opportunity to float in and out of groups unbounded by geographic borders. These interactions have generated a huge data stream that is available to researchers interested in distilling insight into group intelligence. Sports fans have long puzzled on why a team comprised of relatively unknown players can out-perform a line-up of high paid, free agent super stars. Depending on "team chemistry," intuition tells us that the collective skill level can be different than the sum of the individual parts.

Whether debating the madness or wisdom of crowds, the notion of collective intelligence has always been controversial. The cult of IQ is biased in favor of a cognitive elite; our cultural lore lionizes the chief, king, captain or CEO in a manner that minimizes the contribution of the collective. Research contrasting group performance of complex tasks with members found that not only does collective intelligence exist, but it also varies in ways that run counter to what many people might expect. For example, one study found that neither the average intelligence of group members nor the person with the greatest intelligence accurately predicted group performance. Group satisfaction, motivation and unity were unimportant; instead, collective intelligence was directly related to the ability of group members to read each other's emotions. The groups with a strong or overbearing leader unwilling to cede the floor did worse than those with more equitable participation that successfully exploits the talents of all group members.[32] Better engineered groups may be able to someday boost their intelligence and increase productivity.

Cultural, social, political and economic networks combine to form the central nervous system of the collective brain. When these networks wither and regress, so does our collective IQ. But a high collective IQ does not necessarily translate into material well-being. One of the more vexing questions in economic history is why it took so long for an expanding collective brain to translate into a permanent increase in the standard of living for the vast majority of humans.

INTELLIGENCE IS NOT ENOUGH: THE GREAT STAGNATION
Despite the undeniable increase in our collective intelligence before 1800, it did not result in a significant improvement in living conditions for the average person. It is true that there was considerable variation in the standard of living among social groups and there were also epoch periods of cultural advance as evidenced by the golden ages of Rome, Greece, Egypt, Mayans, etc.; but prior to the Industrial Revolution, there was little change in the average living standard. Until about 200 years ago, most of the good things in life remained the prerogative of the wealthy. Average height, a good indicator of material success and absence of childhood disease, was actually greater for some prehistoric populations than many 18th century people. Per capita income as measured by protein consumption and access to light, heat and living space was likely greater for a large variety of hunter-gatherer societies than the average 18th century city dweller or peasant. Life expectancy 200 years ago was about 35 years, the same as it was for the ancient Greeks.

Many hunter-gatherer societies probably enjoyed considerably more leisure time along with a much more varied diet than the average 18th century urban worker, most of whom lived lives of unrelenting drudgery. In regard to material consumption, hunter-gatherer societies tend to be more egalitarian than many 18th century social structures in which a disproportionate share of the wealth was concentrated among a small number of landlords. Witnessing one's family make do with so little while others have so much was beyond the expe-rience of most primitive men. Hobbes was not exaggerating in 1651 when he described the ordinary man's life as "solitary, poor, nasty, brutish and short."

In *A Farewell to Alms* Clark argues that despite the undeniable advances in inno-vation and a flourishing trade, the world economy remained in the clutches of the Malthusian Trap. Named after the 17th century minister and philosopher Thomas Malthus, the Trap is a natural law governing animal populations out-lined in his 1798 *An Essay on the Principle of Population*. The cycle starts with bumper crops and surplus food followed by a temporary improvement in living conditions along with population growth. The food surplus eventually becomes a shortage as a consequence of more mouths to feed and the inevitable crop failures. Population may grow slowly, which was the case for the pre-Industrial Revolution world, but the Malthusian Trap ensures that the average standard of living will not substantially exceed subsistence levels. In Malthus's world pestilence, famine, war and violence had the effect of reducing population pressures and temporarily increasing living standards for those who survived only for the cycle to repeat itself.

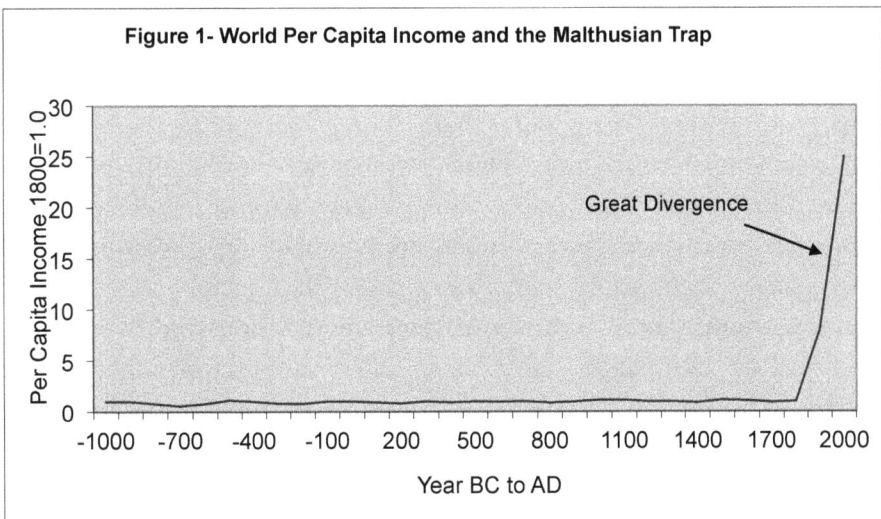

Figure 1- World Per Capita Income and the Malthusian Trap

Many economic historians reject the notion that the pre-industrial world was Malthusian but whatever the cause of the stagnation in per capita output, some-thing miraculous began to happen around 1800. Starting in England, a small group of countries began to produce at an economic level that exceeded previous human experience. Over the next 200 years, per capita income in these countries would increase by a factor of 20. Figure 1 taken from Maddison and Clark neatly summarizes man's economic struggle for much of recorded history. Economic opinion on who benefited most from the Industrial Revolution is divided. Some believe the return to land and capital rose at a faster rate than the return to labor while others argue that the greatest recipient of this economic bounty was the common man and that for the first time labor's share of output exceeded the return to land and capital.

Despite the ability to create dazzling financial derivatives and elegant mathematical models, economists have been unable to answer convincingly some of the most fundamental questions about economic history. What caused the sudden growth rate in economic productivity around 1800? Why did it begin on a small island 20 miles off the European Continent? Perhaps most compelling, why is it that not every country has been able to repeat the process? Indeed, as many people in the world have become richer, the populations of some countries such as Sub-Saharan Africa are poorer than they were in prehistoric times. In numerical terms the order of magnitude between the richest and poorest countries is 40:1. Pomeranz refers to this rich/poor gap that emerged in the 20th century as the Great Divergence.

Explanations for why the Industrial Revolution began in England when it did are many and varied. One popular theory argues that unlike the Malthusian world in which parents produce a large number of children with little investment in the education of each, post Industrial Revolution societies have smaller families but devote more resources to the family's upbringing. Presumably, the increased investment results in more productive children who are much more efficient economic actors. Other theories view the Industrial Revolution as the inevitable consequence of population concentrations that simply reached critical mass and ignited in a kind of spontaneous economic combustion. This theory predicts that all man had to do was survive long enough for the population to reach critical size and that the Industrial Revolution was pre-ordained from the point when the first human walked upright. Finally, the institutional explanation considers the establishment of property rights, the creation of systems for settling disputes and other institutional infrastructure that facilitates social and commercial transactions as having reached a critical confluence in pre Industrial Revolution England. Institutions facilitate and help enforce rules and contracts and along with a sharp decline in social violence contributed to a stable environment more conducive to production.

Clark rejects all of these popular explanations for why the Industrial Revolution happened when and where it did and instead offers a surprisingly elitist, top-down interpretation. He argues that higher population growth among the affluent resulted in the rich passing their "bourgeois values" on to their children. But not all rich prospered and multiplied as Clark suggests. Although a larger proportion of children born into wealthy families survived to adulthood than among poor families, the English landed gentry appears to be an exception. The family line of Thomas Malthus died out because he had no surviving children. In general the aristocracy and gentry were not reproducing at a rate sufficient to replace dying members. Their numbers were replenished from a merchant class that quite literally provided "new blood" and a different perspective on the world.

Clark is less clear whether the transmission of bourgeois values occurred genetically or through socialization although he insinuates that genetics play a role. The "good breeding" argument of economic progress is highly suspect and not that much different from the vision of Herrenstein and Murray. Not surprisingly, Allen takes exception with the genetics/socialization proposition. He maintains that sociobiology is such a "serious and contestable position" that it should be clearly "asserted and defended" if that is Clark's intention: "The problem with either genetics or socialization is that heritability is so low by either channel that Clark's mechanism could not spread middle class values through English society."[33]

Clark's dismissal of the role that institutions played in 19th and 20th century economic development contrasts sharply with the views of many other economic historians and the historical record. The British Empire spent heavily on public infrastructure and colonized large parts of the world providing ready markets for English goods. The decline of interest rates may have partly reflected a change in the "time preference" of British citizens but it also depended on the development of credit markets and financial institutions. Continental Europe developed credit mechanisms for financing land wars during the Middle Ages; England was an Island that confronted different challenges and so the development of financial institutions tended to lag behind the rest of Europe. Modern financial institutions in England emerged around 1689 when William and Mary were invited to assume the throne. William was Prince of Orange and Stadholder of most of the Dutch Republics. The King and Queen brought with them modern banking practices that would lead to the establishment of the Bank of England.[34]

For much of history the economies of the Middle East rivaled those of Western Europe. In the year 1000, the Middle East's share of the world's gross domestic product was estimated to be 10% or larger than Europe's 9%. By 1700 their share had fallen to 2% while Europe's rose to 22%.[35] One reason the Middle East fell behind may be because it failed to produce commercial institutions, such as joint stock companies capable of mobilizing vast quantities of resources that endure over time. In contrast, Europeans inherited the concept of the corporation from Roman law.[36]

Acemoglu and Robinson make the case that the political institutions dictate who holds power in society and how that power is used. Narrow and unconstrained political power results in absolutist political institutions such as monarchies or other authoritarian rulers who establish economic institutions designed to enrich themselves and augment their power at the expense of society. These political institutions are characterized as *extractive*. In contrast, institutions that distribute power across society while at the same time subjecting it to constraints are pluralistic. Rather than power being vested in a single individual or small group, power resides with a broad coalition that is more *inclusive*. Similarly, economic institutions that channel income and wealth to a small group are extractive while those that disburse it over a broader population are inclusive.[37]

In extractive institutions power flows from the top-down and are dominated by elites while inclusive institutions are bottom-up with control disseminated across a much large segment of the population. Clearly, we would expect that inclusive political institutions tend to foster inclusive economic institutions. Once political institutions become pluralistic, a broad based effort to influence and change economic institutions will tend to follow. However, it is possible to have extractive political institutions and a degree of inclusiveness in economic institutions or alternatively, inclusive political institutions and a degree of exclusiveness in economic institutions.

In the case of the Industrial Revolution, the development of more pluralistic political institutions in England was aided by fortuitous circumstance. The rise

of Atlantic trade with the colonies enriched and emboldened the English merchant class causing them to increasingly challenge the authority of the crown.
The 1688 Glorious Revolution in England limited the power of the king and the
executive, while transferring to Parliament the power to determine economic
institutions. This opened the political system to a much broader cross-section
of society that was able to exert considerable influence on the state creating a
more politically inclusive society.

The increase in British trade with the colonies might have progressed quite differently if Spain had continued to control the Atlantic shipping lanes. Exactly
100 years before the Glorious Revolution in 1688, Philip II of Spain dispatched
his much superior Spanish Armada to destroy the English fleet and consoli-
date control of Atlantic shipping with the very real potential of over throwing
the Queen and conquering the British Isles. Shortly before the assault, the
experienced commander of the Spanish fleet died and was replaced with a
less experienced leader. Inexperience along with bad weather resulted in the
British destroying most of the Armada opening the Atlantic seas to British
trade on a more equal footing with Spain.

Wrigley points out that whatever forces may have initiated the Industrial
Revolution it could never have progressed without the substitution of more
energy efficient coal and oil for wood.[38] In this respect, the Industrial Revolution
was also an energy revolution since all forms of production and transport require
energy. In organic economies the primary source of energy is photosynthesis
which is notoriously inefficient since it captures only .5% of the energy in sun-
light. Nevertheless, for most of recorded history, human and animal muscle
power derived from vegetable matter produced by photosynthesis was the
primary source of mechanical energy. Wind and water also generated mechanical energy but their contribution was relatively small. Photosynthesis was
also the source of heat energy which is created by burning wood. If charcoal
had remained the primary energy source for smelting iron, all of the trees in
England would not have been sufficient to provide the metal requirements of
their mid-19th century industrial economy. The solution to the energy constraint imposed by photosynthesis was to exploit the same energy source but
one that was stored over geologic time in the form of coal.

Coal was used as a domestic heat source in Tudor England long before the
Industrial Revolution. Attempts to replace charcoal with coal in many industrial

applications, such as iron smelting, took a very long time to perfect because of the transfer of chemical impurities. Mechanical energy as opposed to heat energy was still supplied by human and animal power until the development of the steam engine made it possible to convert heat energy into mechanical energy giving way to a wide variety of applications in production and transport.

The substitution of fossil fuels for trees is apparent even in the so-called post-industrial world characterized by today's information society that stores data in the "cloud" rather than paper files derived from wood pulp. *Facebook* stores more than 100 petrabytes (100 million gigabytes) among a handful of data centers in three states. The newest data center in Oregon is a 300,000 square foot facility that uses 28 megawatts of electricity or enough to power 28,000 homes. *Google* is an even bigger user of fossil fuel derived power with 11 data centers using 260 megawatts or 260,000 homes. Data storage in the cloud consumes 1.3% of world electricity or more than the total electricity consumption of Mexico or Australia.[39] Most of the electrical energy required to run the cloud still originates in fossil fuels. Whatever other factors precipitated the Industrial Revolution, it could not have progressed without the extraction of energy from fossil fuels and much the same can be said for the information age.

It is unlikely that the reason why the Industrial Revolution began in England will be explained by one grand theory; rather, it was a slow accretion of circumstances along with a dash of good luck. This combination of factors contributed to a process that began much earlier than 1800 and included the development of inclusive political and economic institutions with greater property rights. Along with the growth in knowledge and its dissemination, England experienced a prolonged period of relative stability. There was a marked decrease in social violence with an increase in literacy and numeracy. The decline in interest rates also reflected an altered time preference among the general population suggesting a greater willingness to work harder and delay gratification into the future. All of these changes are consistent with an increase in social trust. Whatever combination of forces ignited the revolution, an efficient alternative to wood energy was essential to keeping the economic machine running.

What is most notable about one of the signature events in human history is that it happened not as the result of a constructivist top-down mandate by a king or emperor, but by a spontaneous bottom-up transformation. The elite contributed to the Industrial Revolution but it was mostly a triumph of collective man. Along with increases in the standard of living, people began to live longer. Death from infectious disease such as tuberculosis began declining in Britain with the onset of the Industrial Revolution in the early 1830s with 86% of the drop in the tuberculosis death rate taking place before streptomycin was introduced in 1947. About 68% of the reduction in death from bronchitis, pneumonia, and influenza; 90% of the decline in whooping cough; and 70% of the decrease in death from scarlet fever and diphtheria occurred before sulpha drugs appeared in the 1930s. Deaths from food and water born diseases, such as cholera, dysentery, typhoid and typhus, also lessened decades before they could be medically treated thanks primarily to improvements in hygiene.[40] By the time medical care as a proportion of the gross national product began its steep ascent in 1952, about 92 percent of the decline in mortality for the 20th century had already occurred.[41] In addition to immunization and improvements in hygiene, much of the remaining increase in life expectancy is probably attributable to improved nutrition. Regardless of the precise proportions, the average person owed most of their longer life to the economic bounty that derived from their collective effort. Unfortunately, not all countries and peoples would share in the abundance or longer life expectancy.

THE GREAT DIVERGENCE AND COLLECTIVE IQ

If explanations for why the Industrial Revolution happened when it did have been less than satisfactory, the same could be said for the Great Divergence. Beginning in the late 19th century, a noticeable gap in per capita output between the most and least productive economies became apparent and continued to widen throughout the 20th century. Experts at organizations such as the World Bank and the International Monetary Fund have expended considerable effort and untold billions of dollars in a futile attempt to reverse the gap between the haves and the have-nots.

Why has the substantial foreign aid awarded many less developed countries failed to establish sustainable growth? Calls for debt forgiveness to less developed countries have been challenged by some who maintain that the remedy has been used repeatedly since WWII without much success. The culture of dependency created by domestic welfare initiatives has parallels with foreign aid programs. William Easterly distinguishes two types of development experts: the first is the top-down "planner" who imposes grandiose development schemes, while the second is the "searcher" who looks for bottom-up solutions to specific problems.[42] Easterly believes the more modest and less expensive remedies proposed by searchers have a much better chance of success. His characterization of planners is consistent with their being big picture experts who, despite their good intentions, lack the local knowledge that is disbursed among the indigenous population. The qualifications of planners often derive from the acquisition of credentials or celebrity rather than extensive on-the-ground experience in the subject country. In contrast, searchers attempt to harness bottom-up knowledge by mobilizing the local population in the pursuit of modest projects that improve living conditions one village at a time.

Easterly's view contrasts sharply with Jeffrey Sachs, who can be characterized as a planner. Sachs believes Africa "can be saved" with $75 billion per year in Western aid.[43] Critics of foreign aid are skeptical; they tend to think that the present generation of white philanthropists is no more likely than the previous one to succeed in the self-appointed and often imperial mission of saving the Dark Continent. Others take a more middling view but still believe that the West can play a more active role in the development of lagging countries.[44]

Despite the careerism and strident disagreements over policies, the economic difference between very rich and very poor countries manifests itself as a gap in labor output. The difference was first apparent in the textile industry in the mid 19th century and has continued to grow. New production methods since the Industrial Revolution have raised the wage premium for high quality labor. "Shallow" production techniques in the pre-industrial world were less precise, involved fewer steps and were more forgiving of error than the "deep" methods of the post-industrial world which are characterized by process precision. Over time, shifts in the best practice technologies cause many less developed countries to fall further behind. Failure to adopt new technologies can result in such large differences in worker output that even countries with very low wages can be at a cost disadvantage.[45]

Differences in labor productivity between the richest and poorest countries may also reflect a more sinister problem. There is evidence that modern medicine in some of the poorest regions has substantially reduced subsistence income, which allows populations to continue growing at wage rates below the average of the pre-industrial world. Despite lower income, life expectancy in some of the poorest countries is higher than it was during the pre-industrial era. The increased life expectancy derived from modern medicine has not increased labor productivity sufficient to raise per capita output.

Development economists have long speculated on the role that "disease gradients" play in the health and output of those living in less developed countries. It is argued that the heat and humidity associated with equatorial climates cannot help but influence productivity of human labor. Indeed, the "economic dualism" that once distinguished the American north from the southern states has largely disappeared. Some believe that the widespread adoption of air-conditioning played no small role in this convergence.

Acemoglu and Robinson characterize the role of climate differences as a "geographic" explanation of economic development and reject it out of hand. They insist that failure to establish inclusive institutions remains the dominant explanation for lagging economic development. Anyone who has spent a summer in Memphis or New Orleans without air conditioning followed by one in Cambridge, would find it difficult to believe that climate has an insignificant influence on labor productivity and economic development given its influence on health and stamina.

The brains of newly born children require 87% of their body's metabolic energy. The proportion declines to 44% for five-year-olds but even adult brains, which comprise 2% of body weight, consume 25% of our energy. Parasites and pathogens compete for the body's scarce energy by feeding on the host's tissue, derailing systems that absorb food and provoking a response in the immune system that diverts nutritional energy from other processes.[46] Researchers have used World Health Organization and IQ data for 192 countries to examine the relationship of average country IQ relative to the prevalence of infectious disease, which they characterize as the "disease burden." Countries among the lowest in mean IQ such as Equatorial Guinea, St. Lucia, Cameroon, Mozambique and Gabon, experience the greatest burden of infectious disease such that the correlation between IQ and the disease burden averages -.67. Of course, correlation is not causation but the authors make a compelling case that alternative explanations such as income, education, climate, agricultural output, etc., are small or insignificant when the consequence of disease are considered.[47]

Parasitic diseases and malaria have long been known to affect cognition in children, but diarrhea may cause the most insidious damage since it accounts for a sixth of all infant deaths and occurs at a time when the brain is growing rapidly. Conversely, some health problems increase with economic development. An unintended consequence of prosperity is a predicted rise in asthma and allergies in the more developed countries. Some scientists speculate that these conditions are increasing because infantile immune systems, unchallenged by infection, are turning on cells they are supposed to protect.

Contrary to earlier research that assumed differences in mean IQ among countries accounted for differences in economic development, under development accompanied by assorted health problems may largely explain low average IQ. Clearly, the argument can lapse into a chicken versus egg conundrum and the Great Divergence is much more complex than a single correlation suggests. Eradicating infectious disease requires clean water and adequate sewer systems, infrastructure investment that can cost billions of dollars. However, the research does suggest that foreign aid policies designed to address public health in countries with the largest burden of infectious disease may have the greatest long-term net benefit assuming health improvements can be sustained long enough to increase labor productivity.

Personal freedom plays a key role in development. Amartya Sen observed that no country with a free press and working democracy has ever suffered from famine. Authoritarian top-down cultures that subjugate women experience greater social violence and lagging economic development because they fail to fully exploit the knowledge and experience of half their population; essentially lobotomizing the collective brain. Much the same can be said for societies that practice widespread racial and ethnic discrimination. If development is a bottom-up process that derives from harnessing the fragmented tacit knowledge of everyone in society, then Western experts will likely have no more success engineering development than planners within the lagging country. Reversing the Great Divergence depends not on a cadre of cognitive elite, but on fostering bottom-up inclusive processes conducive to growing the collective intelligence while rewarding individual effort. The lesson of history is that social and economic advancement depends critically on individual liberty.

CHAPTER 2

WHAT DO WILLIAM SHAKESPEARE AND LEE HARVEY OSWALD HAVE IN COMMON?

Our popular fixation with individual expertise even extends to history's villains. Stalin, Hitler and bin Laden have each been described as an "evil genius." If chance and the will to dominate largely explain how such men achieve power, history invariably reveals a garden-variety thug lurking behind a thin veneer of religion or ideology. Mass murder requires no special talent. Its perpetrators are unique not for the possession of extraordinary human qualities, but for their lack. Hannah Arendt coined the phrase "the banality of evil" to describe the unremarkable Adolph Eichmann and his minions. Some think Arendt's expression has been over-used; perhaps this is because it so succinctly captures the vacuous nature of the unquestioning follower as well as the fact that there seems to be so many of them among us.

If collective behavior is responsible for much of the good in life, it must also bear the blame for much that is bad. Victims of evil are usually self-evident but its' perpetrators typically extend beyond those who pull the trigger or fire the ovens. The "evil genius" simply cultivates seeds that have already sprouted. In his biography *Hitler*, A. N. Wilson argues that the Fuhrer has long been mistakenly portrayed as evil incarnate, destined to fulfill his role as "the Demon King" of modern history. Instead, Wilson maintains that Hitler's extremism and fanatical racism were not that much out of step with prevailing cultural norms in Germany and much of Europe following World War I, "albeit an exaggerated embodiment of the beliefs of the average modern person." Rather than an aberration, Wilson portrays Hitler's rise to power as the predictable result of a more secular world, an unavoidable manifestation of "the Enlightenment's cloven hoof."[1] To Wilson, Hitler personified "more than anything else the futility of the 'modern' or 'scientific' outlook on life."

On issues such as belief in the benefits of vegetarianism, opposition to hunting, rejection of religion, support of both abortion and euthanasia, and indifference to the historical past, Wilson draws eerily familiar parallels between Hitler's beliefs and many of the prevailing mores of the contemporary world. He asks whether the Nuremberg rallies are really that much different than the contemporary world's affinity for "spectacularly large football stadiums, pop festivals and open air religious festivals."[2]

The distinguished biographer Carl Rollyson believes that Wilson's effort to write a "Hitler, our contemporary polemic" places him "at odds with a legion of Hitler biographers and historians who have studiously documented the unique historical and cultural conditions responsible for his rise to power."[3] But even Rollyson admits that Wilson exhibits provocative insight into Hitler's artistic sensibility, especially his understanding of the power of speech, noting that *Mein Kampf* was dictated rather than written. Wilson refers to Hitler as the "most hypnotic artist of [the] post-literacy" world. Like modern talk radio "entertainers," he understood that the spoken word could be used to animate millions.

If Hitler was the unavoidable product of the malevolent stew simmering throughout post-World War I Europe, what can be said of Joseph Stalin and what are the chances that the reigns of two "Demon Kings" would overlap? If Hitler is the inevitable consequence of "scientific" modernity, the Enlightenment's right cloven hoof as it were, then Stalin surely represents the left. Speaking of the Russian people, the historian Mikhail Gefter wrote, "We should not be afraid of our spiritual kinship with Stalin. We must see and realize it in order to eliminate all that is Stalin in us."[4] Adam Hochschild asks how tens of millions of Russians could perish in the collectivization of Soviet agriculture and the gulags of Siberia without widespread cooperation of the Russian people.[5] Russia was the epitome of a top-down society with a long tradition of passive obedience at the bottom of the social structure and absolute power at the top. Until outlawed by Peter the Great, Russian citizens in the capital would lie totally prostrate in the street when the Tsar passed in his carriage. When serfdom officially ended in the middle of the 19th century, about half of all Russians were serfs. Many believe that the profound passivity engendered by the system persisted long after it ended.

Hochschild argues that this deep passivity was combined with a Russian culture that cultivates "millenarian" scenarios that promise deliverance from suffering, a theme that is present in the schismatics of the medieval Russian Orthodox Church and the writing of Dostoevsky.[6] The early Bolsheviks exploited belief in the millenarian while at the same time appealing to a more sophisticated audience by framing their arguments in the jargon of "scientific socialism." Bolshevik theorists displayed the technical certainty and arrogance typical of 20th century experts. In a visit to Russia shortly after the revolution, Bertrand Russell wrote, "The governing classes had a self confidence quite as great as that produced by Eton and Oxford. They believed that their formulae would solve all difficulties."[7]

If coordinating the production of a simple wooden pencil without the help of markets to mobilize the factors of production is a devilishly complex task, imagine the literally millions of decisions required by planners to produce a single locomotive. Stalin's efforts to transform a technologically backward agricultural country into a modern industrial machine in just a few short years, encountered endless problems— raw material shortages, bottle necks in the production of spare parts, railroad tracks that stopped short of the factory, precision tools that were imprecise and canals that were too small for the ships that they were supposed to convey. There were shortages of bread and house-hold items from soap to toilet paper along with frequent work stoppages due to industrial accidents caused by unsafe work conditions.

This was not the way a revolution based on the principles of scientific socialism and choreographed by the party's intellectual elite was supposed to proceed. The only rational explanation was that counter revolutionaries and saboteurs had conspired to thwart the will of the people. A 1937 edition of *Pravda* ominously intoned: "Assembly lines do not stop by themselves, machines do not break down by themselves, boilers do not burst by themselves... Somebody's hand is behind every such action. Is it the hand of an enemy? This is the first question we should ask."[8] Convinced by the Party that traitors and conspirators were everywhere sabotaging the rightful destiny of Mother Russia; even honorable citizens began to interpret innocent actions as suspicious behaviors and alert the authorities. The architects of this brave new world were stead-fast in their intellectual certainty; as Chesterton noted, "only materialists and madmen never have doubt."[9]

Of course, undaunted confidence in one's cause and the suspicion that ene-mies conspire against one, pre-date the Stalinist era and appear throughout literature and history. When humans first organized into groups, they likely questioned one another's motives and spun conspiracy scenarios. What is sur-prising is the degree to which conspiracy theories persist over time and have even proliferated in our presumably more rational age. The time worn expres-sion that "two people can keep a secret if one of them is dead" has more than a grain of truth. Few endeavors demand greater organizational expertise than the perpetuation of a bona fide conspiracy involving more than a handful of conspirators. Yet, large numbers of people are convinced that politicians as well as government and corporate bureaucrats possess expertise sufficient to hide secrets that include the landing of alien space ships and the true identities of political assassins. According to *The Economist*, 75% of all Egyptians believe that the 9/11 Twin Towers attack was a conspiracy organized by both the U.S. and Israeli Intelligence to stoke Western hatred of Islam.[10] If true believers consistently over estimate expertise, they have also been known to deny the presence of technical proficiency and even genius if the person's credentials fail to meet their standards. Both William Shakespeare and Lee Harvey Oswald have been the focus of elaborate conspiracy theories motivated by their respec-tive "credential failure."

In his book *Contested Will* James Shapiro confronts the long, simmering "author-ship controversy" surrounding William Shakespeare. For more than 150 years a diverse group of Shakespeare experts have maintained that he was simply a "front man" in a conspiracy that has successfully hid the true identity of the author or authors. In 1785, James Wilmot, an Oxford-trained scholar who lived near Stratford-Upon-Avon, attempted to locate Shakespeare's papers without success. Wilmot burned his notes before dying but shared his doubts about Shakespeare with James Corton Cowell, a member of the Ipswich Philosophical Society. In two lectures delivered in 1805, Cowell would reveal his reserva-tions concerning the authenticity of Shakespeare's work.[11] Both Cowell and Wilmot based their opinion on what they considered the obvious disconnect between the literary skill and depth of human understanding revealed in the plays versus the presumed author's limited education and experience.

Shapiro explains that the controversy would remain dormant for fifty years before being resuscitated by an Ohio schoolteacher named Delia Bacon (1811–1859). Ms. Bacon devoted much of her early life to the study of Shakespeare and was convinced that no person of low birth could possibly be endowed with the refined sensibility that resonates throughout such a remarkable body of work. She believed the real authorship resided with a group of defeated politicians led by writer/philosopher Sir Francis Bacon (no relation to Delia Bacon). She would later claim that the clues to the real identity of the authors were hidden in the plays although Ms. Bacon would die before sharing the secrets necessary to decode the text.[12]

Unlike Ms. Bacon who was born in America, John Thomas Looney (1870-1944) was a British subject who belonged to a group that studied and revered feudal culture in England. Like Ms. Bacon, Mr. Looney also detected an aristocratic sensibility in Shakespeare's writing that caused him to believe that the real author had to have been a blue-blooded member of the aristocracy. Mr. Looney would settle on Edward de Vere, the Earl of Oxford, as the most likely candidate. The Earl was an educated, well traveled literary man who possessed the intellectual and social credentials sufficient to qualify him as a likely candidate.[13] Because he would have been fatherless when he wrote *Hamlet*, Sigmund Freud became an adherent of the Looney theory (no pun intended). It was an explanation that fit nicely with Freud's Oedipal interpretation of the play and is a good example of how experts across disciplines reinforce one another's misguided expertise.[14]

Over time the conspiracy became more bizarre culminating in a "cipher wheel" for decoding the text that revealed Francis Bacon as Queen Elizabeth's son. Mr. Looney was also known to resort to séances in an effort to expose the truth behind the cover-up. Like a literary precursor of the *Da Vinci Code*, a little artificial complexity added mystery to the conspiracy and enhanced the expertise of those shrewd enough to decipher it.

Shakespeare was the son of a humble glove maker with limited education; how could a man possessed of such narrow social and intellectual credentials possibly be the creator of so much timeless literature? After all, the list of Shakespeare doubters reads like a Who's Who of 19th and 20th century artists and intellectuals that includes Ralph Waldo Emerson, Henry James, Helen Keller, Charlie Chaplin, Orson Welles and Mark Twain to name a few. Notwithstanding their credentials, critic Terry Teachout believes the literary conspiracy theory reveals more about the skeptics than it does about the Bard. He writes, "Time and again, the world of art has been staggered by yet another 'Mr. Nobody from Nowhere' (to borrow a phrase from *The Great Gatsby*) who, like Michelangelo or Turner or Verdi, strides onto the stage of history, devoid of pedigree and seemingly lacking in culture, and proceeds to start churning out masterpieces. For mere mortals, especially those hard-working artistic craftsmen who long in vain to be touched by fire, few things are so depressing as to be reminded by such creatures of the limits of mere diligence." [15] Undoubtedly, there are many more Salieris than Mozarts.

True genius exists but it resides beyond the realm of mere expertise and the faux measurement of IQ tests. If we believe that literary genius cannot exist unless accompanied by certain education and/or social credentials, then the same reasoning can cause us to deny minimum standards of technical proficiency in others. Lee Harvey Oswald satisfied the modern definition of a loser. His father died before he was born and at the age of two his mother temporarily surrendered him to an orphanage. A frequent truant, Oswald was assessed by a New York City reform school psychiatrist as exhibiting a "vivid fantasy life" along with "passive-aggressive tendencies." He would later be examined by two Soviet psychiatrists following a failed suicide attempt in 1959.[16] By the age of 17, when he dropped out of high school to join the Marines, he had lived in 22 different places and attended 12 different schools. The Marines sent Oswald to radar operator training but consistent with The Marine Corps Rifleman's Creed, every Marine is trained first and foremost as a rifleman. In his first test he scored high enough to qualify as a sharpshooter. Given his background it was not surprising that Oswald did not adjust well to military life. He was court-martialed twice, once for fighting and once for accidentally shooting himself with a pistol, and was disciplined for discharging his weapon while on guard duty.[17] Oswald was granted a hardship discharge that would later be changed to undesirable.

Obsessed with the former USSR, Oswald indulged in frequent political fanta-sies and moved to the former Soviet Union when he was 20 years old but soon grew bored with the drab life of a Minsk lathe operator. He never formally renounced his U.S. citizenship and returned to the U.S. in 1962 with his young Russian wife but without the public attention he craved. Having no civilian skills, he held a series of menial jobs and in March 1963 bought a mail order

6.5 mm Carcano rifle using an alias. In April of the same year, Oswald likely attempted to assassinate former U.S. General Edwin Walker by shooting him through a window in his home.[18] The bullet struck the window frame with fragments entering Walker's arm, inflicting minor injury. A substantial quantity of evidence implicating Oswald in the Walker shooting was discovered after the Kennedy assassination but it was largely dismissed by conspiracy buffs.

Oswald returned to New Orleans after the attempt on Walker's life and would eventually travel to Mexico in September of 1963 with the ostensible purpose of proceeding on to Cuba. After an extended delay, he was granted a Cuban visa but inexplicably returned to Dallas, perhaps getting cold feet given his unsuccessful attempt to garner public attention with his defection to the USSR. Running a lathe in Minsk was one thing; cutting sugar cane in the Cuban countryside was something else. On October 6, almost two months before Kennedy's visit to Dallas and the public notification of the infamous motorcade route through Dealey Plaza, Oswald took a job at the Texas School Book Depository. On the morning of the assassination he was seen carrying a long paper bag that he said contained "curtain rods." Another witness reported seeing him on the sixth floor where the rifle was found after the shooting. Oswald's wife admitted taking the infamous picture of him holding the 6.5 mm Carcano rifle months before the assassination but conspiracy buffs continue to maintain that the picture is a phony. [19]

By any standard, Oswald was a failure in life. Because of his last name and furtive manner he was nicknamed *Ozzie Rabbit* by his fellow marines. The results of his childhood psychiatric exam, attempted suicide, frequent fighting, incessant travel, political fantasies, the inability to hold a job and his reported sexual performance problems all suggest a maladjusted young man with a very tenuous hold on life. The heart of the assassination conspiracy rests on the premise that such a person is incapable of formulating, much less executing, a successful plan to assassinate the President of the United States, particularly a President whose manner and appearance contrasted so sharply with the hapless Oswald. Jack Kennedy was everything that Ozzie Rabbit was not. Sinister forces had to have placed Oswald at the Book Depository; his whole life suggests a disturbed personality moving inexorably toward the fateful day when he would fulfill his destiny as a "patsy."

Foremost among conspirator objections is the assertion that Oswald did not possess the necessary skills as a marksman to have fired the fatal bullet using the antiquated Caracano rifle. Posner employs his forensic skill to provide an almost second by second rundown on how Oswald, acting alone, carried out the assassination. Despite failing at almost everything he attempted in life, the one thing Oswald was eminently qualified to do was fire a rifle with above average accuracy. As for questions about other gunmen positioned elsewhere in Dealey Plaza, one reviewer described Posner as "running a high-powered leaf blower over the Grassy Knoll."

Posner explains the conspiracy theory this way: "strong psychological reasons prompted the public's early embrace of conspiracy theories. The notion that a misguided sociopath had wreaked such havoc made the crime seem senseless and devoid of political significance. By concluding that JFK was killed as the result of an elaborate conspiracy, there is belief that he died for a purpose."[20] Life is more random than we like to admit and sometime even losers get lucky.

CREDENTIALISM AND THE RISE OF THE EXPERT

If credentials validate expertise then their absence must invalidate it. That is the reasoning associated with the conspiracy theories surrounding both Shakespeare and Oswald. Of course, performance should be measured by *output* not *input* represented by credentials; unfortunately, many of us are prone to misinterpret cause and effect. During the late 20th century a surge in credentialism reflected popular attempts to advertise expertise and block entry into a number of careers.

Millions of people pay for investment advice dispensed by a variety of experts who boast fancy credentials. In most instances, the value of the advice is as questionable as the credentials. Does your financial advisor have a CPA? How about a CRFA, CSA, CFP, CFA, CSFP, CMA, CPFC, CPWA, CPM? This brief list of acronyms represents just a few of the "professional" investment advisor credentials beginning with the letter C in an alphabet soup of designations that has increased from 45 in 2005 to over 95 in 2010.[21] With a half dozen exceptions, most of these credentials are not worth the paper they are written on. Why are the organizations that churn out fancy credentials able to not only survive but prosper? Credential inflation reflects the bubble economy but it is mostly a manifestation of the public perception that expertise derives from these designations no matter how obscure or easy to acquire. Rather than an indicator of skill, credential inflation renders all certifications suspect and reveals the designation business as pretty much a sham industry.

In general, no one is forced to pay for the services of investment advisors who brandish worthless credentials but this is not the case for all industries. In some instances, groups have been successful in establishing what Kling calls "credential cartels." In *Life on the Mississippi* Mark Twain explains how riverboat pilot's pay stagnated at the very time westward expansion was causing a sharp rise in company profits. The reason was that anyone could sign on as a riverboat pilot apprentice. A surge in the number of riverboat pilots depressed wages until they conspired to form an association that would monopolize information on the location of hazards, snags, sandbars, etc. The association would only share this information with other members. As the number of groundings and accidents among non-association pilots increased, steamboat insurance companies insisted that pilots be members of the association. Since the existing pilots were able to limit the number of new pilots admitted into the association they were able to extract a wage premium from the steamboat companies who simply passed the increase on to their customers. The cartel worked well until the overpriced steamboat industry was replaced by railroads. According to Twain, "the association and the noble science of piloting were things of the dead and pathetic past!"[22] Faster and not confined to natural waterways, railroads extended the network comprising the collective brain.

The reign of the riverboat pilot association was short lived but other cartels have survived longer by enlisting government assistance to control the distribution of their service. In 1998, a California woman was fined $1,000 for operating a hair-braiding salon without a cosmetology license.[23] Hair braiding is a form of ethnic art passed down from mother to daughter and involves no chemicals or processes that pose a danger to the customer. More disconcerting is that instruction for a cosmetology license in California did not include any training in hair braiding. If hair braiding posed no threat to customers, it did threaten state cosmetology cartels that try to preempt control of any revenue stream that is even vaguely related to their industry. In the wake of legal challenges and a rash of negative national publicity, many states now exempt hair-braiding from a cosmetology license that can require 2,000 hours of training and cost over $10,000. In most cases, state licensing boards are run by the industry that they are supposed to regulate and much like the riverboat pilots association, a major objective is to block entry into the profession.

In a weak economy, the push to award more licenses coincides with anxiety over government growth. In 2008 about 23% of U.S. workers were required to obtain a state license compared to 5% in 1950. In the mid-1980s there was 800 regulated professions; the number today is over 1,100 according to the Council on Licensure, Enforcement and Regulation. Some states require a license to be a florist, tree trimmer, locksmith, interior designer, conveyer belt operator, retailer of frozen desserts as well as a "shampoo specialist" that can involve 150 classroom hours of instruction, including 100 of them devoted to the "theory and practice" of shampooing.[24] States are receptive to the licensing of different occupations because the regulatory bureaucracy creates patronage jobs. After paying all of the inspectors and administrators who enforce occupational requirements, state regulatory agencies can even generate a profit. In fiscal year 2008-2009, the state of California's general fund borrowed $96.5 million from the state's licensing reserve fund. Best of all for the politicians, licensing is a hidden tax that citizens don't even know they are paying. One study estimates that occupational licensing adds at least $116 billion to the cost of services.[25]

The 1950s were the glory days of organized labor when the union card represented one of the most coveted credentials and 35 percent of all U.S. workers belonged to a labor union. In 2009, the Bureau of Labor Statistics reported that only 7.2% of private sector workers were union members. Global economic forces and technological change are largely responsible for the decline. In contrast, union membership among public sector workers exceeds 37% and has been rising until very recently. There are now more union members in the public than private sectors despite the latter being four times larger. Government budget deficits along with un-funded pension liability have caused popular political sentiment to turn against public unions in some states.

Despite the Great Recession, the two sectors with the largest growth in consumer spending between 2007 and 2010 were education and healthcare, which grew at rates of 13.4% and 10.8%, respectively.[26] They are the only industries in which spending is rising faster than income. Each has been criticized for poor performance and both are dominated by credential cartels. Large increases in public education spending show little or no improvement in learning while studies suggest that much of the spending on healthcare is wasted. Medical schools graduate fewer general practitioners and gerontologists despite projected demand in these areas. Credential cartels prevent registered nurses from hanging out a shingle and treating minor illness such as the flu or hemorrhoids at a lower cost than medical doctors while hospitals continue to invest in expensive equipment rather than low-cost processes that could improve care.

The delivery methods in both education and healthcare have changed very little when compared to the revolutionary application of information technology in other sectors. Possibly, this is because incumbent producers use licensing, accreditation and other credentials to construct barriers to creative entrepreneurship thus preventing the kinds of innovation found elsewhere and government helps enforce these barriers which perpetuate inefficiency.

Primary, secondary and higher education may be the most credential driven of all industries. The teaching certification process for grades K-12 is a multibillion dollar franchise granted to thousands of education colleges located on university campuses throughout the U.S. Once teachers are certified and tenured in their jobs, work rules can make it very difficult to remove low performance teachers. Lagging test scores suggest that the current system has failed many U.S. school children, particularly those attending the poorest inner city schools. Politically controversial, attempts to address these problems via charter schools, alternative certification, vouchers and greater teacher accountability have achieved limited success. In the worst instances, school performance is so dismal that there is little risk to the students from implementing radical institutional reform.

Some claim that a college degree simply screens the more talented and hard working segment of the population from those who are less tenacious. Rather than building "human capital," colleges identify those with preexisting cognitive ability who are likely to be more receptive to training by prospective future employers. Critics of formal instruction argue that much of the most important lifetime learning, such as the acquisition of speech, occurs in a non-classroom environment that places responsibility on the learner rather than the teacher. Adults teach themselves golf, auto repair, chess, a second language, how to play a musical instrument, a computer program, home improvement, etc. They establish their learning objectives in response to frustration, curiosity or economic need in a process that can be more effective than formal instruction. It works because they are self-motivated and take responsibility for their learning rather than transferring it to teachers. When learning is costly and primarily motivated to acquire credentials, the student tends to assume less personal responsibility while assigning more to the teacher.

One study examined the daily work effectiveness of psychotherapists based on "output" measured as changes in the patient's condition rather than "input" measured as time spent by the therapist, how much he charges or how long he attended school. "Contrary to much professional opinion" the skills that make a superior therapist are mainly common sense human skills such as warmth, empathy, lack of pretentiousness, etc., which are the same qualities "one looks for in a good friend."[27] Scientific training was only important in establishing that the patient's problem did not arise from chemical imbalances, injury and other problems such as a thyroid condition or tumor. Once those were eliminated, extensive formal training counted for little in restoring the patient's mental health.

Another study conducted for the Federal Aviation Administration attempted to isolate the factors that contributed most to the competency of a few hundred highly proficient air traffic controllers. Conventional wisdom suggests that such a complicated job might require many of the technical skills conveyed by training in management, engineering and mathematics along with a disciplined mind that allows the controller to juggle multiple tasks. Presumably, technical proficiency correlates closely with the personal qualities that are reinforced by formal education such as responsibility, motivation, dependability, ability to make quick decisions, etc. The study concluded that education was not a factor in the performance of one of the most demanding decision-making jobs in America.[28]

CREDENTIALS, MERITOCRACY AND SOCIAL CLASS

Some occupations employ formal rules and enlist the aid of government to enforce credentialism but it can also be enforced by informal status arrangements. In his book *Bobos in Paradise,* David Brooks makes the case that education credentials have replaced more traditional class indicators in American society. Brook's book is a sometimes humorous examination of the self-absorbed cupidity of the educated elite and provides a more revealing examination of class differences than other more serious books.

To make his point, Brooks compares the current wedding pages of the *New York Times* to the 1950s. Today's "mergers and acquisitions" as many know it, gives a detailed account of the bride and grooms educational pedigree beginning with prep school followed by under graduate degree and proceeding to graduate or professional school. Education background is typically followed with information on the respective careers of the young couple as well as their parents. [29]

In 84 percent of the weddings both bride and groom have a parent who is a business executive, lawyer, professor, doctor or belongs to the professional class. They tend to marry late, age 29 for the bride and 32 for the groom. Brooks breaks the newlyweds into predators versus nurturers. Predators are the people whose careers revolve around money or negotiations involving money such as lawyers, bond traders, investment bankers, etc. In contrast, nurturers are liberal arts majors who work as academics, foundation officials, activists, journalists, artists or facilitators. He found that about 50 percent of the unions involved two predators hooking up; about 20 percent involved a combination of two nurturers; and the remaining 30 percent were mixed marriages. [30]

The contemporary account of bride and groom appearing in the *Times* contrasts sharply with the 1950s. The wedding coverage of yesteryear did not emphasize jobs or advanced degrees. Often, the career of the groom was not even mentioned and the bride's career was almost never listed. When the bride's job was noted it was almost always identified in the past tense. Instead of emphasizing education and career, the weddings of this bygone era reported on the couple's ancestors, social connections, club memberships and the bride's debutante history. This was typically followed by an exhaustive description of the wedding gown and flower arrangements as well as the names of the groomsmen, bridesmaids and ushers. [31]

The *Times* did not list ages in the 1950s but clearly the average age of the couples was much younger. Today, graduate and professional school combined with the long hours required to cultivate a high-powered career necessarily delays the nuptials. In pre-Vietnam America the military was a more acceptable career track for established young men, accordingly, many more of the males attended West Point or one of the service academies. Digby Baltzell coined the acronym WASP to describe the ethnic background of the era's dominant social milieu.[32] Brooks notes that in the1950s the couples featured in the *Times* wedding pages were much "WASPier" with about one half exchanging their vows in an Episcopalian ceremony compared to less than one in five doing so today. [33]

In many respects, the wedding pages of the 1950's mirrored the familiar class stereotype appearing in the novels and short stories of writers like John Cheever. Picture a sunny terrace where patrician, middle-aged couples are polishing off a pitcher of martinis. The men discuss the stock market and the women talk of fashion and coming out parties in the familiar lock-jaw speech of Northeastern WASPs. Enter Buffy and Brad in tennis whites, radiating the vibrant good health that comes from good breeding and expensive prep schools; they will soon begin their senior year at Wellesley and Yale. If it were a late 1940s movie, the perky June Allyson might have been cast as Buffy while a young Peter Lawford is a dead ringer for Brad who also speaks with a faint English accent despite being born and raised in Connecticut.

Who would have guessed that the mechanism for the demise of the WASP establishment would originate on college campuses rather than the voting booth, union halls or in the streets? In less than two decades the old money elite at much of the Ivy League would be displaced in favor of a new "meritoc-racy" of young strivers. Between 1950 and 1960 the number of female students at Harvard increased 47 percent and an additional 168 percent from 1960 to 1970.[34] In response to the large number of highly qualified Jewish applicants, the Presidents of Harvard and Columbia Universities had restricted their admis-sion but in the 1950s, elite universities reversed course and established new admission standards that were based more on academic achievement than family connections.

In *The Big Test* Nicholas Lehman argues that the social transformation from old establishment to modern meritocracy began when James Bryant Conant became President of Harvard University following WWII. Conant feared that America in general and Harvard in particular had evolved into a hereditary aristocracy. [35] He did not set out to displace the WASP establishment but to admit a small group of high achieving students in the hope that they would repay their debt by devoting themselves to public service.

The first order of business was to develop a method for selecting the new elite. To help solve the selection problem, Conant turned to Henry Chauncey a Harvard alumnus schooled in "social science" and endowed with a righteous belief in the merits of standardized testing. The passionate intensity with which Chauncey pursued his life's mission would culminate in the founding of the Educational Testing Service and the creation of the first SAT or Scholastic Aptitude Test.[36] The rest, as they say, is history.

In 1952, two thirds of all applicants were admitted to Harvard and there was a 90 percent admission rate for those whose fathers had attended the school. Between 1952 and 1960, the mean score on the verbal portion of the SAT increased from 583 to 678 with a similar change in math SAT scores. The average freshman from the 1952 class would have placed in the bottom 10 percent of the 1960 class.[37] This transformation occurred not just at Harvard but was reflected in entry requirements across the Ivy League. By the early sixties, college enrollments were exploding as the first members of the baby boom generation arrived on campus. The huge increase in the number of college students made it much easier for the highly selective schools to implement higher admission standards. Between 1960 and 1980, the number of higher education institutions increased by 60 percent while the ranks of college professors rose by 190 percent. [38]

The growth in U.S. higher education reflected the parental hope that their children would enjoy a better life but it also derived from a new appreciation for the power of science and technology. The story of the Manhattan Project and the scientists who developed the first atomic bomb that shortened the Pacific war and saved hundreds of thousands of American lives became part of popular lore. If scientists can reproduce the power of the sun what else awaits discovery? The launching of the Sputnik satellite by the Russians shocked a country whose citizens assumed their technological preeminence was unassailable. Science and all education would soon be portrayed as an integral part of national defense as billions of dollars in federal and private research money was funneled to the elite private universities and the best state schools. Private philanthropists, many of whom made their money selling tobacco, steel and oil while battling their workers, were eager to cleanse their reputations by bequeathing a part of their fortunes to universities. The accumulated treasure from these philanthropic baptisms would further cement the role of elite universities in the new leadership system.

Kennedy, and later Johnson's circle of policy advisors, epitomized the ascendancy of the credentialed expert in the new meritocracy. Culled from the most prestigious universities, the Kennedy men were labeled the Best and Brightest. The phrase appears in the poem *To Jane: The Invitation* by Shelley, but David Halberstam is credited with first using it to describe Kennedy's inner circle. Robert McNamara was a charter member and personified the modern technocrat able to apply the principles of scientific management he once taught at Harvard to problems in the auto industry and national defense. After listening to President Johnson brag on the brilliance of his advisors, House Speaker Sam

Rayburn remarked: "I just wish one of them had ever run for sheriff, Lyndon." [39] Rayburn's misgivings were well founded; the over confidence and bad advice proffered by the Best and Brightest would help ensnare Johnson in a war that transformed a minor skirmish in an obscure Southeast Asian country into an American nightmare and accentuated a class cleavage that John Fogerty made famous in his song *Fortunate Son*.

As the Vietnam War escalated, many learned that the privileges of the new meritocracy had much in common with the old WASP establishment. Its bipartisan members would send the young of the poor and politically disconnected into the belly of the beast at a much faster rate than their own children. The sons of Defense Secretary Robert McNamara and Governor Ronald Reagan both received medical deferments, as did Nixon speechwriter and Presidential candidate Pat Buchanan. At the war's peak, the U.S. granted medical deferments at a rate three times higher than other NATO countries and whites were twice as likely as blacks to be excused for medical reasons. A letter from the family physician or a doctor friend at the country club was often sufficient to ensure someone else took Junior's place.

Credentials and membership in the meritocracy can increase wages and cement job security but they can also save your life. The corresponding college deferment allowed many future politicians who came of age during the Vietnam War to avoid service. The list includes Newt Gingrich, Phil Gramm, Bill Clinton, Joe Biden, Mitt Romney and the world champion of college deferments, Dick Cheney. Cheney received a total of five of them and like many other members of the meritocracy, made it clear that he "had other priorities in the 60's than military service." "Chickenhawk" became a popular epithet used by the left to describe the members of meritocracy who supported the Iraq War but stood down when it was their turn to serve their country in combat. [40]

Even after college, the meritocracy found ways to avoid jeopardy. Rumors persist that George W. Bush was able to leap frog the waiting list for the National Guard at a time when Guardsmen were deployed exclusively state side. Of the 1,200 men in the 1970 graduating class of Harvard, only 56 saw military service and only two went to Vietnam. MacPherson quotes a 1970 report in her book *Long Time Passing* that notes of the 234 sons of senators and representatives that came of age since the beginning of the Vietnam conflict, more than half received deferments. Of the 28 who went to Vietnam, one was wounded and none was killed—*fortunate sons*, indeed. [41]

The not so fortunate sons were expected to kiss mom and dad good-bye and report for service all in the name of defending an expert policy idea that had to do with dominoes falling on the other side of the world. Richard Nixon was no stranger to class resentment. As a freshman Congressman on the House Un-American Activities Committee, Nixon fashioned his political brand in opposition to Alger Hiss, a handsome, urbane, Eastern educated diplomat. Despite overwhelming evidence that Hiss was a traitor, the cognitive elite never wavered in Hiss's defense or Nixon's vilification. Nixon's role as "the heavy" would be reprised in the 1960 Presidential campaign. After the first fateful debate, he would forever be portrayed as the sweaty and sinister counterpart to JFK's cool and patrician persona. Once the lottery closed loopholes in the draft, Nixon knew that the elite would never allow their sons to be sacrificed in the name of arcane theories promulgated by Washington policy wonks. It was only a matter of time until the more politically astute foreign policy experts readjusted their opinion allowing the President to engineer a face saving exit. Of course, the Watergate scandal intervened leaving Gerald Ford to decide the timing of the departure.

A rough and tumble politician of the old school, there was nonetheless a palpable element of tragedy attached to Johnson's downfall. That this folksy politician with the pronounced Texas twang would be hung out to dry by the new meritocracy that made him the frequent butt of their jokes strikes some as poetic justice. Johnson spoke with a different accent and he may have matriculated from an obscure state teachers' college but he displayed the same hubris and over confidence as his pedigreed advisors.

It's hard to imagine a pre-meritocracy President like Harry Truman falling victim to the same plague of experts. Truman respected intelligence but he also had a low tolerance for BS. His joke about the one armed economist encapsulated his disdain for intellectual doublespeak. After Senator William Fulbright, a favorite among establishment intellectuals, advised him to appoint a Republican Secretary of State and resign the Presidency, Truman started calling him "Senator Half-Bright." The last President to not graduate from college, Truman was a self-taught historian who understood the benefits and limitations of formal education. He admired the self-effacing George Marshall more than anyone, not so much for his intelligence, which was formidable, but for what are too frequently regarded as old-fashioned virtues like integrity, honesty and fidelity to duty—traits that often appear lacking among the modern meritocracy. Some surveys count Truman among our greatest Presidents. Given his lack of credentials, it is highly unlikely that a modern day version of the plain speaking haberdasher would have ever made it out of Kansas City. In a world of expert political spin, plain speaking is an anachronism that has been replaced by the legalese of the meritocracy.

What can be said for a meritocracy that allows its own to opt out when their country needs them? During WWII, George Bush Senior and many other young men from affluent families dropped out of college and volunteered for combat service without a moment's hesitation. WASP society may have been racist and socially rigid but there was also the recognition that privilege was accompanied by obligation. In contrast, members of the meritocracy are led to believe that they own their success. Would Vietnam have turned out differently if more of the credentialed elite had answered their country's call? Probably not, the failure of Vietnam resides not with the courage or ability of the American GIs who fought the war and bore the cost, but with the bad advice proffered by the plague of experts who largely avoided it.

Radical student movements in the sixties challenged the meritocracy but the revolution would be short-lived. As the number of students setting their sights on admission to elite colleges grew, a far greater threat to the institutions was preserving the integrity of the admissions process. High school courses, especially advanced mathematics, can accurately predict the probability of successfully completing college but elite universities can glean little information from high school GPAs since virtually everyone who applies has an A average and there are large differences in academic rigor across secondary schools. Despite legitimate criticism of cultural bias, the greatest advantage of "the big test" is that it probably provides the single most objective standard for rationing elite college admissions.

By arraying applicant scores from the highest to the lowest and proceeding downward until the freshman class is filled, the university could deflect charges of favoritism but blind acceptance is problematic for two reasons. First, the difference between the scores of those admitted versus a substantial number of those rejected is not significant in any statistical sense. The vast majority of "elite students" who score at the 95 percentile or above do not attend elite universities. The number of elite students attending non-elite schools relative to those attending elite schools is so large that Herrnstein and Murray declined to graphically compare the data in *The Bell Curve*. The second and more troublesome problem is that admissions based exclusively on "the big test" are unlikely to result in a student body that meets the university's financial goals while providing acceptable diversity. Because a substantial number of freshmen openings are earmarked for legacies, children of donors, athletes, etc., it becomes even more critical that schools appear to be fulfilling their public duty by admitting a smattering of minorities.

Critics contend that in an effort to achieve financial goals and diversity, admission criteria have been expanded to include non-academic standards and that discretionary admissions based on non-academic metrics are incompatible with a true meritocracy. The first legal challenge to race based college admissions was the 1978 Bakke decision.[42] The Supreme Court ruled that it was unconstitutional to use fixed quotas for minority applicants at professional schools. At issue was a state medical school's affirmative action program that required a certain number of minority admissions and had twice denied entrance to an otherwise qualified white candidate. Though the court outlawed quota programs on the grounds that they violated the equal-protection clause of the Constitution, it allowed colleges to use race as a factor in making college admissions decisions.

Bakke and subsequent decisions helped spawn a new field of higher education expertise. Admission experts able to implement "comprehensive review" standards that meet legal and financial goals while achieving the targeted degree of ethnic diversity, can command six figure salaries. They claim that the standards supplement "the big test" with more subjective information on leadership, motivation and the student's ability to translate opportunity into achievement that takes into account the student's background. Rather than expanding the discretionary power of the university and diluting the meritocracy, they maintain that comprehensive review simply considers additional admission criteria.

Most elite universities are private and able to establish admission standards independently while state schools are more constrained by law. A 2003 Supreme Court ruling upheld the University of Michigan's affirmative action policy for the Law School but struck down the undergraduate admissions policy as unconstitutional. The University of Michigan employed a 150-point "Selection Index" to score and compare applicants. The Index assigned points for GPA, SAT, quality of school, strength of curriculum, in-state residency, alumni relationships, essay, personal achievement and race. Black, Hispanic or Native American applicants automatically had 20 points added to their score. The 20 points rendered a Black, Hispanic or Native American B student equivalent to a straight A Asian or white student. The Selection Index awarded just 12 points for a perfect score on the SAT or ACT, 8 points for choosing a demanding high school curriculum and 1 point for writing an outstanding admissions essay for a total of 19 possible points. Minority applicants started with 1 point more than they could possibly earn through high school coursework, SAT exam and an admissions essay combined. In 2006 Michigan voters passed a state-wide referendum to the constitution that bans public affirmative action programs. The Supreme Court is scheduled to revisit affirmative action policies among public universities.[43]

In 2004, the chairman of the University of California Board of Regents claimed in an article in *Forbes* magazine that UC-Berkeley was admitting Latino and African-American students at the expense of Asians. The Chairman wrote that the university was "discriminating so blatantly against Asians."[44] Some have compared the difficulty accommodating the large number of highly qualified Asian applicants at Berkeley and Stanford with the "Jewish problem" referenced by the Presidents of Harvard and Columbia Universities in the 1920s. Others argue that some critics of affirmative action are being disingenuous. Sumi Cho uses the phrase "racial mascotting" to describe the process by which diversity opponents often champion the interests of Asian-Americans in an effort to lend legitimacy to their political agenda.[45] One study found that the elimination of affirmative action programs at three elite universities would substantially reduce African-American and Hispanic enrollment while significantly increasing the enrollment of Asian Americans but would have only a negligible impact on white student admissions.[46]

In his book *The Price of Admission* Daniel Golden argues that the seedy underbelly of the meritocracy is not affirmative action but admissions for sale. Golden won a Pulitzer Prize in 2004 for a series of articles on college admission boards that challenges the assertion of a blind meritocracy. He recounts prominent families such as former Senate Majority Leader Bill Frist (Republican, TN) whose son was accepted to Princeton because his father "lavished tens of millions of dollars on a new student center." He claims that a large number of prominent families routinely buy their child's entry into an elite university through donations to the school or a prominent politician who is willing to make a telephone call on their behalf. Golden estimates that it costs approximately $2.5 million to purchase a spot at Harvard not including legal or illegal political contributions to the politician placing the call.[47]

Generally, membership in Harvard's Committee for University Resources requires a donation of at least $1 million. He found that of the 424 COUR members at least half or 218 have had at least one child at Harvard. In the late 1990s Duke University embarked on a strategy to systematically increase its endowment that included admitting a significant number of students over a period of years that would have been rejected had their families not made large donations. It is a common practice for the development office to flag the application of the well connected. Golden estimates that in high demand years as much as 60 percent of freshman openings at some elite schools may be spoken for and that on average 25 percent of students at these schools circumvent the merit process either as progeny of donors, legacies or athletes. Others estimate the percentage is closer to 15 than 25 percent. Patrician sports such as rowing and horseback riding can allow elite schools to camouflage donor children as athletes. Golden identifies the California Institute of Technology as an example of a legitimate meritocracy and asserts that rather than a meritocracy the current system in "America looks increasingly like imperial Britain." [48]

Legacies may be more controversial than admissions for sale but both strategies serve the same purpose which is to circumvent the meritocracy in order to generate donations to the college. Alumni of selective colleges who have children give more to their alma mater than childless alumni and the giving increases as the children near the age of eighteen. Giving drops off after the child is accepted and declines even more sharply if the child is rejected.[49] University alumni offices understand the timing of the process and cynically exploit the dynamic to maximize the sums they extract from anxious parents.

Legacy admissions are regarded as a legal prerogative of universities although many people believe they should not be allowed at public colleges. Carlton Larson argues that the Constitution prohibits legacy preferences at public universities through its nobility clauses. In separate clauses, the Constitution bars the federal government and the states from granting titles of nobility. The clauses reflect a principle that the Constitution's framers believed fundamental to the ideals of the American Revolution. John Adams wrote in 1788, "legal distinctions, titles, powers and privileges are not hereditary." *The New York Times* quotes Larson in an interview arguing that public universities "have always been, much more than private universities, engines of upward mobility." As a matter of policy, principle and constitutional law, he said, they should not be handing out benefits "based solely on ancestry."[50]

Codevilla believes that the French meritocracy has more legitimacy than the U.S. system. "To see something closer to an academic meritocracy consider France, where elected officials have little power, a vast bureaucracy explicitly controls details from how babies are raised to how to make cheese, and *people get into and advance in that bureaucracy strictly by competitive exams.* Hence for good or ill, France's ruling classes are bright people – certifiably." Unlike elite U.S. universities that manage admissions, "getting into the Ecole Nationale d'Administration or the Ecole Polytechnique or the dozens of other entry points to France's ruling class requires outperforming others in blindly graded exams, and graduating from such places requires passing exams that many fail."[51]

The multiple admission criteria along with legacies, donors, affirmative action, athletes, etc., certainly complicate the process for parents. One mother compares the trials and tribulations of getting a kid into an elite U.S. college as an "escalating arms race." She recounts the uncertainty along with thousands of dollars she and her husband spent on SAT tutors, *de facto* required campus visits, college counselors and test retaking, not to mention the tens of thousands of dollars expended on private school tuition for K-12. Given special admissions, she concludes that the whole process is "so unjust that it makes the House of Lords look like a New England town meeting."[52]

The real issue is not whether elite schools conform to some idealized admissions policy but whether or not the meritocracy has devolved into a more sophisticated version of Mark Twain's riverboat pilots association. Has the meritocracy become *extractive*? If growth in the collective brain drives human progress, is the current system making us collectively smarter? In a frequently referenced article in *The Atlantic* titled "The Case Against Credenitalism," James Fallows argues that there are essentially two tracks to success in American life: the entrepreneurial track or the professional meritocracy. Celebrated in the writing of Horatio Alger, with pluck and luck, the hard working, risk-taking entrepreneur competes in the market place to build a product or deliver a service that customers are willing to buy. He charts his own course and must prove himself on a daily basis. Entrepreneurs are largely unconcerned with the acquisition of credentials since their reward depends on output rather than input. Except for top managers who enjoy golden parachutes that guarantee lifetime financial security, most private sector employees whose career prospects depend on their daily production can be classified as part of the entrepreneurial class.[53]

To Fallows, the credentialed meritocracy has become synonymous with the professional class. These are the lawyers, physicians, professors, accountants, architects, upper level managers and other careers that require the acquisition of credentials as a pre-condition for entry but Fallows' definition probably does not go far enough. Also included among the "professional meritocracy" are those with lower status credentials such as teachers, civil service employees and workers whose job requires credentials as a condition of employment. The informal enforcement of credentialism is reflected in any job that establishes artificial standards by requiring a college degree or specifying that only "graduates of top tier universities" need apply. With few exceptions entry into the professional meritocracy is front-loaded, meaning that once one has obtained the appropriate credential, its maintenance becomes largely perfunctory in comparison to those who must struggle daily to survive on the entrepreneurial track. Fallows is especially contemptuous of the MBA degree which he regards as a misguided attempt to "professionalize" the entrepreneurial function.

Of course, the two-track career concept is a broad generalization. Certainly, many in the professional meritocracy work grueling hours and are required to meet demanding production schedules that are rewarded by entrepreneurial incentive systems. Some entrepreneurs may become college professors and vise versa. However, in most instances movement between the two tracks tends to be one directional. Members of the professional meritocracy have the option of becoming entrepreneurs but because of credential requirements many entrepreneurs are barred from the professional meritocracy. In most instances, there is little love lost between the respective camps.

The plague of experts largely originates among the professional meritocracy with the upper echelons of the most prestigious fields dominated by the graduates of elite universities. In contrast, most of those who work in corporate

America's entrepreneurial positions attend state universities. *The Wall Street Journal* surveyed the companies that hired over 43,000 college graduates in 2009 and found that the most sought after graduates were from large state universities with Penn State, Texas A&M and the University of Illinois topping the list. Corporate recruiters said that the graduates of these "top public universities were the most prepared and well rounded academically" and "fit well into our corporate culture." When queried why no Ivy League schools made the list, the lead researcher who is a professor at Harvard explained: "We have none of the basic bread and butter courses that serve you well in industry."[54] About 55% of Harvard graduates go on to earn a PhD and a substantial number attend a professional school. Essentially, Harvard like most elite institutions prepares their graduates to assume positions in the professional meritocracy. Outside of their MBA programs whose graduates enter consulting and finance in disproportionate numbers, the elite schools training tomorrow's leaders are largely indifferent, if not openly contemptuous of industry and commerce.

The institutional transformation that opened the doors of elite universities to women and minorities helped foster a cultural and economic renaissance that enriched our lives and spurred unparalleled prosperity, but it is not clear that the so-called meritocracy continues to foster the same economic and social dynamism. President Conant may have implemented "the big test" but he also opposed the GI bill that allowed 2.3 million WWII veterans to attend college including a half-million whose backgrounds suggested they were not college material. The Harvard President called the bill "distressing" because it did not "distinguish between those who can profit most by advanced education and those who cannot." Robert Hutchins of the University of Chicago warned that, "Colleges and universities will find themselves converted into educational hobo jungles." Fortunately, these higher education experts were ignored. Returning soldiers would distinguish themselves as more mature and academically successful than the average student.[55]

Doubts persist about a system that measures status and prestige by the number of students who are turned away. Nor can questions be dismissed as the sour grapes of losers who covet the status of their betters. William Deresiewicz argues that while there is nothing wrong with taking pride in one's intellect there is something amiss in the smugness and self-congratulation that elite schools foster among their students. "From orientation to graduation, the message is implicit in every tone of voice and tilt of the head, every old-school tradition, every article in the student paper, every speech from the dean. The message is: You have arrived. Welcome to the club. And the corollary is equally clear: You deserve everything your presence here is going to enable you to get because your SAT scores are higher." [56]

Despite the privileges an elite education bestows, Deresiewicz thinks that it can also have a corrosive influence. Getting in is tough but once you are embraced by the system there is almost nothing that you can do to get kicked out. Elite schools may nurture excellence but they also nurture a sense of "entitled mediocrity" among those who choose to simply get by: "you may not be all that good, but you're good enough." Choosing to be a teacher is perceived as "wasting" an expensive resume. It is especially distressing at the twenty-year reunion when the low status teacher has to confront former classmates who are high paid lawyers and investment bankers living in Manhattan. Better to be another mediocre Wall Street lawyer than a great high school teacher. When young adults are constantly reminded that they are special, they can become terrified of failing and more willing to embrace the conventional choice. In contrast, entrepreneurs regard resilience in the face of inevitable failure as a learning opportunity rather than a risk that should be avoided at all cost.

Highly selective schools pride themselves on their diversity but it is almost entirely a matter of ethnicity and race. Class boundaries persist among student enrollments that are increasingly homogeneous. The *Century Foundation* estimated that only 3 percent of freshman at elite colleges came from the bottom socioeconomic quartile, compared to 74 percent from the top quartile.[57] Social separation along with growing income inequality has become a pervasive element of American life. In a *Saturday Night Live* skit titled *What's That Name,* two members of the professional meritocracy are game show contestants; the first is a CFO and the second a law partner. They know the names of the guy in the *Subway* sandwich commercial and the second lead in the movie *Saving Silverman* but despite several years in the same apartment and work place don't know the names of "Norman the doorman" in their building or Mary who cleans their office. The subtext of the comedy skit is clear: my position derives from personal merit, so why should I bother with non-meritorious persons in low status jobs?

Still relatively rare, friendships across social class seem to be more common among those on the entrepreneurial track. Members of the professional meritocracy are more likely to have a social life that is an extension of their career network. Local chapters of national credential cartels frequently congregate at conferences in resort locations to discuss career concerns as well as methods to protect and promote their professional status. Unlike members of the professional meritocracy, the social life of entrepreneurs is less likely to be an extension of their career network. Entrepreneurs identify more closely with employees and customers; their peers are often viewed as hostile competitors.

No one wishes to return to the misogynistic ways of yester year but "assortative mating" is partly responsible for the greater social segmentation. In 1970 only 9% of those with a bachelor degree were women, so the vast majority of men with a college education married women without a college degree. Today the proportion of women earning college degrees is greater than men and the increase in female participation in the labor force reflects the trend. Since people tend to marry those with similar educational background, it reinforces inequality in household income and contributes to social separation. In the last thirty years there has also been a sharp increase in the number of children born outside marriage. Depending on the time period examined, as much as 20 to 40 percent of the observed increase in income inequality can be attributed to an increase in single parent households. Small towns tend to have greater social class interaction in church and school but their numbers have declined relative to sprawling urban suburbs that sort themselves by home real estate values. Changes in workplace technology and the elimination of mandatory military conscription have also reduced social class interaction.

THE GALES OF CREATIVE DESTRUCTION

Fallows believes that meritocracy fosters an insular, "play it safe" approach to life: "From college and graduate school I know lawyers, consultants, and analysts aplenty, but few people who have started their own businesses or created jobs for anyone beside themselves." Very few professionals become truly rich but rarely do they fall from the top tier of American society. "In addition to depressing the "unmeritorious" a meritocracy can corrupt its professionals, making them care more about keeping what they have than creating something new." He asks whether American society can afford "a swelling class whose chief ambition is one day to "make partner?"[58]

The answer to Fallows question is "probably not," but even socio-economic systems that are fatally flawed can limp along indefinitely. Despite the brutality of the system, Soviet society functioned at a reasonably high level of performance throughout WWII as well as the early post war years and was even able to launch the first satellite into space—creating what President Obama described as "a Sputnik moment" in America. Social trust, particularly among Russians old enough to remember life under the Czar, was still sufficiently high to warrant behavior consistent with the collective welfare. However, by the 1970s corruption was endemic. The old ideologues were dying, social trust was eroding and replaced by a collective cynicism. Communist party members became the new elite and took advantage of their status to plunder the system. By the time the Berlin Wall fell in 1989, any residual social dynamism derived from Marxist ideology had long since dissipated.

Countries with top-down extractive political and economic institutions like the former Soviet Union, can experience high growth rates in the early years by shifting resources from a less productive sector like agriculture to a more productive industrial sector. Much of the economic growth in China likely derives from a similar redeployment of resources. However, once the gains from reallocation are realized, societies with top-down institutions do a very poor job creating additional wealth. Communism was destined to fail because there was no self-correcting mechanism to replace the old and worn out with the new and vibrant. The decline of the British Empire coincides with a leadership class that disdained commerce and industry. Similarly, the WASP establishment contributed mightily to the economic growth of the late 19th and early 20th centuries but had grown complacent with their place in society. Has the dynamism of the meritocracy been replaced by a credentialed miasma?

In 1917, *Forbes* constructed a list of the top 100 U.S. companies based on asset size since market capitalization was not available and they republished the list in 1987. Sixty-one of the firms on the original list no longer existed. Of the thirty-nine remaining companies only eighteen were able to remain among the top 100 firms in asset size. As a group, the 1918-1987 returns for the thirty-nine surviving firms were 20% less than the market. Only two companies, Eastman Kodak and General Electric, beat the market. Unable to transition easily into the digital age, Eastman Kodak has since sold many of its patents and filed for bankruptcy while GE Credit Corporation was a major beneficiary of the government engineered bank bailout. The transformation that occurred in the Forbes 100 also applies to other indices such as the Dow and the S&P500. Of the five hundred companies included in the 1957 S&P index, only seventy-four remained in 1997 and only twelve out-performed the index for 1957-1998.[59]

Joseph Shumpeter referred to this process of company birth and death as "the gales of creative destruction." Markets facilitate a sometime painful process that replaces ossifying companies in decline with vibrant upstarts in a continuous cycle of renewal. In contrast, mechanisms of creative destruction among not-for-profit organizations and institutions often appear minimal or even non-existent partly because they have learned how to use government to secure their status. Since 1957, turnover in the S&P500 was on the order of approximately 85% while the top fifty elite universities today are pretty much the same as the 1957 top fifty. Extractive institutions can still be productive but they also tend to be very much concerned with maintaining the *status quo* rather than cultivating creative alternatives that jeopardize their status.

Sixteen of the top universities in the country have joined a venture that provides free Internet courses worldwide through a for-profit company called Coursera. The schools began offering 111 mostly introductory courses in the summer of 2012. Initially, the classes will not offer credit though some of the participating schools may award certificates for successful completion. Co-founder of Coursera, Andrew Ng said, "It gets us one step closer to where anyone in the world can have a connection to the best universities."[60] The best students deserve more than just an Internet "connection." Online technology now makes it possible for millions of deserving students to gain low cost access to elite university degree programs. Unfortunately, there is no incentive for elite schools to open the virtual door and voluntarily surrender their credential cartel.

Codevilla goes further than either Fallows or Deresiewicz when he writes, "Our ruling class recruits and renews itself *not* through meritocracy but rather by taking into itself people whose most prominent feature is their commitment to fit in" thus does it "stunt itself through negative selection. But the more it has dumbed itself down, the more it has defined itself by the presumption of intellectual superiority."[61]

"Fitting in" and being a "team player" may be a condition of entry and continued membership but the professional meritocracy, as represented by credential cartels like the American Medical Association, The American Association of Trial Lawyers, the American Federation of Teachers and many others, has proven to be very clever at extracting "economic rent" from the political process. It is no accident that the four richest counties in the U.S. surround Washington DC or that politics has become more of a family business. Since John Quincy Adams, politicians with the same surname have been a feature of the political landscape but elective office is becoming even more of a legacy enterprise. In 1986, at least 24 U.S. Senators or Representatives were closely related to governors or other members of Congress; by 2006, there were more than 50.[62] Like the brand recognition associated with *Taco Bell* or *Subway,* names such as Kennedy, Bush, Gore, Romney, Clinton, Paul, etc., have become family political franchises. Concern over franchise value can prevent brand owners from making unpopular choices or influence decisions in other ways. Ron Paul probably declined to run as the Libertarian candidate because he didn't want to jeopardize the political fortunes of his son and Bush Junior's decision to invade Iraq was likely colored by Bush Senior's first Gulf War. Like Hollywood's dependence on sequels, political legacies and the power of incumbency reveal a lack of creative destruction in the elective process.

A large share of educational resources is devoted to the production of experts within the professional meritocracy. Yet, the bumper crop of expertise has failed to reverse the upward drift in education and healthcare costs or America's declining competitive advantage in a variety of industries. The U.S. now ranks near the bottom of developed nations in measures of social mobility between generations. Stiglitz points out that three quarters of Danes born in the lowest earning 20% of the population go on to escape poverty in adulthood. In supposedly class conscious Britain, seven out of ten children accomplish the same feat; however, in the U.S. fewer than six out of ten do so. In America, it is much less common for children born into the lowest economic quintile to move to the top quintile than it is in Britain or Denmark.[63]

The income "churning" frequently used by economists to measure the dynamic nature of American society occurs to a much greater extent among entrepreneurs and other private sector business and industrial workers. Like the tenured professors who compile the churning data, the experts who reside within the professional meritocracy are largely sheltered from creative destruction or other self renewing mechanisms. Whether or not we choose to recognize it, systems that fail to foster internal renewal will experience externally imposed change. The process of creative destruction applies not just to companies but also to leadership networks, institutions and nations.

The Arab Spring began when a young street vendor in Tunisia set himself on fire because the police confiscated his scales and fined him more than a month's earnings for selling vegetables without a license. In September 2012, heavily armed terrorists in Libya used the cover of a religious protest over a *You Tube* video to murder the American ambassador. Riots spread to other Middle East countries like Egypt where unemployment among young men is estimated to be 50%. Weak local leaders responded half-heartedly to the demonstrations because they would rather have these idle young men demonstrating against the U.S. than their own bankrupt and fragile regimes. Many countries like Egypt spent heavily on higher education but it did not translate into economic growth or boost employment. Credentials without opportunity only exacerbate frustration.

Given current growth rates in GDP, China will surpass the U.S. in 2018 to become the world's largest economy. Despite uncertainty surrounding the future of the euro, the status of the dollar as the world's dominant "reserve currency" will continue to decline imposing greater fiscal constraint on the American economy. The economic and political stature of the European Union is unlikely to be restored any time soon causing the U.S. to shift more of its attention to Asia. Indications of a new global order that have long been in evidence have accelerated. In the five years from 2005 to 2010, the U.S. share of publicly traded equity in world financial markets shrank from 45% to 24%. In this new order, output will matter more than input. Rather than rationing opportunity based on credentials, the global economy will reward countries with a more flexible and liberalized work force that are able to enfranchise and economically exploit the total stock of human capital within and between national borders.

When large numbers of young men avoid serving in a bloody and dangerous war because they are the recipients of "college deferments," it cannot help but tarnish the image of an unbiased meritocracy. Affirmative action, admissions for sale and legacy admissions have had a similar corrosive effect. The meritocracy is still alive but if the U.S. economy fails to return to the growth path of previous decades, many young people who played by the rules and assumed large student loans in a bid to join the middle-class will find it tough going. Even lower status jobs such as teacher and civil service worker will become much more competitive. As admission to the professional meritocracy becomes more expensive, arbitrary and credential driven, the system will be subjected to more intense criticism and the public trust in the model, especially among the young, will dissipate.

If America is to restore its social dynamism, avoid growing income inequality and reverse the dominance of an increasingly extractive and calcifying "credentialed elite," it must once again nurture bottom-up mechanisms of creative destruction among the professional and leadership class.

CHAPTER 3

THE LIBERAL TRADITION:
NO COUNTRY FOR OLD EXPERTS (OR YOUNG ONES)

When it comes to creating new knowledge, bottom-up liberal science has zero tolerance for top-down expert opinion. But before the skeptics revolutionized critical inquiry, Plato believed that only the cognitive elite could be trusted to sort through new ideas and judge which ones should be discarded versus those that should be added to the growing body of human knowledge. Since only a very few were deemed intellectually fit enough to join the fraternity of sorters, the vast majority of the population played no role in the process and were expected to defer to the judgment of their betters. In *The Republic*, Plato argued that the ruling class's personal interests should be subjugated to the good of the state, which would be charged with controlling marriage, procreation and carrying out a policy of euthanasia to preserve genetic purity. Private property and family would be abolished and children would be raised collectively "so that we can count on their being free from the dissentions that arise among men from the possession of property, children and kin."[1]

In an effort to instill the appropriate values, Plato believed the state must exert strict control over speech and written communication, including poetry and music. In addition to the censorship of speech and writing, all artists and craftsmen would have their work vetted by the appropriate authorities. But who should head the state? Only eminent philosophers "are capable of apprehending that which is eternal and unchanging, while those who are incapable of this, but lose themselves and wander amid the multiplicities of multifarious things, are not philosophers."[2] Plato believed that only people like himself could discriminate between true knowledge and the false knowledge propagated by the mass of conflicting opinion. "To them by their very nature belong the study of philosophy and political leadership, while it befits the other sort to let philosophy alone and follow their leadership."[3] The "motley hoard" that wishes to participate but fails to meet Plato's standard would only disrupt the ship of state and must be "compulsorily excluded."

It is not surprising that people would be inclined to depend on a wise and benevolent leader to ferret out truth in our ongoing attempts to make sense of the objective world. As modern man knows all too well, the clash of ideas and beliefs can cause social strife that will ultimately consume "a house divided." A sober leader can reconcile differences and prevent minor disputes from escalating into major conflicts. He acts as a referee to monitor and preserve some ideas and discard others.

Of course, the problem with such an arrangement is that the wise and benevolent leader is likely to be wrong part of the time; in which case, truth may be assigned to the trash bin while falsehoods grow and multiply. Skeptics, including Socrates, recognized the problem inherent in Plato's model, but throughout much of history, critics were constrained by authoritarian rulers or the dominance of Divine Will as represented by the Church. Fissures appeared when Martin Luther declared that all Christians, not just those at the top of the church hierarchy, were granted the power to judge right from wrong in matters of faith. Long quieted over the years, skepticism reemerged in the 17th and 18th centuries in the writings of Descartes, Hume, Locke and others.

Skepticism as it is applied to liberal science does not require that we refrain from reaching conclusions based on available knowledge; it only requires we recognize that our conclusions may be wrong and subject to correction. All knowledge is tentative and even the smartest among us is likely to be wrong part of the time. Since even Plato's wise philosopher is subject to error, the skeptical school of thought dethroned forever the authoritarian top-down interpretation of how knowledge accumulates. When the skeptical ethic is extended from liberal science to social interaction, the principle of public criticism emerges. If all of us err, then all disagreements concerning the objective world must be exposed to ongoing scrutiny and no dispute is permanently settled. If a society accepts skeptical principles then sincere criticism is always legitimate.

Jonathon Rauch summarizes the liberal model this way: "If any belief may be wrong, then no one can legitimately claim to have ended any discussion—ever. In other words: **No one gets final say**." There is a second conclusion that follows from the first: "If any person may be in error, then no one can legitimately claim to be above being checked by others—ever." If anyone can be wrong then no one has "any unique or personal powers to decide who is right or wrong. In other words: **No one has personal authority**."[4] These two principles formed the foundation for liberal science. Other principles such as consistency and parsimony are also characterized as criteria to be applied to the construction of any hypothesis but are considered to be of lesser importance.

Initially, it might appear that the rules create more confusion than they resolve; if no one gets final say and no one has personal authority, then how can we distinguish "right" from "wrong"? It may be impossible to demonstrate *certain* knowledge but *uncertain* knowledge, knowledge that is false, is readily apparent. The physicist Freeman Dyson wrote:

"The Royal Society of London in 1660 proudly took as its motto the phrase *Nullius in Verba*, meaning 'No man's word shall be final.' The assertion of papal infallibility, even in questions of faith and morals having nothing to do with science, grates harshly upon a scientist's ear. We scientists are by training and temperament jealous of our freedom. We do not in principle allow any statement whatever to be immune from doubt."[5]

Compared to Plato's expert philosopher, our experience of the previous two-and-half centuries of *Nullius in Verba* has revealed a system for accumulating knowledge and resolving disputes that outperforms all others by a country mile. It would be difficult to challenge Rauch's assertion that these rules are two of the most successful social conventions that have ever evolved.

The skeptical rule that *no one gets final say* renders all knowledge provisional; a statement becomes knowledge only if it withstands attempts to discredit it, a process frequently referred to as falsification. Liberal science does not attempt to prove statements are true but to systematically disprove false ones. In practice, it may be quite difficult or impossible to falsify a statement but the rule requires action; we are bound to make an effort. "If you do not try to check ideas by trying to debunk them, then you are not practicing science," you are doing something else.[6] Even principles that are most revered because they have withstood checking still remain tentative, no matter how much time has passed.

Rauch refers to the second rule of liberal science as the empirical rule: *no one has personal authority*. No matter how sincere, sympathetic or certain one might be, everyone is held to the same standard regardless of their reputation or stature in society. A statement can claim to be established as knowledge "only insofar as the method used to check it gives the same result regardless of the identity of the checker, and regardless of the source of the statement." No one enjoys an exalted status: "The views of experts, no less than those of laymen, are expected to withstand checking."[7]

When liberal science is practiced correctly, it is a powerful mechanism in the advancement of human knowledge and one of our best defenses against the plague of experts; unfortunately, it is not always practiced correctly. In 1998, a British physician named Andrew Wakefield published a paper in the prestigious medical journal *Lancet*. The paper claimed that the measles-mumps-rubella (MMR) vaccine may cause autism. Dr. Wakefield's study involved eight children who developed symptoms of autism one month after receiving their MMR shots. He hypothesized that the measles vaccine virus causes intestinal damage that allowed brain damaging proteins to enter the bloodstream of the children. Needless to say, Dr. Wakefield's "study" did not meet modern standards of scientific testing. Clearly, he should have examined a much larger sample of children who did and did not receive the MMR vaccine, a methodology that has been employed by more than a dozen subsequent studies carried out by independent researchers around the world. None of the subsequent research found a link between the MMR vaccine and autism.[8]

Later investigation revealed that some of the eight children in Dr. Wakefield's study developed symptoms of autism before receiving the vaccine while others never actually developed autism. A UK reporter found that Dr. Wakefield had accepted large sums of money from a personal injury lawyer who was involved in law suits against pharmaceutical companies. When *Lancet* found out about the payments, the journal retracted his paper but the damage had already been done.

Thousands of parents in Britain and Ireland chose not to vaccinate their children based on the publicity generated by Dr. Wakefield's study and hundreds of children were subsequently hospitalized. In 2008, for the first time in more than a decade, measles was declared endemic in England and Wales and at least four unvaccinated children were reported to have died from measles. In the U.S., there have been epidemics of mumps, measles, whooping cough and bacterial meningitis following parental decisions not to vaccinate children. California experienced the largest whooping cough epidemic in the U.S. in more than a half century.

Jenny McCarthy, a Hollywood celebrity and the mother of an autistic son, wrote a book and formed an organization known as Generation Rescue that promoted Dr. Wakefield's hypothesis. Pandering to public fascination with celebrities, the popular media helped to publicize the discredited vaccine/autism connection and bears some of the blame for the consequences.[9] But it is the editors of *Lancet* that shoulder the greatest responsibility. Wakefield's paper was sent to six referees, four of whom rejected it; however, the editors still decided that the paper was provocative and published it despite the majority decision of the reviewers. Consistent with liberal science, the premise that the MMR vaccine does *not* cause autism remains tentative knowledge despite the accumulated evidence. Dr. Wakefield was eventually stripped of his license to practice medicine. Ms. McCarthy's celebrity status does not grant her personal authority in autism research but it does cause the popular media to disseminate her opinions much more widely than someone less celebrated, even when she is wrong. Despite the growing body of evidence to the contrary, liberal science *would not* and *should not* discourage Ms. McCarthy and her organization from supporting *legitimate* inquiry in a *responsible* effort to debunk the research that debunked Wakefield's hypothesis.

A fair system of "checking" would evaluate any new research on the vaccine/autism connection and publish or reject it depending on its merit, but what happens when the system of peer review is called into question? Austin Smith and Robin Lovell-Badge, both scientists conducting stem-cell research, went to the BBC with their complaint that the process of peer review is frequently unfair and corrupted. They charged that much flawed and inconsequential research is published and promoted while more substantive and imaginative work can be delayed indefinitely or even rejected. This happens because some scientists working in the same field will attempt to sabotage their competitors in an effort to be first in the publication of important findings[10]

When journal referees reject or accept papers based more on politics or careerism than merit, liberal science is threatened. The "Climategate" scandal resulting from the disclosure of hacked emails at the Climate Research Unit of the University of East Anglia in the UK reveals the degree to which ideology can creep into science. Certainly, receding ice and temperature data for the last century support global warming but some of the evidence has been miscon-strued in an irresponsible manner. In 2009, The U.N. Intergovernmental Panel on Climate Change retracted their forecast that the Himalayan glaciers would disappear in a few decades. It turns out that there was no scientific evidence supporting the original estimate. Such apocalyptic projections may energize a part of the climate science base, as they say in politics, but they do nothing to advance our understanding of global warming and its causes. Hyperbole has no place in science and in this case only served to provide ammunition to those who deny the planet is warming.

Michael Mann, author of *The Hockey Stick and the Climate Wars,* has been at the center of the climate debate for the last fifteen years. In 1998 and 1999, Professor Mann published research papers that included a graph of global tem-peratures for the last 1,000 years. The illustration took the shape of a "hockey stick" showing relatively stable temperatures up until the 20th century when they began to rise, primarily as a consequence of carbon emissions caused by humans. Professor Mann has been a leading advocate for immediate reduc-tions in U.S. carbon emissions and global cap and trade.

"Hockey stick" skeptics argue that attempts to establish statistically significant trends in temperature from proxy data can be exceedingly difficult and that, given the significant economic consequences of some climate policy proposals, such research should be subjected to rigorous scrutiny. Mathematical models of time series data can be exceedingly sensitive to model specification. Projections may be even more suspect when most of the time series observations are proxy estimates derived from historical documents such as letters and private dia-ries along with "paleoclimatology" estimates gathered from analyses of tree rings, fossil pollen, sediments, corals and ice cores.[11] This does not mean that proxy temperature data are incorrect or provide no information content. Such data should be interpreted with caution relative to the 140 years of recorded temperatures, at least until its accuracy can be more precisely validated, since small errors in the data and model specification can have a large impact on the precision of climate forecasts.

The burning of fossil fuels has increased CO_2 levels in the atmosphere from pre-industrial levels of 280 parts per million to the current readings of 395; but there is disagreement over the extent of the detrimental effects of CO_2 levels since life on earth has flourished at much higher levels than those existing today. Complicating matters is disagreement on the exact relationship between CO_2 levels and global temperatures. Some scientists estimate that direct warming due to a doubling of CO_2 levels in the atmosphere will increase global warming by one degree Celsius. The United Nations Intergovernmental Panel on Climate Change (IPCC) predicts three times that amount and even more since their computer model also assumes that changes in water vapor or clouds amplify the direct warming from CO_2 in a positive feedback loop, an effect that may be exaggerated. There appears to be a widespread consensus among scientists that global temperatures have increased by about one degree Celsius since the "little ice age" of the early 1800's but decomposing how much of the increase can be blamed on rising CO_2 levels attributed to man, is still subject to disagreement since temperatures were already rising before large increases in CO_2 emissions occurred. [12]

Over the last ten years, the warming trend predicted by the IPCC model failed to materialize leading some to suggest that rising CO_2 has caused weather patterns to become more "extreme" despite little hard evidence supporting this assertion. The winter of 2010 was very cold but it was followed by an unusually warm 2011 winter in the continental United States while winter temperatures in the U.S. were unseasonably mild, it was a bitterly cold winter in Europe, Asia and Alaska. Drought conditions have afflicted the Midwest and Plains States in the summer of 2012 but many parts of the country experienced heavy rainfall. Ubiquitous CNN and Weather Channel footage of hurricane and tornado damage might suggest to the casual viewer that the extreme weather hypothesis has merit; but Andrew Revkin of the *New York Times Blog*, dotearth.com claims that "there is no evidence of any trend in the number of potent tornadoes (category F2 and up) over the past 50 years in the United States, even as global temperatures have risen markedly." [13]

Some maintain that the climate debate has been politicized because the stakes are so high and that "bad" science is a consequence of both sides pandering to a largely uninformed public audience; but the rise in fraudulent or inaccurate science is independent of the acrimony surrounding the global warming debate. The total number of articles published in scholarly journals has surged over the last dozen years but so have the number of retractions. [14] Between 2006 and 2010, medical journals experienced the largest number of retractions followed by biology and chemistry with some of the most prestigious journals experiencing some of the highest numbers. The time between publication and retraction has also been lengthening from an average of 5.25 months in 2002 to 31.6 months in 2009.[15] Current research builds on the past so that when an article is retracted it calls into question all subsequent studies that have incorporated findings from the retracted paper. Millions of dollars in research can be wasted and, in some instances, has resulted in the loss of life. In one prominent example at the Mayo Clinic, a decade of cancer research that was partly funded by taxpayers was essentially wasted when seventeen research papers published in nine scholarly journals were retracted.[16]

Some see the increase in retractions as a "glass half full" proposition—arguing that critics and journals are doing a better job of rooting out mistakes partly because of the increased use of computer software that makes it easier to check for plagiarism and other factual violations. Still others maintain that publication in the more prestigious journals can make or break a career and so there is a temptation to fudge results even at the risk of getting caught. Honest mistakes occur but there has also been a marked increase in fraud over the last decade. One study that examined a sample of 742 withdrawn papers in the medical field found that nearly 27% were retracted due to fraud by the authors.[17] Some partly blame the surge in retractions on ambitious journal editors who hope to further their own careers by publishing papers with spectacular results in an attempt to make their journal appear "cutting edge" and on the research frontier—an attitude that renders them more susceptible to high-risk papers. On the other hand, a "low risk" editorial policy often results in accepting papers only from established "experts," an editorial approach that comes close to granting personal authority based on credentialism.

The scramble by scientific journals to extend their influence has caused many to try and "game" the system that is partly responsible for ranking their status. A ranking measure that quantifies the number of journal citations known as the Impact Factor (IF) ranking has been around for more than fifty years and serves as a relatively straight forward method for ranking scientific journals. The IF is used by professors to help determine the most significant articles in their area and by university tenure/promotion committees as an indicator of quality. Thomson Reuters publishes the IF and calculates it by dividing the number of citations of research papers in a given journal in one year by the total number of papers published in the same journal over the previous two years. While the IF quantifies the citation rate of a journal over the previous two years, it does not vouch for the veracity or quality of individual manuscripts.

Despite the shortcomings, the IF is frequently used as a mechanism to grade scientists; institutions in some countries offer bonuses to those who publish in journals with a favorable IF rating. Some scientists believe that such incentives reward fashionable research and may divert articles away from journals more appropriate for the issue under investigation but have a less favorable IF. More disturbing is that the IF can be manipulated by journals in a manner that artificially increases their rating. Editors frequently request that citations appearing in their journal be cited in a submitted paper as a condition of acceptance even if the citations are related to the topic in a tangential manner.[18] Thomson Reuters recently penalized *Scientific World Journal* and *Cell Transplantation* with a two-year suspension for artificially manipulating their IF rating. *Scientific World Journal* retracted two papers on regenerative medicine because the authors excessively cited *Cell Transplantation* in a manner that was intended to pump up the latter journal's rating. A writer at the science blog, *The Scholarly Kitchen*, noted that a review article in another journal had 490 article citations with 445 from *Cell Transplantation* alone thereby raising its IF rating by 21%. *Cell Transplantation* is not the worst offender; between 2009 and 2010 the *Journal of Biomolecular Structural Dynamics* increased its IF rating from 1.0 to 5.0 largely because of self-citations.[19]

Academics in a number of disciplines reported being coerced by editors to pad their papers with non-essential citations of articles appearing in the same journal.[20] The problem has become serious enough that the Australian government announced that it would no longer use the IF in evaluating grant applications. It's not just about science anymore; grants and patent applications that can generate billions of dollars in licensing fees can influence scientists desperate to keep labs open and research assistants working, not to mention filling their own bank accounts. For those who would give scientists a pass on the pervasive self-interest that afflicts the rest of us, think again.

The threat to liberal science as a consequence of misguided celebrity, fraud, incompetent peer review, manipulated IF and lack of editorial oversight are serious, but manageable compared to what Rauch calls the Fundamentalist and Humanitarian Threats.[21] The threats discussed above occur around the edges as a consequence of a lapse in vigilance; the bottom-up core principles of "no one gets final say" and "no one has personal authority" remain intact. In contrast, the Fundamentalist and Humanitarian Threats represent a top-down assault on core principles. The fact that these threats originate among people who are essentially motivated by good intentions does not render them any less dangerous.

The debate surrounding the teaching of creationism/intelligent design versus natural selection in public schools is the most familiar example of the Fundamentalist threat. "Intelligent design" or ID was conceived as a strategy to circumvent court rulings which found that the teaching of "creation science" in public schools violated constitutional principles regarding the separation of church and state. Variations of the phrase "intelligent design" can be found among the writings of creationist authors in the 1960s but the principle itself can be traced to the 13th century writing of St. Thomas Aquinas who framed his argument for the existence of God as a syllogism. To paraphrase St. Thomas: complex systems require a designer; nature is complex; therefore, nature must have an intelligent designer. The first modern and systematic presentation of ID, as distinct from creationism, is attributed to a 1989 biology textbook called *Of Pandas and People* that was intended for use in public high schools and published with the support of the Discovery Institute.[22] Charles Thaxton, the editor of *Of Pandas and People*, claimed to have borrowed the phrase "intelligent design" from a NASA scientist because it sounded like "a good engineering term" that conveys the impression of technical sophistication.[23]

In the 2005 decision *Kitzmiller vs. Dover Area School District*, the court rejected ID and barred it from being taught in the Pennsylvania middle district public school science classes. It is noteworthy that the leaders of the movement have attempted to frame the public debate as an example of liberal science falling victim to an activist judge. The associate director of the Center for Science and Culture at the Discovery Institute was quoted as saying:

"The Dover decision is an attempt by an activist federal judge to stop the spread of a scientific idea and even to prevent criticism of Darwinian evolution through government-imposed censorship rather than open debate, and it won't work. He has conflated Discovery Institute's position with that of the Dover school board, and he totally misrepresents intelligent design and the motivations of the scientists who research it."[24]

Of course, the charge fails the smell test. ID advocates have yet to publish a single peer reviewed research article in a scientific journal. The reason is clear, as explained by the court: ID fails the two most basic tests of liberal science. The ruling states that ID "is not *falsifiable*" since its existence is typically asserted without sufficient conditions to allow a falsifying observation. "The designer being beyond the realm of the observable, claims about its existence can be neither supported nor undermined by observation."[25] The decision goes on to state that "intelligent design is not a *provisional* assessment of data, which can change when new information is discovered. Once it is claimed that a conclusion that need not be accounted for has been established; there is simply no possibility of future correction."[26] In the science of ID, God is granted both personal authority and final say, a circumstance that is acceptable for a *belief* system but not a *knowledge* system. Rather than play the science game, advocates of ID seek to establish their arguments by alternative venues such as lobbying public opinion, political donations and legal challenges.

The Humanitarian threat originates on the opposite side of the political spectrum from the Fundamentalists but it is no less worrisome. Similar to the creationists, radical humanists approach their task with a devotion that can border on the religious. Paul Rubin makes the case that one sect of this movement, radical environmentalists, display the fervor and *a priori* beliefs that render it very similar to religion. He notes the following traits shared by religion and radical environmentalism:

A Holy Day—Earth Day

Food Taboos—Instead of fish on Friday or avoiding pork, Greens eat organic foods or only locally grown food.

Self-sacrificing Rituals—The debate over the benefits/costs of recycling are ongoing but in the long-run, recycling to save trees may actually reduce the number planted.

Conflicting Belief Systems—Greens embrace belief systems without logical basis such as acceptance of the dangers of global warming but rejection of the best solution to the problem, which is nuclear power. Beliefs that co-exist based on faith rather than reason.

Proselytizing—Environmental skeptics are not merely people with a different opinion but often portrayed by Greens as infidels. [27]

Rubin lists other similarities but you get the picture. He maintains that environmentalism like religion has creation stories and ideas of original sin; and like religion, it also provides its adherents an identity within a larger group. Evolutionary psychologists believe that in addition to explaining our origins—albeit in non-scientific terms—religion can fulfill our need to belong to a "tribe" which is an innate part of evolved human nature. The universal God of modern religion has replaced individual tribal gods. As self-identification with religion has become less pervasive, people have substituted alternative "tribal creating identities" that lead them to "define themselves as being Green rather than being Christian or Jewish." [28]

Rubin's comparison may be partly satirical but it does illustrate an important point concerning the humanist threat: similar to the Fundamentalists, it follows a *belief* system rather than a knowledge system. Like the Fundamentalists, the Humanists have tried to promote their political agenda within the educational system; but unlike Fundamentalists, they have enjoyed considerably more success. A survey of environmental education by the Arizona Institute of Public Policy Research found that much of the environmental curricula used in public schools are written by political advocacy groups and concluded that "unbiased materials are a rare exception."[29] Even science textbooks from mainstream publishers tend to take an activist rather than scientific approach to environmentalism. When textbooks combined science class with social studies in interdisciplinary programs for fifth graders, science was subjugated to the interests of "diversity politics" and "global interdependence." [30]

The multicultural agenda has on occasion promoted dubious historical revisionism, such as Afro-centrism as well as "hate speech" restrictions that can compromise first amendment rights and have a chilling effect on discourse.[31] Some of the more exclusive groups on college campuses are those whose expertise partly derives from their multicultural standing. In some fields, professors who possess an appropriate multicultural credential occupy an exalted status since they are presumed to be imbued with greater insight into the cultural milieu that pertains to their respective identity group vis-a-vie the oppressive tradition of Western civilization. Being a *bona fide* minority can be a valuable trump card but the moral high ground can be forfeited if one's ethnic credentials are found to be false.

Elizabeth Warren, a Harvard University law professor, was listed by the University as a minority faculty member on the basis of her claim that she is one-sixteenth Cherokee Indian. When her Indian ancestry and minority status was questioned, Ms. Warren initially denied self-identifying as a Native American and Harvard dismissed any assertion that her ethnicity played a role in her hiring. Professor Warren later admitted that she listed herself as a Native American in the American Association of Law Schools Directory because she hoped to "meet others like me," i.e., one-sixteenth Native American, Ivy League law school professors who earns in the mid six-figure range.[32] Professor Warren was absolved of her multicultural misstep and went on to run for the U.S. Senate. Ward Churchill was not so fortunate. Another member of the academic "Wanabee Tribe", Professor Churchill also claimed Native American ancestry. Best known for calling 9/11 World Trade Center bombing victims "little Eichmanns" and referring to the attacks as "chickens coming home to roost," Churchill parlayed a master's degree in communications from Saginaw State into a full professorship and chair of the Ethnic Studies Department at the University of Colorado before being fired. Ostensibly, he was terminated for committing plagiarism but his supporters claim it was for expressing controversial opinions about 9/11.[33] Many in the University community defended Churchill's assertion that his firing violated academic freedom; but his support quickly evaporated and his moral status as an expert in ethnic culture was withdrawn shortly after the discovery that his Native American credential was fabricated. [34]

On the heels of the Civil Rights Movement and the Vietnam War, campus radicals argued for a more "relevant" course of study. Higher education's response to political demands was to create an essentially political curriculum that presumes to represent those disenfranchised from a male dominated Eurocentric culture. In addition to now familiar fields such as African-American Studies, Chicano Studies and Women's Studies, young scholars are blazing new trails in the cutting-edge fields of White Studies, Disability Studies and Fat Studies.[35] A defining principle of such identity scholarship is that all facets of human nature should be examined through the lens of group politics in a world divided between oppressors and victims. Anyone can pursue identity studies but only official members of the respective groups can fully comprehend the brutality and nuance of genuine victimhood. In his book *The Victim's Revolution*, Bawer notes that for the people who choose to study these fields it's "all about personal pain, personal confession, personal grievance" rather than shared experience.[36] Special insight into the human condition cannot be conferred by virtue of ethnicity, race or gender no matter how genuine or sincere the feeling of personal injury. To quote Locke: "The strength of our persuasions is no evidence at all of their own rectitude."[37] Not surprisingly, the Brahmins of the identity movement do not feel constrained by Locke's warning nor by the liberal tradition. Bawer points out that much of what passes as contemporary Women's Studies denounces objective knowledge and rationality as "masculinist" oppression. He quotes one prominent textbook author who cautions students to resist men's "separate knowing" that demands "the mastery of relevant knowledge and methodology."[38]

The skeptical revolution that enshrined liberal science was really a gradual evolution involving countless persons who struggled from one proposition to the next in a valiant effort to enhance our understanding of the objective world. When the rules of science are extended to the broader culture, they establish an environment of liberal democracy and public criticism. Locke never explicitly connected his philosophy of knowledge with politics but the link is obvious. To Locke "good men are men still liable to mistakes, and are sometimes warmly engaged in errors, which they take for divine truths, shining in their minds with the clearest light."[39] Locke goes on to ask "for where is the man that has incontestable evidence of the truth of all that he holds, or of the falsehood of all he condemns?"[40] If the wise and good men of science must subject themselves to relentless checking by others, then kings and rulers who are no more perfect should be required to do the same. Just as a system of open criticism and endless correction can be used to further science, a similar model could be applied in the public domain to sort able leaders and worthy ideas from the less able and unworthy among them.

More than anyone else, Locke is responsible for enshrining rule by law instead of rule by person. Despite Locke's death three quarters of a century before the American Revolution, the reference to the "long train of abuses" detailed in the Declaration of Independence was taken verbatim from his Second Treatise. The Declaration also borrows from Locke's "state of nature" idea that declares all men equal with the right to "life, health, liberty or possessions" which the Founding Fathers would paraphrase as "life, liberty and pursuit of happiness." In his Letters Concerning Toleration, Locke formulated his classic liberal argument for religious tolerance and it was this idea along with his defense of natural rights that most influenced the First Amendment in the fledgling Republic's *Bill of Rights*: "Congress shall make no law respecting an establishment of religion, or prohibiting the free exercise thereof; or abridging the freedom of speech of the press; or the right of the people peaceably to assemble, and to petition the government for the redress of grievances."

Like propositions in science, the laws of a democracy are tentative and subject to repeal or amendment but only after following a rigorous process. Whether one is a prince of industry or the village pauper; anyone can participate and no one gets more than a single vote. Those who win elections deserve our respect but their status derives not from their personal authority but from the office and the people they represent. Elective turnover strengthens democracy precisely because it illustrates the absence of personal authority. Unfortunately, the logic of the liberal tradition does not always reflect political reality.

Despite Congressional approval ratings in the low double digits, getting reelected to a seat in the House of Representatives is a cakewalk compared to the uphill battle confronting a challenger. Approximately 95 percent of all House members who sought reelection from 1982 through 2004 were reelected. If the time horizon is altered, the numbers change slightly but the results remain the same. According to the *Center for Responsive Politics*, between 1964 and 2010, those who were incumbents in the House were elected between 85 and 98 percent of the time with the majority of those election cycles resulting in incumbent reelection rates of 90 percent. A House seat essentially belongs to the incumbent unless he or she dies, quits or retires. What has caused the system of liberal democracy to grant "final say" and "personal authority" to the overwhelming majority of politicians able to capture a seat in the House?

It has been said that money is the mother's milk of politics; incumbents certainly dominate campaign spending. Campbell reports that in the 1992 House election cycle incumbents spent 86% of total campaign spending; they outspent challengers by a ratio of more than 6 to 1. In the 2000 elections cycle, the percentage of total campaign spending by incumbents increased to 93%; a ratio of 13 to 1 against the challenger. For contested elections in the four House cycles of the 1990s, incumbents spent approximately 90% of total campaign expenditures to capture about 65% of the vote. Since these numbers examine only the contested elections, they understate the actual power of incumbency. In the five House election cycles that include 1992 through 2000, there were 261 uncontested elections. [41] Essentially, these were elections in which the odds of successfully challenging the incumbent were so remote that the opposition party did not even bother to mount a nominal challenge.

The high reelection rate for House incumbents has been accompanied by a toxic polarization in American political discourse. Political pundits suggest these two trends are related, but attempts to identify causality or correlation between the two have largely eluded investigators. Gerrymandering, which consists of redrawing congressional districts in order to substantially increase the electoral advantage of one party's candidate relative to the other, has had only a marginal influence on the rising rate of reelection among incumbents as only a small percentage of districts are redrawn. Incumbents already enjoy reelection margins in the range of 60 percent plus, given such an overwhelming advantage, most would likely characterize an even favorable redistricting as disruptive to their reelection plans. Increased stridency along partisan lines is unlikely to drive elective margins much higher even in gerrymandered districts.

One study concludes that gerrymandering does have a negative influence on electoral competition but it does not appear to have contributed to increasing polarization.[42] Other research found "districts that have undergone significant changes as a result of redistricting have become even more polarized."[43] However, the gerrymandering effect is characterized as relatively modest, which "suggests that redistricting is one among other factors that produce party polarization in the House and may help to explain the elevated levels of polarization in the House relative to the Senate."[44]

The historical record suggests that political polarization in the U.S. runs in cycles. There was intense disagreement and several violent rebellions over the governing principles that would ultimately come to define the United States. Certainly, the period before the Civil War was probably the most politically polarized time in U.S. history. Factions vehemently disagreed on everything from state's rights to slavery. Numerous historical examples have illustrated just how far some politicians will descend if they can enhance their chances of winning an election. In elections past, candidates who practiced nasty tactics were often denounced by others in their own party—an occurrence far less common today. During the two or three decades following the end of WWII, there appeared to be a much stronger political consensus, perhaps as the result of the Cold War and a common enemy. Political polarization increased during the 1970s and has pretty much continued unabated to the present day.

In liberal science, strident disagreements can actually motivate participants to work harder in an effort to establish new propositions that will withstand "checking" by peers and ultimately emerge as tentative additions to the body of knowledge. As long as the system functions as intended, much the same could be said for liberal democracy. Instead of "peer review", democracy is "checked" by the three branches of government, the electorate and an unbiased free press that holds a candidate's feet to the fire. Electoral checking has been compromised by low voter turnout and the economic domination of incumbency while many in the press have followed the lead of the dominant political parties and sort themselves along partisan lines. Television viewers tune into *Fox News* or *MSNBC*, not for unbiased "fact checking" in an effort to cull the best ideas or most promising candidates, but to have their partisan opinions reinforced by others who share their world view. Meanwhile, the Internet and information technology have eviscerated newspapers and print media. Blogs may help fill the newspaper gap on the national stage but it is still important for a local reporter to inform citizens that the asphalt contract for the bypass went to the brother-in-law of the county commissioner – the kind of unglamorous fact checking that is critically important to the functioning of liberal democracy but will never appear in the *Huffington Post* or the *Drudge Report*.

Despite its problems, such is the power of the liberal tradition that almost half of the world's population now lives in a democracy with the number having increased steadily since the end of WWII.[45] Many of these new republics are still testing their wings, barely a generation or two removed from rule by iron fist rather than by rule of law. Not everyone has been so sanguine about democracy's prospects; some of those most concerned about its future numbered among the Founding Fathers. Madison feared that democracy would lead to "a rage for paper money, for an abolition of debts, for an equal division of property and for any other improper and wicked projects."[46] Madison was not alone; John Adams feared that because the majority in a democracy have the power to redistribute the wealth of the rich through onerous taxes "the idle, the vicious, the intemperate would rush into the utmost extravagance of debauchery, sell and spend all their share, and then demand a new division of those who purchased from them." [47]

The Economist maintains that given the rise in income inequality, Madison and Adam's concerns about confiscation of private wealth have not come to fruition. But there may be a more insidious problem afflicting the system. Democracy creates political stability but this stability encourages sovereign creditors to lend more than they would lend to a less stable authoritarian regime unlikely to survive the passing of its dictator. Access to easy credit can contribute to some democratic nations spending beyond their means. Government in modern democracies has grown much larger than the Founding Fathers could have anticipated and politicians have become wishing wells of political patronage. To the beneficiaries, government pork is large enough to justify the effort to capture it, but the cost is spread out over a large number of taxpayers so that the pain to any one citizen is relatively small, or seemingly non-existent, if financed by borrowing from sovereign creditors. Over time, democracies can find themselves burdened with growing debt and a commitment to make good on a mountain of contingent liabilities commonly known as "entitlements."

The very meaning of the word "entitlement" has been the subject of disagreement. Some claim to resent the word since it suggests government largesse in cases where there is a contribution made by individuals to public "insurance" programs like Social Security or unemployment compensation. This view asserts that every developed country provides a "social safety net" for its citizens and many are more generous than the one in the U.S. Regardless of terminology, U.S. government payments for Social Security, Medicare, Medicaid, Unemployment Insurance and Income Maintenance have grown at an exponential rate over the last 50 years. Since 1960, such entitlement spending has increased from about one third of the total federal budget to about two thirds today with the greatest growth coming from the health related categories of Medicaid and Medicare—spending categories that were non-existent in 1960.[48]

It is conventional wisdom among many people that the current growth rate is unsustainable but we seem powerless to address the problem. Perhaps it is because 49.1% of the U.S. population lives in a household in which at least one member receives some form of government benefit with the number expected to surpass 50% in the not too distant future, a circumstance that presents a special challenge.[49] If entitlement programs contribute to the income of a majority of households, then one need not be an expert in political strategy to conclude that the way to get elected is to side with this majority and against those who would cut benefits. One suggestion to overcoming the electoral log jam has been to remove fiscal policy from the hands of elected officials, a strategy that was used in Greece and Italy in response to the Euro crisis. The U.S. appears to favor "independent commissions" to deal with politically explosive problems, such as closing military bases or reforming Social Security.

Even if reform takes place, paying for entitlements will require a cut in spending, an increase in taxes or some combination of the two but the federal income tax system has a problem similar to entitlement programs. "The percentage of people who do not pay federal income taxes, and who are not claimed as dependents by someone who does pay them, has jumped from 14.8% in 1984 to 49.5% in 2009."[50] Despite the accuracy of this data, Presidential candidate Mitt Romney failed miserably to articulate its meaning and suffered the political consequences. By characterizing non-payers of federal income tax as victims fixated on feeding at the public trough, he potentially alienated half of the U.S. population—many of whom are registered Republicans. As someone who paid less than 15% in federal income tax on $23 million in income and is rumored to have off-shore accounts in the usual tax havens, Mr. Romney was on unstable ground.

Many Americans who pay no federal income tax spend a much larger percentage of their income on other taxes such as payroll, sales and excise taxes (certainly larger than Mr. Romney). But the statistic Romney quoted does point to the same issue that was raised by Madison and Adams two hundred years ago: can a democracy that grants growing benefits to an increasing proportion of its citizens while funding them from a decreasing proportion of taxpayers remain solvent? Economists have long observed that people tend to overuse anything that is free, e.g., water, air, wild buffalo. Do the people who do not pay federal income tax perceive federal government services as "free" and, if so, does that mean they will always vote for more services? If the answer is in the affirmative, then one might argue on economic principle that even low income wage earners should pay a "nominal" federal income tax.

Is the growing entitlement dilemma beyond the power of a post-industrial liberal democracy? The problem is likely to be dumped into the lap of a "bipartisan commission" similar to Bowles/Simpson; a group of experts who will be given the unpleasant task of resolving a dilemma that has eluded our elected leaders. Politicians defer to commissions, not so much for their expertise, but as a way to outsource intestinal fortitude, a character trait that is in short supply among elected officials. Whether they admit it or not, everyone in Congress appreciates the magnitude of the fiscal problem but taking a tough stance could jeopardize incumbency and the personal authority that congressional representatives have worked so hard to build.

The liberal tradition represented by science, democracy and markets has literally turned the world upside down. Instead of the goods things in life trickling down at the discretion of authoritarian rulers, all knowledge, freedom and wealth emanate from the bottom-up in mutually reinforcing systems that often appear to be teetering on the verge of collapse yet have proved to be more resilient and adaptable than any of the alternatives. When practiced in the manner intended, this tradition allows everyone to have a chance to participate and no one is indispensable. The liberal tradition truly is no country for experts, old or otherwise.

CHAPTER 4

WELCOME TO THE JARGON JUNGLE: EXPERTS IN BUSINESS

"A wesome" was a word reserved for the truly breathtaking before people started using it to describe everything from a tsunami to a cup of coffee. In the business world, *innovation* is the new awesome. Many companies have *innovation officers* who develop *innovation strategies* in concert with *innovation teams* and some of their activities take place on *innovation day*. *The Wall Street Journal* found that in 2011 the word "*innovation*" was mentioned 33,528 times in company quarterly and annual reports.[1] An *Amazon* search revealed that during a three-month period in early 2012 there were 255 books published with the word *innovation* in their title. A survey of over 700 business schools found that twenty-eight percent use variations of *innovation* in their mission statement with many of the same schools sponsoring "*innovation* centers." Amidst all the talk, little *innovation* actually takes place.

Cartoonist Scott Adams has fashioned a lucrative career lampooning contemporary office life and the pseudo-scientific jargon perpetuated by business experts. When the boss says, "Let's schedule a scenario-based round table discussion ...We'll use our infrastructure survey tool to architect a risk-based tiering system." *Dilbert* responds, "That almost meant something."[2] As every cubicle dweller knows, business jargon fueled by the latest management fads come and go, but on occasion a real *innovation* appears that permanently alters our lives. Few inventions influenced the texture of 20th century life more than the automobile.

The car was not only a potent symbol of post-WWII manufacturing; it validated our personal freedom as Americans. TV personality Dinah Shore urged the nation to "see the USA in your Chevrolet" and we eagerly accepted the invitation to travel across the country on President Eisenhower's new interstate highway system. Presumably, Ike had such a difficult time deploying troops in Europe during WWII that he envisioned a network of interstate highways as an essential component of national defense should America ever need to defend itself against a foreign invader. Urban legend contends that the minimum overpass clearance was designed high enough to allow a Nike-Ajax missile to pass beneath.

The network of interstate highways may have paved the way, but it was the romance of the automobile that beckoned us to the open road. *Route 66* was a popular TV series about the adventures of two young men traveling around America but the real star of the show was a Corvette convertible. Few of us are fortunate enough to begin our driving career behind the wheel of a new Corvette but, however old and dented our first car, not many experiences in life evoke the same sense of excitement and limitless possibility. Because the automobile allowed people to live a greater distance from their work, sprawling suburbs soon surrounded every major city, thus adding a third category to the rural/urban taxonomy of American culture.

If suburbia forever altered the social and geographic landscape, the culture of corporate America was also changing. Ford Motor Company had steadily lost money since the great stock market crash of 1929. By 1945, losses averaged about $100 million per year, an astronomical figure for the time. Henry Ford was still the boss but he was getting old and his health was failing; the company's lagging performance was not helped by the aging tycoon's public image. His anti-Semitism, pacifist political views and aggressive anti-unionism during a time of unprecedented growth in the labor movement did not endear him to Jews, veterans or factory workers. It has been rumored that Ford's wife and daughter-in-law presented the patriarch with an ultimatum: either he appoint his grandson as the company's president or his mother would sell her controlling share of company stock to the highest bidder. The elder Ford relented and his grandson took charge of the company. Henry Ford II immediately hired a group of "Whiz Kids" known for their application of scientific management principles to business problems. Robert McNamara emerged as the most prominent Whiz Kid and was eventually named CEO before graduating to become a member of John F. Kennedy's "Best and Brightest."

Ford prospered during the post-WWII years but it was General Motors with a 50 percent market share that dominated not only automobile manufacturing, but all of industrial America. In the early 1950s, GM was the largest private employer in the world with revenues equal to nearly 3% of Gross Domestic Product. It was the first company to pay $1 billion in taxes at a time when total federal tax revenues were $70 billion. In 1953, Eisenhower nominated GM President Charles Erwin Wilson for Secretary of Defense. When Wilson was asked by the Senate Armed Services Committee if as Secretary of Defense he could make a decision contrary to the interests of GM, he replied that he could not conceive of such a circumstance "because for years I thought what was good for the country was good for General Motors and vice versa."[3] Wilson's reply would later be shortened and quoted out of context as: "what's good for General Motors is good for the USA."

An early adoptee of the "stakeholder model" that elevated the interests of employees, customers, community, etc., to equal status with shareholders, GM was lionized as the "poster child for responsible capitalism." Stakeholder advocates maintained that the company may have earned monopoly profit but a substantial portion of those earnings were shared with Uncle Sam, managers, hourly workers, cities like Detroit and a dealer network that encompassed all of North America. Fast forward twenty-five years: higher gas prices as a consequence of the OPEC oil embargo would precipitate a surge in fuel efficient Japanese imports causing the domestic market share of The Big Three auto makers to dwindle from 82% in 1970 to 57% by 2005. Increased energy prices in the early 1980s coincided with tight monetary policy and large fiscal deficits that pushed the trade weighted value of the dollar to new highs. Combined with generous union wages and high manufacturing costs, U.S. automobile producers were at a serious disadvantage relative to Japanese companies. Over the next three decades there would be many ups and downs; but in 2009, the company whose managers once believed that their interests were inseparable from America's would file for bankruptcy.

The rise of Japan, accompanied by the decline of U.S. manufacturing in general and the auto industry in particular, elicited a barrage of criticism from politicians eager to capitalize on the fear and resentment of the electorate. In

1980, former Texas Governor John Connally warned the Japanese they had "better be prepared to sit on the docks of Yokohama in your little Datsuns and your little Toyotas while you stare at your own little television sets and eat your mandarin oranges, because we've had all we're going to take!" [4] In his campaign for the White House, Walter Mondale asked free trade advocates: "What do we want our kids to do? Sweep up around Japanese computers?" [5] And in 1985 on the 40-year anniversary of the Hiroshima bombing, Tennessee Senator Howard Baker made two observations: "First, we're still at war with Japan. Second, we're losing." [6]

Rather than engage in "Japan Bashing," business experts were more inclined to express admiration for the Japanese miracle. Peter Drucker referred to the Japanese experience as the "the most extraordinary success story in all economic history" [7] while futurist Herman Kahn believed that "it would not be surprising if the 21st century turned out to be the Japanese century." [8] Given that imitation is the sincerest form of flattery, a good many business experts suggested that we should strive to emulate the Japanese and essentially "beat them at their own game."

In 1989, Drucker published *The New Realities* which was followed in 1992 by Lester Thurow's *Head to Head: The Coming Economic Battle Among Japan, Europe, and America* and by Laura Tyson's *Who's Bashing Whom?: Trade Conflict in High Technology Industries*. Drucker was a business guru and management icon; Thurow was dean of the business school at MIT; and Tyson was on the Council of Economic Advisors in the Clinton Administration and would go on to become dean of business schools at The University of California-Berkley and The London School of Economics. All of three of these books found a large popular audience and each prophesied the eventual economic dominance of the Japanese approach. Drucker, Thurow and Tyson were marquee names but if Japanese imports caused a bust among The Big Three auto makers, it spawned a boom for experts on Japanese business. In pre-Internet America, newspapers, magazines and book publishers could not get enough commentary on the Japanese miracle. Recognizing an opportunity, many college professors redefined themselves as specialists in Japanese business practices in efforts to cash in on the bubble. Every business school or cow college worth its salt boasted a few such experts scattered among their faculty. In response to the growing trade gap in manufacturing, the business school accreditation agency known as the Association to Advance Collegiate Schools of Business added a production course to the core business requirement which was often heavily flavored with cases and anecdotes about Japanese industry.

Japan was said to replace "competition with cooperation" by fostering a high degree of vertical integration among many large firms that were interlinked via industrial groups in a system known as *keiretsu*. Presumably, the system allowed Japanese companies to realize three important operating advantages: the ability to cross-subsidize weak or new product lines from more profitable segments, a guaranteed internal demand when external global markets faltered, and a reliable supply of critical inputs, including low cost financial capital.

The interlocking shareholder arrangement among group members and other institutions is a feature of *keiretsu* that is believed to foster an ownership struc-ture that results in low turnover in the stock of Japanese member companies. Among the 300 largest U.S. and Japanese manufacturing companies in the early 1990s, seventy-nine percent of Japanese company shares were held by relationship investors compared to 34 percent in the U.S.[9] Unlike with Western companies, the interwoven stock ownership structure was believed to insu-late Japanese managers from short-run, day-to-day market fluctuations and allows them to concentrate on growing long-run value.

Inter-locked shareholdings can also restrict foreign companies from acquiring Japanese firms while foreign companies may find Japanese regulatory certi-fication an especially frustrating element of their industrial policy. Because Japanese regulators rely more on design standards than performance charac-teristics, foreign producers have difficulty accessing Japanese markets even when their products perform better than those produced by the Japanese. Regulators and Japanese companies write the design standards and tend to exclude foreign participation.

The final element of *keiretsu* is the main bank system. Most business groups in Japan are associated with a main bank that provides member firms preferential access to low cost financial capital. Rather than the adversarial relationship that frequently characterizes creditor/borrower relationships in Western coun-tries, especially when credit quality deteriorates, main banks pride themselves on supplying a financial buffer to member firms when economic conditions worsen. This was portrayed as a stabilizing force giving Japanese companies the latitude to pursue long-term objectives relative to the short term incen-tives characteristic of their Western counterparts.

In 1989, the Japanese Nikkei Index peaked at 38,916, fifteen times higher than the Dow Jones Industrial Average that was trading around 2,600. Fast forward to March 2012: the Nikkei is at 10,000 and the Dow at 13,000. Property prices that topped out in the early 1990s crashed to earth as Japan's economy experienced a second "lost decade." From 1992 to 2010, real GDP in Japan grew by just 16% compared to 62% in the U.S. In 2011, Japan experienced its first trade-deficit in 31 years; although it was partly the result of the Fukushima tsunami that damaged export industries and forced Japan to increase energy imports to make up for lost nuclear capacity.

Japan is still the world's third largest economy with Japanese companies exporting their skills and bolstering manufacturing in the U.S. and other countries such that Japan's overseas assets are valued at approximately $3 trillion. Contrary to what the experts espoused, Japan's economic success always had more to do with the resilience and productivity of its people than the alliance between industry and government bureaucrats; but there is no doubt that the Land of the Rising Sun is no longer rising as fast as it once did. What happened to the Japanese miracle and how could so many highly esteemed business experts be so wrong?

If *keiretsu* worked miracles for a time in the auto industry, it did not work everywhere and for all time. Two sectors where the long-run failing of the Japanese approach is especially evident are electronics and finance. Sony has been losing money on televisions for eight years in a row, and along with Sharp, recently saw their credit rating downgraded to BBB+, two tics above junk status. Over the past decade Japan's electronic production has decreased by 41% while electronic exports have shrunk by 27%. Between 1990 and 2000, Japan's market share of semi-conductors produced by the top 20 companies has declined from 55% to 24% while over the same period the U.S. share has risen from 31% to 51%. About 70% of Japan's entire electronics output represents parts and components that go into the products of other firms. Unfortunately for Japanese manufacturers, the real profit from electronics accrues to product inventors, not parts producers. Richard Katz argues that the skills and mindsets that led Japan to create revolutionary audio-video products such as the transistor radio, Walkman and VCR have not carried over to the digital era.

Why? Katz believes that the Japanese system failed to foster mechanisms of creative destruction. Emerging technologies in the U.S. are usually promoted by companies that do not have a stake in the old technology; most of the companies in the forefront of the TV and midrange computer era are gone. "Among the top 21 electronics manufacturers in the U.S. today, eight did not exist in 1970 and six were too small to be in the Fortune 500 a decade ago. In Japan, there has been no new entrant into the top ranks of electronics manufacturing for more than half a century." [10] The Japanese approach tends to slow the process of creative destruction, which might not be a big problem in more mature industries with a long life cycle, but it is a systemic failure in the constantly evolving world of digital electronics.

If the daily drama between U.S. banks and regulators in late 2008 appeared to mimic a TV soap opera about a dysfunctional family, then by comparison Japan's banking system was a Eugene O'Neil play for most of the 1990s. Regulators bickered while bankers, unwilling to recognize losses, withdrew from their problems in a futile hope that they would somehow go away. The financial malaise dragged on and, like an emotional grindstone, it slowly eroded confidence in the banking system; as the Japanese economy ground to a halt the country seemed mired in "crisis fatigue."

The industrial policies that worked so well to generate trade surpluses contributed to excess capacity while shielding Japanese banks from international competition. Many bank reforms introduced in the West during the 1980s were delayed in Japan, which contributed to moral hazard. "Too big to fail" was an article of faith among Japanese banks two decades before the 2008 financial crisis and should have supplied U.S. policy experts some insight into conditions here if they had only been paying attention. The delays in implementing Japanese bank reform postponed efficiency gains and created additional weakness that only became worse as fears about contagion and the general collapse in the financial system spread. Because the U.S. depends more on public debt markets, bank loans as a percentage of GDP were more than three times larger in Japan compared to the U.S. Rather than concentrate lending decisions in the hands of a relatively small number of experts in a highly centralized banking system like Japans', public debt markets exploit information and knowledge dispersed across a much larger swath of the population. Less dependence on the banking system also enhances financial diversity should problems in the sector become chronic. *Keiretsu* and the main bank financial system was an evolved form of mercantilism that was designed to manage domestic production and promote exports.[11] Consistent with Milton Friedman's critique of discretionary stabilization policies, *keiretsu* was also pro-cyclical, exaggerating both booms and busts when they reared their ugly heads. The main bank system flooded Japanese businesses with easy credit, contributing to an asset bubble that was followed by a general price deflation at the end of the millennium.

Unlike Western countries, there is no tradition of public criticism in Japan. According to the intellectual historian Masao Maruyama, the word "opposition", as distinct from "enmity" or "antagonism", did not exist in the Japanese language until imported from the West in the last century. The social emphasis on consensus created a climate that regarded criticism as rude. It is difficult to have open debates when many people feel that disagreeing with an idea is tantamount to a personal attack and that the appropriate response is to remain silent. While the public environment is changing, Rauch and Sackett note that in the early 1990s "ideas tend to be traded on a kind of gray market."[12] The Japanese aversion to criticism makes it hard to produce, test and separate useful ideas from the irrelevant, a cultural aversion that imposes a significant economic cost. The Japanese university system lags behind the rest of the developed world while the bottom-up intellectual resources of a highly educated and hard working people are not fully exploited. Much of the intellectual agenda in Japan is established by outsiders in an economy that is skilled at commercially exploiting the innovations conceived by others but not very good at developing their own. Between 1901 and 1985, Japanese citizens won five Nobel prizes in science which is one twenty-eighth of the share won by Americans and one tenth of the number awarded Germans.

The fact that so many prominent experts believed that the U.S. *could* or *should* emulate the commercial culture of Japan while failing to acknowledge fundamental flaws in their system does not engender confidence in business expertise. The 2008 financial crisis in the U.S. evolved in a manner very similar to the bubble in Japan but it would have been much worse if changes advocated by the experts had been implemented. Fortunately, calls for American *keiretsu* never fully materialized. The experts on Japanese business disappeared from university campuses almost as abruptly as they arrived and the popular business press moved on to the next big thing.

MANUFACTURING BUSINESS EXPERTS

The production of business experts is a booming business. For the most part, they are manufactured by universities in MBA programs that have been the subject of criticism for as long as they have been in existence. Like making sausage, the recipe depends on personal taste and is not always pretty to watch. In the late 1950s, the Carnegie and Ford Foundations characterized MBA education as "a vague, shifting, rather formless subject." Critics have argued that MBA programs are too basic, too theoretical, focused on school rankings and guilty of training graduates for careers in narrow specialties like finance. Retention among the elite MBA programs is very high once students have paid their tuition and institutional spending on job placement is substantially more than graduate or professional schools in other disciplines. Elite business schools have in-house placement agencies that employ a significant number of head hunter types who do nothing but place their graduates. This has led some to argue that graduate business programs function primarily as a screening and placement mechanism for employers. [13]

Some studies suggest that the economic return to an MBA is highest for the graduates of elite programs while others are unable to find any evidence that an MBA degree had a significant influence on career advancement or earnings. Many of the most successful and admired business leaders of today such as the late Steven Jobs, Michael Dell, Warren Buffett, Bill Gates and Jack Welsh, did not acquire MBA degrees; however, survey data does suggest that the chief executives of large companies are much more likely to have an MBA degree today than in years past.

If the MBA degree is just a credential that companies use to screen employees, then it can still have value to employers and students but the debate over program curriculum is not especially important. Alternatively, those who challenge the *status quo* in business curriculum typically argue for greater integration of functional fields, more instructional diversity and increased hands-on business experience for students. Some critics believe there is a depressing tendency for schools to avoid the risk of being different.

Business schools frequently announce sweeping changes to their curriculum following a major crisis or the implementation of new technology. In response to criticism and in an effort to emphasize globalization and integrate new technology such as the Internet, many B-schools redesigned their programs in the 1990s. Following the 2008 financial crisis, some emphasized the "social impact" MBA that places graduates in not-for- profit jobs or in the "sustainable energy field." John Fernandes, President of the Association to Advance

Collegiate Schools of Business, is quoted in the *Financial Times* saying: "Even though these jobs don't offer the same upward remuneration that the for-profit sector does, they tend to have better balance of life and they speak to the desire of this new generation of MBAs to do good with their business degree. To many of these students the measure of success is not income, it's more holistic." [14]

In 2011, Harvard's new business school dean announced two "bold" changes to their program. The first-year curriculum added a Field Immersion Experiences for Leadership Development (FIELD) course, which will focus on developing small group learning experiences with the goal of "advancing the schools mission to develop leaders who make a difference in the world." The second change provides faculty and students greater flexibility to design their course schedules in order to promote "significant innovation in experiential learning in management education." [15]

Mintzberg believes changes that purport to address new technology or ethical lapses tend to be more cosmetic than substantive and that most MBA programs remain a coalition of competing functional fields—organized in "silos" of accounting, finance, marketing, management—and the business faculty have little incentive to change the structure. Students often appear more concerned with acquiring the MBA credential to enhance career prospects than they are in grasping the material. Mintzberg believes many students are simply too young and inexperienced to benefit from a MBA and would be better off working and gaining experience. He argues that programs ignore the degree to which management is a craft that requires leadership, enthusiasm and intuition rather than the ability to formulate strategies and analyze data. [16]

Can business schools produce business experts with good business intuition? Certainly, some management techniques along with methods of data analysis are teachable but the rapid pace of change in many industries requires that managers respond more quickly if they are to skim the profit from new ideas. Malcolm Gladwell argues that the best decisions makers are *not* those who process the most information or spend the most time analyzing data, but those able to distill decision criteria into a few manageable factors.[17] Yet, some snap decisions that appear to be intuitive may actually be learned. Like the baseball player who learns to turn away from the inside fastball or the defensive driver who anticipates another driver's mistake, it may be possible to teach future managers to respond more quickly to changing business conditions; but this invariably requires making decisions with less information.

Even if leadership and good business intuition are largely un-teachable, MBA training can provide future managers a framework for decision making along with analytical tools and rules that are applicable to a wide range of business situations. The problem is that in the most dynamic industries, the business environment changes so rapidly that many of the tools will likely have a short effective life. What distinguishes business prodigies like Steven Jobs and Bill Gates is their ability to successfully navigate un-charted ground, writing the rules as they go.

"STAKING" OUT THE MORAL HIGH GROUND

A number of critics claim that not only have MBA curricula failed to instill ethical standards of conduct in graduates, they have contributed to unethical business practice which has become more pervasive as a consequence of graduate business education. In a posthumously published article in the *Academy of Management Learning and Education*, Ghoshal argues that many ethical lapses have their origins in ideas perpetuated by MBA programs. Attempts to make business education a science, "a kind of physics", has resulted in misguided management theories derived from assumptions and methods associated with the Chicago School and Milton Friedman.

Ghoshal is especially critical of Michael Jensen who is known for his work in the development of agency theory, the tendency for corporate managers to pursue their own interests rather than act as "agents" for shareholders. He argues that Jensen's theory teaches students that managers cannot be trusted to do their jobs. When students become managers, they bring the same distrust to their relationships with fellow employees, customers and suppliers that they learned in their MBA courses. Ghoshal is especially critical of "simplistic assumptions" based on the rational, utility-maximizing economic man. When extended to corporate behavior, he believes these simplistic assumptions lead to the mistaken notion that shareholder value is the primary objective of the firm and that this has resulted in elegant mathematical models and empirical analyses that are, in fact, devoid of meaning.

Milton Friedman's well known assertion that in a free society "there is one and only one social responsibility of business–to use its resources and engage in activities designed to increase its profits" is often incorrectly characterized as an invitation to engage in unethical behavior.[18] Reaction to Friedman's assertion has given rise to a multi-objective optimization problem in which shareholders become just another "stakeholder" whose interests are equivalent to the interests of customers, employees, government regulators and the general public. In Classical economics, the price system is sometimes interpreted as overcoming a shortage of ethical behavior. Market participants who pursue their own selfish interests are simultaneously allocating resources in a manner that maximizes social welfare. Hayek did not see the price system so much as a way to resolve a shortage of altruism but as a way to overcome the knowledge deficit of market participants; he perceived markets as a morally neutral method to concentrate widely dispersed knowledge. Many MBA educators portray managers who adhere to the stakeholder model as more "ethical" despite some who co-opt the rhetoric of social responsibility as a means of diverting attention from bad decisions and poor economic performance. GM's adherence to the stakeholder model almost certainly contributed to its declining market share, plant closings, job losses and eventual bankruptcy with many former stakeholders much worse off and no doubt wishing GM had paid closer attention to profits. When it comes to "good business ethics", stakeholder advocates have adopted the credo of William Godwin—"good intentions are the essence of virtue"—while unintended benefits realized in the pursuit of profit are not worthy of notice.

The problem with the stakeholder model is that it encourages managers to substitute their own expert knowledge for the systemic knowledge embodied in share price. While share price is largely unambiguous, the information required to maximize the interests of multiple stakeholders can be confusing, contradictory and open to manipulation. Stakeholder advocates minimize the informational and operational complexity associated with maximizing a multi-objective function that includes an ever expanding group of stakeholders. It is not that the business experts are too unethical to maximize multiple stakeholder interests; they simply are not smart enough to solve the problem given the information available.

If competency is measured by the accuracy of short-run predictions, one of the most competent professions is meteorology. Roll found that the futures market for orange juice concentrate does a better job forecasting weather patterns in Florida than do expert meteorologists.[19] This is because the market combines all available information, including knowledge possessed by weather experts many of whom probably dabble in agricultural futures markets or are employed by companies that do. Even if corporate managers sincerely wish to serve multiple stakeholders, like expert meteorologists, their knowledge is incomplete compared to the aggregated information of market participants.

Critics of markets frequently argue that prices are manipulated by special interests or they lack transparency because of insufficient information. If this is the case, then these problems should be corrected, rather than complicated, by expanding the number of decision criteria to include multiple measures of welfare that depend on information that is even more imperfect. As is often the case, bad ideas by the experts can generate unintended consequences. One unintended consequence of the stakeholder model has been the surge in private equity. Before the onset of the financial crisis, private equity as a percentage of all mergers and acquisitions increased from 5% in 2000 to more than 35% in 2007. *The Economist* reports that a major motivation of private equity is to escape the "different and irreconcilable demands of company stakeholders," including government regulators. [20]

The Republican Presidential candidate Mitt Romney temporarily moved the private equity debate to the forefront. Much of the focus has been on private equity performance rather than why it has become such a popular ownership structure—not that these issues are unimportant. Some research concludes that companies bought by private equity firms remained in bankruptcy for a shorter time with default rates equal to or less than other corporate issuers. [21] Roughly two-thirds of CEOs at private equity companies were replaced in the first four years of ownership, suggesting that private equity owned companies may do a better job aligning management compensation with company performance than public companies. [22]

Whether or not private equity is able to consistently create value remains largely unanswered primarily because companies are not required to disclose performance on buyouts. An analysis of 788 buyouts found that private equity owned firms invested more efficiently than other companies, which the authors attributed to greater access to capital; but the consistent appearance of superior performance among some large private equity firms may occur as a consequence of tax and regulatory arbitrage or the exploitation of debt holders. [23] A study prepared for the *Financial Times* found that 70 percent of private equity earnings from 2001 to 2010 were paid to the firms themselves in the form of fees and not to their investors. [24]

Private equity fund managers share in the profits of the partnership as the equity portion of their compensation. "The tax rules for compensating general partners create a planning opportunity for managers who receive the industry standard 'two and twenty' (a two percent management fee and twenty percent profits interest). By taking a portion of their pay in the form of partnership profits, fund managers defer income derived from their labor efforts and convert it from ordinary income into long-term capital gain. This quirk in the tax law allows some of the richest workers in the country to pay tax on their labor income at a low rate." [25] Because of this "quirk," Mr. Romney's $23 million in 2011 income was taxed at an average rate of 14.5%.

The "irreconcilable demands" of the stakeholder model along with the benefits provided by the tax code have increased the incentive to abandon a more transparent public ownership structure in favor of a more flexible but more opaque private equity. Rather than be surprised that individuals and companies take advantage of loopholes in the law, we should accept self-interest as the norm. The private equity tax "quirk" may be a relatively new convention but the functions these firms perform are as old as the nation itself. The North American colonies were founded by joint stock companies like the Massachusetts Bay Company that hoped to earn a profit on New World ventures. Despite differences in ownership structure or tax status, venture capitalists, distressed asset specialists and closed-end funds often do the same things as private equity firms. As head of Berkshire Hathaway, Warren Buffet frequently bought and restructured companies.

Kohlberg Kravis Roberts (KKR), founded in 1978, acquired RJR Nabisco in 1988 and promptly fired CEO F. Ross Johnson. Mr. Johnson was head of a public company that he ran like a personal fiefdom. His abuse of shareholders was on such a scale that his story is still used in business schools to illustrate the agency problem. Johnson squandered millions on country club memberships and corporate jets and once flew his dog "G. Shepherd", the only passenger appearing on the manifest, cross-country on a company airplane courtesy of RJR Nabisco shareholders.[26] Mr. Johnson's story was told in *Barbarians at the Gates,* a best-seller that was later made into a TV movie starring James Garner as the spendthrift CEO. When private equity companies purge CEOs like Mr.

Johnson, invest in some companies and close others, they facilitate the process of creative destruction and perform a valuable public service.

Private equity also played a minor role in reshaping the U.S. auto industry. Cerberus Capital is a private equity company named after the mythological three headed dog that guards the gates of Hades, a name and image the founder is said to regret. In 2007, Cerberus bought an 80% stake in Chrysler for $7.4 billion. The timing could not have been worse. Because of the financial crisis and the plunge in auto sales, Cerberus would forfeit its investment in Chrysler as part of the bailout; but it did manage to maintain a controlling interest in Chrysler Financial. GM sold a controlling interest in GMAC to Cerberus in 2006 as part of a desperate bid to raise capital and forestall bankruptcy. The image of GM going hat-in-hand to a private equity company would have been unimaginable in the flush years of the 1950s; but in the rough and tumble world of market capitalism, all glory is fleeting.

Before Cerberus' failure to reverse Chrysler's slide there were other "interventions" at the Big Three auto makers but none were able to permeate the industry's dysfunctional culture and change course. Lee Iacocca, the folksy former CEO of Chrysler convinced the Carter Administration and the nation that The Chrysler Corporation Loan Guarantee Act of 1979 "saved" Chrysler from bankruptcy. In fact, federal intervention amounted to a quasi-bankruptcy which required creditors to make "concessions" to Chrysler. Treasury Department Secretary William Miller used the concessions clause to pressure Chrysler creditors into accepting 30 cents on the dollar for $600 million in debt. The company was allowed to convert nearly $700 million of debt into a special class of preferred stock that paid no dividends and was unredeemable until 1983 when Chrysler agreed to redeem it for common shares with less value than the original bonds. [27]

The bailout was supposed to protect Chrysler jobs but it did not prevent the company from firing 20,000 white collar employees and 42,600 hourly workers in the first four years after the law was enacted. Senator William Proxmire (D-Wisc.) complained that the number of employees laid off at Chrysler in this period was probably equal to or larger than the number who would have lost their jobs had Chrysler filed conventional bankruptcy. Responsible stockholders, who were portrayed as benefiting most from the bailout, were the biggest chumps. Shareholders who did their homework and followed Chrysler's long decline had probably already dumped their shares before the 1979 law was enacted. Essentially, the government's action rewarded shareholders who may have had inside information about the forthcoming bailout or simply held on to the stock in anticipation of "too big to fail" government intervention. Economists call this effect "adverse selection" because it rewards the wrong people for the wrong reasons.

When government helps prop up failed businesses, it imposes an unfair "externality" on surviving firms. If Chrysler had been allowed to fail, GM and Ford would have inherited some of their customers. More importantly, it would have provided "a wake-up call" to the managers and union workers at GM and Ford that they best change their ways or face a similar fate. Instead, the auto industry culture remained unchanged, secure in the knowledge that should they fail, government would bail them out like they did Chrysler.

Before GM's government engineered bankruptcy in 2009, there were two notable attempts to inject new thinking into the auto maker's culture and hopefully reverse the slow erosion in market share. In 1985, H. Ross Perot sold Electronic Data Systems Corporation (EDS) to GM and joined their board of directors. To be sure, Perot received a premium price for his EDS stock but he also dreamed of playing a major role in turning around America's most storied manufacturing company. Small in stature but large in ego, Perot built EDS from the ground up fighting for every scrap of market share with industry behemoth, International Business Machines Corporation. In 1979, Perot organized the rescue of EDS workers from an Iranian jail, succeeding where President Jimmy Carter and the Department of Defense had failed. The details of the GM/EDS merger seemed straightforward enough. Presumably, it was designed to exploit each company's strengths; Perot would head-up EDS, which would operate as an autonomous unit within GM and a new security, G.M. Class E stock, was created to ensure that EDS maintained an identity separate from GM in the investment community. [28]

A year later, executives at GM and EDS were feuding over the lucrative stock options paid EDS managers. The entrepreneurial spirit that had endeared EDS to GM Chief Executive Roger Smith from a distance, was much less appealing up close and personal. In a 1986 meeting in Dallas that has become part of GM corporate lore, Smith turned various shades of purple as he unleashed a tirade against EDS officers and executives. Two weeks later, GM engaged McKinsey &

Company to negotiate a peaceful operating arrangement with EDS that Perot characterized as a typical GM ploy—when a crisis occurs, the first thing they do is hire expert consultants. They then have a series of meetings to define the crisis and appoint a committee to talk about it. Perot famously remarked, "If you see a snake, just kill it. Don't appoint a committee on snakes." [29] No one was surprised when GM bought out Perot in late 1986.

Twenty years after Perot, investor Kirk Kerkorian would make a run at GM acquiring almost 10% of shares. GM was still paying a $2.00 per share dividend despite billions of dollars in losses. Kerkorian leaned on GM Chief Executive Officer Rick Wagoner to make substantial reductions in dividends and to scale back executive compensation along with cuts in the pay of hourly workers. He also proposed selling GM's Saab and Hummer brands as a way to raise cash and pushed GM to form an alliance with Nissan and Renault. When GM rejected all suggestions, Kerkorian adviser Jerry York resigned from the GM board. In a letter to GM Chairman and CEO Rick Wagoner, York said he had "grave reservations concerning the ability of the company's current business model to successfully compete with those of Asian producers."[30] In late 2006, Kerkorian dumped his GM holdings.

Since the 2009 government engineered bankruptcy of GM and Chrysler, the industry has partially recovered and many of the workers laid off as part of the bailout agreement have returned to their jobs or to employment at other plants; but the battle to establish the public opinion narrative continues. On one side are those who portray the bailout as an unqualified success with no downside. In the words of President Obama, "the industry is back on its feet and has repaid its debt." According to bailout supporters, if the government had not dictated the terms of the restructuring, GM and Chrysler would have disappeared along with over 1 million jobs. The Administration's narrative contends that the bailout prevented such a disaster and did so at a very reasonable cost.

What is the real cost of the bailout? In late 2008, then Treasury Secretary Henry Paulson loaned GM and Chrysler $17 billion from the $700 billion Troubled Asset Relief Program. In 2009, the Obama administration established an auto task force headed by "car czar" Steve Rattner. Each company was required to file for bankruptcy as a condition for receiving additional loans and rather than a restructuring under conventional bankruptcy rules, each corporation "sold" its assets to a new entity that was established for the purposes of the sale. The $2 billion the new entity paid for Chrysler went to senior lenders to settle the $6.9 billion in debt, roughly 29 cents on the dollar. Fiat did not contribute any money but was given a large stake in the new entity. Despite being lower priority, the sale ensured that Chrysler's retirees would receive a $4.6 billion promissory note and 55% of Chrysler stock. GM's senior creditors fared better than Chrysler's but the "sale" left the government with 61% of GM stock. In August 2012, the Treasury estimated that the taxpayer cost of the bailout would be more than $25 billion but it could be higher or lower based on the price received for the 500 million shares still owned by the government. To break even it would need to sell the shares for $53 per share; in August 2012, they were trading at approximately $20 and unlikely to be sold before the November elections. [31]

In the long run, the real cost derives from the political precedent of government providing debtor-in-possession financing for bankruptcy. The conventional wisdom was that the government engineered rescue of GM was "owed" to blue collar workers as *quid pro quo* for the Wall Street bailout. But not all blue collar workers are equal even when they are members of a labor union. The GM bailout deemed the jobs of politically connected UAW workers higher priority than 2,500 workers at the Moraine, Ohio facility despite the Harbour Report, a productivity measurement service, identifying it as the nation's most efficient SUV manufacturing facility. In 1981, the Moraine plant was converted to automobiles after GM sold its Frigidaire brand. Workers elected to stay with the International Union of Electrical Workers rather than join the UAW but in time accepted contracts negotiated by the UAW. Not only did the bailout sacrifice the Moraine plant but the agreement gave no priority to Moraine workers at other GM plants. The former UAW vice president leading the bailout negotiations with GM said that in the end "we had to take care of our own members."[32] For Moraine workers the lesson is clear: political influence matters more than labor productivity and not all blue collars are the same.

Instead of providing debtor-in-possession financing, the government could have sponsored a real auction of GM and Chrysler and sold them to the highest bidder rather than go through a make believe sale. The notion that neither company would have survived a conventional bankruptcy is highly unlikely. In the future, creditors will be much more reluctant to make loans to companies in industries that have political connections sufficient to subvert the bankruptcy process, which in turn imposes the prospect of even more govern-ment bailouts further down the road. The out of pocket costs of the bailout are insignificant compared to the loss of credibility inflicted on a system allow-ing bankruptcy law to be usurped by an *ad hoc* political process that defines "stakeholder" priority at the whim of whoever occupies the White House. The process of creative destruction must apply to all companies, including large manufacturers and big banks. The 2008 crisis was a "Black Swan" event but the mechanisms that contributed to the downfall of GM and Chrysler were years in the making and go further back than the 1979 Chrysler bailout.

There is an urban legend that the rocket boosters used on the Space Shuttle were shipped from Utah by rail and had to be made small enough so that they could pass through railroad tunnels on route to the launch site in Florida. The U.S. standard railroad track gauge of 4 feet and 8.5 inches followed the gauge of locomotives produced by early British pioneers in the industry. These in turn followed the gauge of horse drawn trams in England, which followed the width of early freight wagons in the northern UK. Presumably, the width can be traced to the carriages of the Middle Ages that were in turn inherited from the old Roman cart gauge of approximately 4 feet, 8-1/2 inches. "Julius Caesar set this width under Roman law so that vehicles could traverse Roman villages and towns without getting caught in stone ruts of differing widths. Over the centuries this became the traditional standard." [33] The gist of the tale is that cart width dictated by Julius Caesar determined the width of the rocket boost-ers used in the Space Shuttle. Some question the veracity of the story but, true or not, it is a good illustration of "path dependence."

The auto industry and GM in particular, were partly the victims of a man-agement environment that was forged in the post-War II era. The executives leading the industry, especially in the latter years, may have made some bad choices but many were "path dependent" decisions greatly influenced by a dysfunctional and bureaucratic corporate culture, a long-term secular increase in energy prices, bad regulations imposed by government, and unsustainable wage and legacy costs.

EXECUTIVE NARCISSISM AND GRATUITOUS COMPLEXITY
Certainly, management hubris played a role in GM's decline but for sheer chutz-pah, criminal behavior and hyper self-esteem, few come close to Bernie Madoff or the business experts who ran Enron. Unlike the architects of traditional

Ponzi schemes who promise exorbitant payoffs, Madoff shrewdly appealed to his victims by fabricating make believe investments with low volatility and reasonably generous returns. The constant vigilance required to sustain an essentially solitary criminal enterprise for such an extended period of time suggests that Madoff never deluded himself into believing he was anything more than a run-of-the-mill embezzler skilled at gaining people's trust. He apparently coped with the knowledge that his scam would eventually destroy the lives of many friends, family and investors by compartmentalizing his own life.

What sets Enron apart from embezzlers like Madoff, is that Enron's financial reporting was very close to Generally Accepted Accounting Principles. For several years, the hollow husk that was Enron hid behind literally millions of pages in complex financial reporting documents and a line-up of smarmy executives who played the experts in the business media like a rented PlayStation. They were so effective in convincing others of their brilliance that they believed it themselves. In a sense, Enron was a Ponzi scheme of bogus expertise. The company paid exorbitant salaries to "brilliant" managers who enlisted consultants and the business media to advertise their expertise sufficient to move the stock price and then used the stock price to justify additional compensation. Enron was a pyramid built on financial complexity and unbridled ego; when a reporter for *The Wall Street Journal* smelled a rat in their reported earnings, the company began its legendary collapse.

The same McKinsey & Company that was hired by Chief Executive Roger Smith to come up with a plan to rid GM of Ross Perot in 1986, was also a favorite among Enron executives. Annual McKinsey billings to Enron topped $10 million and McKinsey consultants often sat in on directors meetings. Jeffrey Skilling, Enron president and later CEO, was a former McKinsey partner. In the 1990s, McKinsey sponsored a study called "The War for Talent" in which thousands of questionnaires were sent to managers at companies across the country. The consultants whittled the responses down to just eighteen companies and spent three days at each firm interviewing everyone from the CEO down to the head of human resources. The purpose of the study was to identify how the top performing companies differed from the mediocre ones in regard to hiring and promotion. The three lead consultants on the project, Michaels, Handfield-Jones and Axelrod, would write a book titled *The War for Talent* based on a summary of the project findings. They concluded that the best companies are the ones that are most obsessive about identifying, hiring and promoting the most talented people. They label this pre-occupation with talent as "the talent mind set" and argue that success in the modern economy requires "deep seated belief that to have better talent at all levels is how you out-perform your competitors."[34]

In his essay *The Talent Myth* Malcolm Gladwell explains that no one embraced "the talent mind set" more than Enron and no one lionized Enron's management more than McKinsey. During the 1990s, Jeffrey Skilling brought "in a steady stream of the best college and MBA graduates he could find to stock the company with talent."[35] CEO Kenneth Lay fully supported Enron's star system explaining that "the only thing that differentiates Enron from our competitors is our people, our talent."[36] Of course, from the perspective of stockholders it is output (share performance) that should differentiate a public company not input (expert talent). Kenneth Lay was a PhD economist by training, hardly the type one would expect to confuse the two; but leading a company that media experts celebrate as a model for the rest of corporate America can blur one's perspective.

Known for creative thinking in weather derivatives and other financial instruments, Enron was no less creative in their financial accounting. Mark-to-market accounting rules allowed Enron to estimate and then report millions of dollars in hypothetical profits that were unrealized. Jonathon Weil, a reporter for *The Wall Street Journal*, was one of the first to successfully permeate the complexity of Enron's mark-to-market accounting. He found that when unrealized profits were deducted from the company's second quarter earnings in 2000, Enron's experienced a substantial loss.[37]

Another part of Enron's gratuitously complex accounting puzzle was the use of *special purpose entities* (SPE). SPEs are partnerships that are formed between the company and outside investors. Enron would place assets in the SPE and then borrow against the assets. If the assets were of low quality, then Enron would promise the lender that they would make good on any shortfall with Enron stock. At the time, the debt borrowed against SPEs was not required to appear on Enron's balance sheet. Although SPE is a common structure in corporate America, Enron introduced a number of variations on the SPE, which included lending partners the minimum three percent interest required to form the SPE and keeping it off Enron's financials. The SPEs were then managed by Enron executives.

Enron's use of SPEs was irresponsible and very close to crossing the line into outright fraud but as Gladwell notes; the company essentially complied with legal disclosure standards. Enron had an internal legal staff of over 100 lawyers and several hundred trained accountants. In 2000, the company paid $50 million to their auditor Arthur Andersen and another $50 million to outside legal counsel. Over the years, this army of financial and legal experts had constructed over 3,000 complex SPEs with paper work for each estimated to average 1,000 pages. Anyone hoping to get a handle on the off-balance sheet liability created by Enron's SPEs would have to wade through approximately 3 million pages of documents. [38] According to some legal authorities, the fraud charges against Enron executives were an incredibly close call. Why commit fraud if it is possible to achieve the same objective by hiding behind gratuitously complex rules that generate millions of impenetrable documents—documents that are not fully understood by the hundreds of accountants and legal experts who prepare them?

The bond rating agencies proved no more proficient in rating Enron than the accounting auditors and financial press. Following the Enron bankruptcy, the rating agencies were targeted by disgruntled investors and an irate Congress. Despite the growing questions about Enron's accounting and use of SPEs, the agencies were slow to downgrade the company in the months leading up to their bankruptcy. Just four days before Enron's collapse, expert bond raters still had Enron bonds rated "investment grade." [39]

The fact that Enron was an empty suit kept alive by largely legitimate but gratuitously complex financial machinations, did not prevent its executives from buffing their public image. In one frequently retold story, Jeffrey Skilling explains how a 29 year-old gas trader at Enron became convinced that the company should construct an on-line trading system. She started working in her spare time until she had over 200 other people involved in the project. Skilling was not informed until six months after the fact. His response: "I was never asked for any capital, I was never asked for any people, they had already purchased the servers. They had already started ripping apart the building. They had already started legal reviews in twenty-two countries by the time I heard about it...exactly the kind of behavior that will continue to drive this company forward." [40] One senior Enron executive bragged to a McKinsey consultant, "We hire very smart people and we pay them more than they think they are worth." [41]

In August 2001, Skilling resigned as CEO and Kenneth Lay assumed the position along with the Chairman of the Board. In November of 2001, the SEC "inquiry" into Enron's financial practices was up-graded to a "formal investigation," a month later Enron filed for bankruptcy. In the months prior to bankruptcy, Skilling and Lay sold $41 million of Enron stock and other corporate insiders sold $71 million. Employees were restricted from selling the Enron stock from their 401(k) retirement accounts unless retiring or leaving employment.

In the end, the stakeholder versus shareholder debate is straightforward. Those who advocate the stakeholder model believe the business experts produced by the meritocracy are talented enough to coordinate and implement a top-down strategy that simultaneously optimizes all competing interests while holding their own self-interest at bay. In contrast, advocates of the shareholder model believe that the maximization of shareholder wealth should remain the primary objective of management because it is relatively easy to implement, utilizes more extensive bottom-up knowledge and is generally consistent with the best interest of stakeholders. Shareholder advocates are much more skeptical of the meritocracy that selects and trains business experts. Time and again the record indicates that self-interested managers need to be aggressively monitored to prevent them from pursuing their own ends at the expense of shareholders and creditors; but even if corporate managers have the best intentions, management science is not sufficiently advanced to produce a top-down solution that is economically superior to one produced by a bottom-up model based on share price.

This does not mean that *all* stakeholders will *always* and *everywhere* benefit by a decision rule that focuses on shareholder value, only that it represents the best trade-off. Accounting and law are human constructs meant to organize and codify rules of conduct rather than obfuscate. No one believes that the accounting rules and tax code needs to be so absurdly complex but we seem powerless to reverse the trend. For markets to operate efficiently, information needs to be cheaper and easier to understand with minimal need for expert translators; but even if the rules are somehow simplified, there will always be people injured by the vagaries of the market place. Some of these inequities can be addressed by policy but many grievances will go unresolved because life is imperfect and there is no one to blame.

If bankruptcy is a fact of life then failure attributable to fraud, malfeasance and managerial hubris is organizational murder. When companies are liquidated, so are the jobs of employees as well as those of suppliers and service providers. Private pension value is often diminished shifting more of the retirement burden to an already strained Social Security System. Erosion in shareholder value reduces tax revenue that supports public schools, programs for the poor and other initiatives that benefit the disadvantaged. Private donations to museums, symphonies, scholarship endowments and a variety of other cultural and charitable organizations suffer when shareholder value declines. [42]

Rather than worshipping at the craven altar of share price, managers who fraudulently destroy business value and justify lining their own pockets on basis of half baked management theories like "the talent mind set" only serve to demonstrate that the self-interested *homo economicus* is alive and well. The failure of agency theory is not that it is predicated on corporate managers pursuing their own interest but that it consistently under-estimates their potential for misconduct. Too often, it naively assumes that mechanisms of compensation, contracts and options have largely solved the problem and aligned the interests of managers with those of shareholders. The CEO and Chairman of the Board positions should be separated to ensure another layer of accountability. Corporate governance rules should encourage greater shareholder activism by mutual funds and pension fund managers in an attempt to restrain irresponsible compensation, and corporate boards should caste a much wider net in recruiting top executives that includes more qualified foreign nationals. If the shareholder model consistently results in economic and social outcomes that are superior to the alternative, it is good business ethics no matter the intentions of managers.

For the record, The Powers Committee investigated the causes of Enron's failure and concluded: "Enron did not communicate the essence of the transactions in a sufficiently clear fashion to enable a reader of its financial statements to understand what was going on." [43] In 2002, Enron auditor Arthur Andersen voluntarily surrendered its license to practice accounting in the Unites States; Kenneth Lay died of a heart attack while awaiting sentencing after being convicted of corporate fraud; Jeffrey Skilling is serving a 24 year-sentence in a federal prison, and McKinsey & Company continues to do a land office business peddling expert advice.

CHAPTER 5

GOOD ENOUGH FOR GOVERNMENT WORK: PUBLIC SECTOR EXPERTS

The larger the canvas on which the expert paints, the greater the potential risk to the rest of us. Big picture government experts, particularly in the foreign policy arena, are especially dangerous since the consequences of their mistakes can resonate for generations. Few judgments are more momentous than the decision to take a nation to war, yet time and again close-knit cadres of foreign policy experts misinterpret intelligence preceding major conflicts.

"Group think" is partly a manifestation of homogeneity in expert knowledge and tends to afflict hierarchal organizations that promote like-thinking persons. When recalling discussions of the Best and Brightest leading up to the Bay of Pigs fiasco, historian Arthur Schlesinger Jr. observed: "Our meetings took place in a curious atmosphere of assumed consensus."[1] Kaufman suggests a similar environment pervaded deliberations preceding the Iraq War.[2] Foreign policy choices frequently give rise to "path dependence" such that today's decisions are inordinately influenced by those made in the past. Intellectual posturing by foreign policy experts can precipitate unnecessary wars that can have dire consequences for future generations, consequences that could have easily been avoided.

The conflagration that followed the assassination of Archduke Franz Ferdinand nearly a century ago is perhaps the best example in the modern era of foreign policy path dependence and the intergenerational repercussions of expert failure. The Archduke was the heir apparent to the throne of the Austro-Hungary

Empire, a quilt work of countries that included nearly a dozen minorities who chafed at the autocratic rule of the dual monarchy. Fifty-years old, overweight and ill-tempered, in the summer of 1914, he and his wife Sophie had traveled to Sarajevo, the capital of Bosnia, to participate in ceremonial activities and review military exercises that were intended to intimidate the trouble makers. Next door to an independent Serbia, Bosnia was home to a number of ethnic Serbs, including a contingent of nationalists who entertained the dream of a Greater Serbia. One such dreamer was Gavrilo Princip, a tubercular, twenty-year-old aspiring poet who read the works of Friedrich Nietzche and the Russian anarchists and who, along with other Serbian nationalists, concocted a scheme to assassinate the Archduke during his visit.

Austria-Hungary and Germany were bound together by a military alliance going back over thirty years. Germany, under the rule of Kaiser Wilhelm II, was by far the more economically and militarily powerful of the two and dominated the alliance. There was a measure of democracy within the German states and a Chancellor who presided over the imperial parliament known as the Reichstag, but foreign policy, defense and the declaration of war were the prerogatives of the Kaiser and the army.[3] Wilhelm assumed the throne at the tender age of twenty-one following the death of his father Frederick III. The Kaiser was born with a withered arm. He shared a difficult relationship with his mother, a daughter of Queen Victoria, but idolized his father despite Frederick's relentless bullying. Wilhelm's father died of cancer after being unsuccessfully treated by English doctors summoned by his mother causing the young Kaiser to blame her and, by extension, the British for his father's death.

The newly unified Germany was an emerging economic power on the European continent and many Germans were anxious for their country to assume what they considered to be its rightful place on the world stage. Easily influenced by military advisors and powerful industrialists, the Kaiser coveted a blue-water navy. Historically preoccupied with domestic problems, Germany had limited access to the world's oceans and had never developed the extensive network of overseas colonies common to many other European countries. Because the army was cobbled together from the old German states, it had diverse loyalties while the new navy owed its allegiance only to the Kaiser. By the start of the war in 1914, Germany had built the second most powerful navy in the world.

Mostly to counteract Austria-Hungary and Germany, Russia and France formed an alliance in 1891. Britain wanted a balance of power on the Continent but remained aloof from European alliances, a stance that could be maintained because of the English Channel and Britain's stature as the world's dominant naval power. Their main interest in Continental Europe was access to channel ports in Belgium, a country that was essentially a British creation and whose neutrality they guaranteed. It wasn't until the dawn of the 20th century and the rise of potentially powerful rivals that Britain modified its position and entered into ententes with Japan in 1902 and with France in 1904. In 1907, Britain signed a treaty with Russia that was intended to prevent a Russian threat to India via Afghanistan. These accords were only understandings, none of which required the British to become involved in a European war.

Immediately following the assassination of the Archduke and his pregnant wife Sophie, European opinion sympathized with Austria but events would quickly spiral out of control. In late July, Austria issued a diplomatic message to Serbia that accused the Serbs of conspiring with subversive elements to incite hatred of the dual monarchy and its institutions in an attempt to detach part of the Empire. An Austria-Hungary investigation claimed to have uncovered evidence that the assassination was planned in Belgrade and that the assassin had been inserted into Bosnia by Serbian authorities. The dual monarchy issued a general order to the Serbian army that required they admit culpability in the assassination and provide an expression of regret to be published in the official Serbian press. All views hostile to Austria-Hungary were to cease and anyone in the universities or government departments expressing subversive sentiments were to be removed. Serbian army officers and other officials accused by Austria of fomenting dissent against the empire were to be dismissed. The dual monarchy also demanded that they be allowed to participate in the prosecution of conspirators conducted in Serbian courts and they gave Serbia forty eight hours to respond.

Germany claimed to have no prior knowledge of the Austria-Hungary ultimatum but history suggests that the government and the Kaiser had assured their ally of Germany's unconditional support. There were harried, last minute attempts at mediation by Russia, presumably acting on behalf of fellow Slavs, as well as by Serbia, Britain, Austria and belatedly by the Kaiser himself to forestall a military confrontation or at least ensure that it remained localized.

Historians have studied the months leading up to the Great War in greater detail than any period in modern history in an effort to understand how a series of cascading events and bad decisions transformed the "unnecessary war" into a political inevitability. In 1910, Norman Angell published a book called *The Great Illusion* that argued such a war was impossible because it violated economic rationality. Angell used numerous incontrovertible arguments to demonstrate that the economic interdependence of European nations had rendered war unprofitable, causing the victor to suffer in equal measure to the vanquished. Translated into eleven languages, Angell's book was studied by groups at universities in Glasgow and Manchester that formed to discuss and promote the rationality theme, thus causing the book to achieve a kind of cult status. Viscount Esher, Chairman of the War Committee, assigned the task of reforming the British Army after its disappointing performance in the Boer War, was an advocate of Angell's hypothesis. In speeches at Cambridge University and the Sorbonne, Esher argued that "new economic factors clearly prove the inanity of aggressive wars" because 20th century war would be on such a scale that it would result in "commercial disaster, financial ruin and individual suffering" of unprecedented magnitude.[4]

At about the same time that Angell had marshaled economic science to prove why the Great War would never happen, German military expert General von Bernhardi advanced the proposition that war was a "biological necessity." His book *Germany and the Next War* contained provocative chapters with titles such as "The Duty to Make War," "Germany's Historical Mission" and "World Power or Downfall" that characterized war as an unavoidable choice for nations that are destined to assume greatness.[5] Bernhardi was a member of the German intellectual elite and had served in the Military History Section of the General Staff. He studied Clausewitz, the German philosophers and was a fan of Darwin. The general reasoned that war is an inescapable form of natural selection given that Germany "is in social-political respects at the head of all progress in culture" but is "compressed into narrow, unnatural limits." Bernhardi provided Germany 'scientific' justification for the Great War, all that remained was for military strategists to devise an operational plan of attack and for Providence to supply creditable provocation, such as a political assassination.

When Bernhardi published his book in 1911, the German attack plan was already in progress. The architect of their strategy was Count Alfred von Schlieffen, Chief of the General Staff from 1891 to 1906. Cold and distant in his immaculate uniform and obligatory monocle, Count von Schlieffen was a Prussian officer straight from Hollywood central casting. Like Clausewitz, Schlieffen was convinced that "the heart of France lies between Brussels and Paris" a perilous path toward fulfillment of its biological destiny since Germany, along with four other European powers, had agreed to Belgian neutrality in perpetuity. The "biological necessity" of Bernhardi became a "military necessity" to the Count, sufficient to justify the violation of Belgium neutrality. His plan of attack was borrowed from the Battle of Cannae in which Hannibal employed a classic double envelopment strategy to encircle the Romans. Like Hannibal, Schlieffen envisioned a sweeping action across Belgium into France with the bulk of the German forces concentrated in the West: "let the last man on the right brush the channel with his sleeve."[6] The Count would retire in 1906 but until his death in 1913, he continued to improve on and promote his plan to those in power.

On August 1, 1914, barely one month after the Archduke's assassination, General Helmuth von Moltke launched the German attack on the Western Front but, true to his nature, the Kaiser had last minute reservations and asked the general to reverse direction and march the army east to engage Russia. Moltke refused on the basis that once set in motion, ten years of detailed planning involving the mobilization of 1 million men and 11,000 trains could not be reversed. It was as if Moltke had fallen in love with the plan's clock-work precision and could not bear to see its technical beauty disrupted. Of course, his assertion that the attack "once settled, cannot be altered" was patently false since there were alternative plans in the files of the German General Staff going back to 1905 in which the attack was routed eastward.[7]

Like many other conflicts before and since, the Great War began with military plans wagging the dog of foreign policy. Commander of Britain's Staff College, General Henry Wilson learned of Schlieffen's envelopment strategy as early as 1909 and commiserated with General Foch, his counterpart in the French army, on how best to respond.[8] In the weeks leading up to war, virtually all of the experts anticipated a short engagement, none more than the Kaiser who in August of 1914 told departing troops "you will be home before the leaves have fallen from the trees."[9] The German strategy was predicated on quick victory over the French so that a substantial portion of the troops in the West could be redeployed against the Russians who were not expected to achieve full mobilization for several months. Experts such as Norman Angell and the German General Staff reinforced the notion that the war would be a brief one; almost no one dissented from the quick war scenario or planned for what would prove to be a prolonged war of attrition.

After the Battles of the Marne and Ypres, the coming winter saw the fighting on the Western Front from Switzerland to the English Channel sink into the slow, deadly stalemate that was labeled trench warfare. Every day for four years, soldiers would fight valiantly to gain the next mud filled trench as the line moved back and forth over a few hundred yards grinding up young men by the tens of thousands. Before the Armistice was signed in November of 1918, it is estimated that more than 4 million French, British and German soldiers were killed in all theatres of war.[10] In contrast to more contemporary conflicts, there were few *Fortunate Sons*. About 12 percent of all British soldiers who participated in the war were killed but among the officer corps that drew from the upper classes the percentage was 19 percent. Of all men who graduated from Oxford in 1913, nearly one in three or 31 percent perished in the war. The German Chancellor lost his oldest son as did British Prime Minister Herbert Asquith. Future Prime Minister Andrew Law lost two sons as did Herbert Lawrence, chief of the British general staff on the Western Front. Lawrence's counterpart in the French Army, Noel de Castelnau sacrificed three sons to the war.[11]

Many more people, including civilians, were killed in WWII. Yet, the Great War may be the single greatest human folly of the 20th century, not just because of the casualties and expenditure of treasure, but because it was an unnecessary war motivated by German hubris. The Great War set the stage for WWII and its consequences resonate to the present day. The Versailles Treaty of 1919 required that Germany pay onerous war reparations in either foreign exchange or gold. Attempts by Germany's Weimar government to monetize the payments by printing marks to purchase foreign currency ignited a hyperinflation that John Maynard Keynes described in *The Economic Consequences of the Peace*. "The inflationism of the currency systems of Europe has proceeded to extraordinary lengths. The various belligerent Governments, unable, or too timid or too short-sighted to secure from loans or taxes the resources they required, have printed notes for the balance."[12]

The hyperinflation eroded trust in liberal institutions, especially among the now impoverished German middle-class who held their savings in bonds. Some Germans blamed the crisis on banks or financial speculators and referred to the worthless Weimar banknotes as "Jew confetti." The inflation was followed by economic collapse and civil unrest which provided fertile soil for the rise of National Socialism whose leaders would convince a significant portion of the German population that their Fatherland had not been defeated on the field of battle but had been betrayed by spineless politicians, Bolshevism and international Jewry. Keynes observed: "Lenin was certainly right. There is no subtler, no surer means of overturning the existing basis of society than to debauch the currency."[13] The greatest fear of Keynes and many others was that burdensome war reparations would unleash a Bolshevik revolution in Germany that would spread to the rest of Europe. The popularity of Keynes' essay in Britain fostered the perception that Germany was treated unfairly and may have later contributed to public support for Chamberlain's policy of appeasement.

The Austro-Hungary Empire collapsed after the Great War creating Yugoslavia and Czechoslovakia, but the Versailles Treaty would fail to reconcile the religious and cultural differences in the Balkans which led to future conflicts. Even if there had been no Great War, Russia was ripe for revolution and, despite the absence of a democratic tradition, the war likely provided greater opportunity for the more radical Bolsheviks who eventually claimed victory. The Balfour Declaration of November 2, 1917 was an attempt by the British Foreign Secretary Arthur Balfour to gain the backing of some influential Americans to enter the war in exchange for promising the establishment of a Jewish homeland in Palestine. Despite Chamberlain's abrogation of the declaration in 1939, it would eventually lead to the establishment of the State of Israel a decade later and a subsequent dispute that has been in the forefront of Middle Eastern politics for much of the post-WWII era.

Monarchy was presumed to foster international stability by creating blood alliances via the cross-country marriages of royal families. At no point in modern history has there been a greater number of interlocking monarchies than existed prior to the Great War. Rather than promoting stability, this web of family connections seemed to fan petty jealousies that would further erode the status of royalty in post-war Europe. The Kaiser would end his days in exile at Doorn in Holland and while he rejected overtures from the Nazis, he could not resist sending a congratulatory telegram to the German army when it occupied Paris. He died in exile in 1941; his son, a dissolute alcoholic, would expire in the arms of his Italian mistress ten years later.[14] The Russian Czar and his family were executed by the Bolsheviks and while other European monarchs were more fortunate, most would be rendered relatively powerless symbols of a bygone age.

The Great War gave us the phrase "shell shock" which was displaced by "battle fatigue" in WWII and is now described as "traumatic stress disorder." This psychological condition was known to officially afflict over 80,000 British soldiers between 1914 and 1918 but there were undoubtedly many thousands more. Some men became catatonic; others would break down in prolonged periods of uncontrolled sobbing; still others simply refused to return to the trenches. Britain executed over 300 of their own men by firing squad, many of whom were experiencing psychological disorders that the military dismissed as "cowardice." With little public understanding of battle induced stress disorders, tens of thousands of returning veterans would struggle the rest of their days to readjust to civilian life.[15]

The Great War is the war that keeps on giving. Over 700 million artillery and mortar shells were fired on the Western Front with approximately 15 percent of them estimated to constitute "unexploded ordinance" that every year yields a deadly "iron harvest" to farmers tilling in the fields.[16] When France excavated a rail bed for a new high speed train in 1991, 36 people were killed by these old explosives. Since 1945, more than 630 Frenchmen employed as bomb disposal workers have died in the line of duty.[17]

Barbara Tuchman maintains that Schlieffen and Moltke may have engineered the Great War's attack plan but one hundred years of German hubris had a hand in its making. It could be blamed "on the hand of Fichte who saw the German people chosen by Providence to occupy the supreme place in the history of the universe, of Hegel who saw them leading the world to a glorious destiny of compulsory *Kultur*, of Nietzsche who told them that Supermen were above ordinary controls, of Treitschke who set the increase of power as the highest moral duty of the state, of the whole German people, who called their temporal ruler the All-Highest. What made the Schlieffen plan was not Clausewitz and the Battle of Cannae, but the body of accumulated egoism which suckled the German people and created a nation fed on the desperate delusion of the will that deems itself absolute."[18]

The intellectual glorification of both war and the martial tradition was not exclusive to Prussian officers and the German army. Colonial apologists and jingoists among the Allies also contributed to the popular 19th century notion that war built character and that military service was the preferred path to a fulfilling manhood. A stanza of Kipling's poem *The Young British Soldier* written in 1895 mirrored popular sentiment among many late 19th century Brits:

> When you're wounded and left on Afghanistan's plains,
>
> And the women come out to cut up what remains,
>
> Jest roll to your rifle and blow out your brains
>
> An' go to your Gawd like a soldier.[19]

Such an ending was portrayed as an admirable conclusion to a young life spent in service to Empire but the Great War would not only strip away romantic notions of cavalry charges in exotic lands, it would forever change the way people view modern warfare. After sacrificing a son whose body was never recovered, Kipling's writing assumed a much more somber tone.

The young man in Erique Remarque's novel *All Quiet on the Western Front* is not engaged in a romantic struggle; none of the battles even have names. Instead, Remarque tells the story of a young German soldier who navigates the filth and deprivation of the trenches in a life that alternates between mind numbing boredom and the terror of unremitting artillery bombardment. One by one the young soldier's friends are lost in battle. When he is finally killed on a day that is described as "all quiet on the Western Front" there is no glory, only release from a living nightmare and respite from complete mental and physical exhaustion. Predictably, the Nazis hated *All Quiet on the Western Front*. Goebbels banned all of Remarque's work and sponsored public book burnings falsely claiming that the author had never seen action in the Great War and was descended from French Jews.

As the Paris Peace Conference convened in the aftermath of the Great War, the Irish poet W.B. Yeats was working on *The Second Coming*, one of the 100 most anthologized poems in the English language. In the body of the poem Yeats observed that "Things fall apart, the centre cannot hold" and in the last line foretells of a "rough beast, its hour come round at last, Slouches toward Bethlehem to be born?"[20]

Many firsthand witnesses to the carnage of WWI were subsequently swept-up in the encore performance of WWII or what some began calling The Great War of 1914-1945. Understandably, a prevailing view among European elites

who came of age during the first half of the 20th century was that no matter what price had to be paid, it should never be allowed to happen again. The
most obvious antidote to resurgent nationalism was to build closer political
and economic ties among European countries. Perhaps more than anyone else,
Konrad Adenauer, the first Chancellor of the Federal Republic of Germany
from 1949-63, changed the face of post-war German and European history.
Together with French President Charles de Gaulle, Adenauer worked to reconcile historic differences between their two countries and in 1963, Germany
and France signed a treaty of friendship, which became one of the milestones
on the road to European integration. In 1957, Germany, France, Belgium, Italy,
Luxembourg and the Netherlands would sign the Treaty of Rome creating the
European Economic Community or Common Market. Denmark, Ireland and
the United Kingdom would join in 1973. Portugal later joined the Common
Market following the overthrow of Salazar; Spain applied for admission after
the death of Franco. The collapse of the former Soviet Union and the fall of the
Berlin wall redrew the map of Europe to include a unified Germany.

With the free movement of goods, services, money and people, along with a
common currency, the dawn of the new millennium ushered in feelings of
economic and political exuberance until the financial crisis of 2008 exposed
the Euro's shortcomings. In hindsight, the exuberance bordered on the "irrational" since many knowledgeable observers recognized from the beginning
that monetary union was incompatible with fiscal autonomy. Critics like Milton
Friedman, who predicted a looming crisis, were cognizant of the fact that the
experts had replaced fiscal discipline enforced by financial markets with a system of rules known as the European Stability Pact, as everyone knows, expert
rules beg to be broken.

The crisis in Greece and Spain deflated the recovery and threatened to drag the
world back into recession; there was a palpable sense of 'schadenfreude' among
EU opponents. The same feeling was discernible among many conservative
economic commentators in the U.S. media who sought to use the European
experience as a cautionary tale to combat growing public debt and the gradual encroachment of the welfare state in America. As the dominant "partner,"
German insistence that the road to prosperity requires austerity, unleashed a
wave of anti-German sentiment. Editorials in member newspapers accused
their partner of finally gaining "economic hegemony" of Continental Europe
after failure to establish it militarily. Effigies of German Chancellor Angela

Merkel in a Nazi uniform have been burned on the streets of Athens amid signs of "Heil Merkel" and demands for "War Reparations."

Political tension among EU countries was not helped by the publication of *Europe Doesn't Need the Euro*. The author, former Bundesbank director Thilo Sarrazin, makes the case that the euro has brought more financial risk to Germany with few tangible economic benefits. German trade with nations outside the euro zone is growing faster than trade with other members. A currency union without political union was a pipe dream and now Germany is under increasing pressure to accept bailout measures that will ultimately lead to an increase in German debt and rampant inflation. Sarrazin argues that if other EU nations are unable to accept German discipline they should either leave the euro or Germany should; otherwise the "transfer union" many Germans feared will soon become a reality.[21] Sarrazin disputes Angela Merkel's assertion that "if the euro fails, then Europe fails." Instead, he views the common currency as a source of instability and argues that the grand experiment of European integration would be more successful without it. Sarrazin's most controversial claim is that German politicians, in bailing out other euro nations, abrogated the national interest because of guilt over the Holocaust and WWII. The former bank director is undoubtedly verbalizing what some Germans are thinking but it did not prevent a number of politicians from accusing him of pandering to German nationalism, a prospect that still frightens many of Germany's neighbors. [22]

A number of Germans adhere to the assertion that their *real* guilt derives *not* from the Holocaust and a war that ended 67 years ago but from the fact that their national economy operates at a much higher level of efficiency than other Euro members, especially their partners to the south. But the contention that Germany has given more to other Euro members than it has received in return and that their economic success can be attributed exclusively to Teutonic know-how and self-discipline, is somewhat disingenuous. Without the euro, it is unlikely that Germany would have enjoyed the same export bonanza since the mark would have appreciated considerably in the face of their trade surplus. Indeed, because a soaring currency would result in lower growth and big losses in overseas balances, some financial models predict that the country with the least incentive to exit the euro is Germany.[23]

There may be widespread public resentment against Euro bailouts but Germans should have known what they were getting into when they admitted such a diverse group into the single currency union. A decade ago, the experts allowed many countries in fragile fiscal health to essentially "cook their books" as a means to qualify for Euro membership. Both Germany and France were fore-warned that Greece, Spain and Italy were fiscal accidents waiting to happen but in an environment of "irrational exuberance" they chose to ignore the warn-ing signs. As long as times were good and there was an abundance of cheap money, no one in Berlin or Paris complained, let alone Athens, Madrid or Rome.

Did guilt over the Holocaust and WWII play a role in the creation of the European Union? Certainly, but the common currency will not sink or swim on the basis of residual guilt from a war whose perpetrators are all dead or dying. Instead, it will depend on Germany's willingness to assume the inflation risk associ-ated with the issuance of Eurobonds or other "lender of last resort financing" provided to member nations by the European Central Bank. Germany's leg-endary aversion to inflation has less to do with the Holocaust or WWII guilt than with the hyperinflation that followed the Great War. The consequences of the Weimar government's "debauched currency" are seared into the German consciousness. For Europhiles, the political symbolism of a common currency dwarfed economic reality and blinded them to the inevitable day of fiscal reckoning. Along with the fiscal/monetary disconnect, euro architects failed to consider the collective memory of its largest partner and now the future of the common currency depends on the willingness of the German people to finally put that memory to rest.

INTELLECTUAL HUBRIS AND AMERICAN WARS OF CHOICE

Since the Great War ended a little less than a century ago, the U.S. has par-ticipated in a surfeit of military conflicts around the world. Some, like WWII, Korea, Dessert Storm and the war in Afghanistan, were unavoidable responses to naked aggression. Others, most notably Vietnam and Iraq, were wars of choice motivated by intellectual arguments advanced by foreign policy experts.

U.S. policy in Vietnam was an extension of George Kennan's concept of "con-tainment" that was laid out in the famous "long telegram" of 1946 while he was working as Chief of Mission and Consultant to Soviet Ambassador Averell Harriman. A summary of the long telegram was published in a 1947 issue of *Foreign Affairs* titled "The Sources of Soviet Conduct" with Kennan writing under the pseudonym "X." In the essay, Kennan described Moscow's strategic behavior as a "fluid stream" that has "filled every nook and cranny available to it in the basin of world power." He suggested that Soviet designs be "contained" by the "adroit and vigilant applications of counterforce at a series of constantly shifting geographical and political points."[24] At the time, Kennan was referring to Soviet ambitions in Eastern Europe but the containment policy was extended to include Communist China and its designs on Southeast Asia.

As early as 1950, President Truman committed to helping the French maintain its hold on Indochina as a way of thwarting Chinese Communist expansion in the region. U.S. aid to France in Indochina was also tied to greater French support of the U.S. containment policy in Europe. By supporting France, the U.S. failed to exploit two thousand years of enmity between China and Vietnam and the fact that Ho Chi Minh was a less than enthusiastic ally of the Chinese. America went "all in" as it were on the "domino theory," which maintained that if the communists prevailed in Vietnam all of Southeast Asia would succumb. The toppling dominos metaphor may have been visually pleasing and helped to drum up public support for U.S. policy, but its literal interpretation ignored complex cultural and ethnic differences among countries in the region that could have been exploited to further American objectives. The application of counterforce at a series of constantly shifting "political points" was an important but subtle element of Kennan's containment policy but in Southeast Asia the doctrine was increasingly interpreted in military terms, an over simplification that helped drive the North Vietnamese into the arms of their historic enemy.

The partitioning of Vietnam into North and South according to the Geneva Conference was intended as a short-term solution that provided the French the opportunity for a graceful exit. When the Soviets suggested that each half be recognized as an independent country, the U.S. rejected the overture and lost an opportunity for a political solution, however tenuous. When hostilities resumed after the French departure, the non-communist South was led by Diem, a devout Catholic who was politically unskilled and no match for the hardened communist leadership in the North. Despite Diem's high moral character, his government was corrupt and undisciplined, leading Ambassador Lodge and President Kennedy to conclude that they were backing a losing horse. A bungled military coup orchestrated by the U.S. government would result in the unintended assassination of Diem, which would reinforce the perception that U.S. complicity in the incident increased America's moral obligation to help turn South Vietnam into a viable nation. Kennedy was assassinated three weeks after Diem was killed.

In the summer of 1964, Lyndon Johnson was facing a November election against Barry Goldwater, an arch-conservative with impeccable anti-communist credentials. Johnson was eager to burnish his image as being "tough on communism;" so, when a minor naval incident occurred in the Gulf of Tonkin, Johnson seized the opportunity as an excuse to bomb North Vietnam. There were actually two incidents, but the bombing was based on the second one which most historians now believe never took place. Instead, the "torpedoes" identified on radar were probably caused by unstable weather patterns in the Gulf.[25] The bombing would set the U.S. on a path of escalating military entanglement in a conflict that could only be resolved politically. Never really losing an important battle but never completely winning in decisive fashion, the Vietnam War would divide a generation of Americans as one by one most of the pro-war experts eventually admitted the error of their ways.

In late September of 2012, the Vietnamese government was less concerned with the teaching of Chairmen Mao and Ho than how to prevent the rating agencies from downgrading their bonds deeper into junk status. A banking scandal, along with deteriorating loan quality and declining profitability, prompted the bond downgrade. A contrite government spokesman promised to do everything necessary to restore confidence in the banking system. Perhaps, if General Westmoreland had Moody's on his side the U.S. might have prevailed.

Vietnam may have been a war of choice but even intellectually motivated wars based on foreign policy theories require provocation. Johnson embraced the Gulf of Tonkin incident as an election year opportunity. In Iraq, provocation consisted of Saddam Hussein's manufacture of weapons of mass destruction (WMD) and, like the Gulf of Tonkin incident; it also proved to be a canard. Instead of "containment" and the "domino theory," the neo-conservative principles of "regime change" and "benevolent hegemony" would provide the intellectual justification for invading Iraq. Where did these foreign policy intellectuals come from and why did we fight their unnecessary war?

Neo-conservative roots can be traced to a group of intellectuals who attended the City College of New York during the 1930's and 1940s. Their unifying principal was an intense anti-communism and distaste for liberals unable to recognize the inherent evil of the Soviet system. Much has been written about University of Chicago professor Leo Strauss and his role as intellectual mentor. Drury argues that Strauss was "the inspiration behind the reigning neo-conservative ideology of the Republican Party"[26] and although her interest in Strauss predates the Iraq War, her books provide the most informed attempt to link Strauss with neo-conservatives.

In their book *The Truth About Leo Strauss*, Catherine and Michael Zuckert claim that depictions in the media of Straussian influenced neo-conservatives are little more than caricatures. In *America at the Crossroads: Democracy, Power, and the Neoconservative Legacy*, Fukuyama similarly contends that more nonsense has been written about Leo Strauss and the Iraq War than on virtually any other subject. Strauss was a classicist. His contribution to neo-conservative thought was the idea that "regimes" matter in foreign policy, particularly in regard to how aristocratic, autocratic and democratic regimes influence the character of people who live under them.

Most knowledgeable observers believe it was Albert Wohlstetter, the Rand Corporation researcher and University of Chicago professor, and not Strauss who would influence future advisors in the Bush Administration. Wohlstetter opposed Henry Kissinger and the realists who dominated foreign policy and held the Straussian view that regimes influence the identity of their citizens. He rejected the 1970s conventional wisdom of "mutually assured destruction" arguing that the Soviet Union was eminently capable of launching a nuclear first attack. Accordingly, he was an advocate of precision targeting, including the use of nuclear warheads. During the 1980's, Wohlstetter turned his attention to the Persian Gulf and nuclear proliferation in the Middle East. Many of his ideas on the deployment of a lighter, more mobile combat force would come to fruition in the first Gulf War.

Kagan and Kristol outlined the neo-conservative view on "benevolent hegemony" and "regime change" under American leadership in *Foreign Affairs* and in their book *Present Dangers*. The policy called for an active effort to undermine foreign dictators and hostile ideologies in "support of American interests and liberal democratic principles" while providing assistance to those struggling "against the more extreme manifestations of human evil."[27] In September 2000, a year before the 9/11/01 attacks, the neo-conservative Project for the New American Century (PNAC) released a report titled *Rebuilding America's Defenses*.

The report states, "the United States has for decades sought to play a more per-manent role in Gulf regional security. While the unresolved conflict with Iraq provides the immediate justification, the need for a substantial American force presence in the Gulf transcends the issue of the regime of Saddam Hussein."[28] WMD supplied provocation and the neo-conservatives provided intellectual justification for what was essentially a foreign policy experiment to test the principles of "regime change" and "benevolent hegemony."

Seymour Hersh contends that neo-conservatives relied on Straussian philoso-phy to gain intellectual permission for their duplicity.[29] In fairness, Strauss did not invent the plague of experts or the top-down model of human progress that tolerates subterfuge if it serves a higher purpose. Plato thought that "our rulers will have to make considerable use of falsehood and deception for the benefit of their subjects."[30] Lofty ideals have always been distilled from the current crop of fashionable doctrines and as Shumpeter observed, "the first thing a man will do for his ideals is lie."[31] Members of the foreign policy elite are probably no more duplicitous than other public sector experts such as those in the judiciary. Constitutional scholar Alexander Bickel wrote that dissimula-tion" is sometimes "unavoidable" and urged "statesmanlike deviousness" in pursuit of the public interest.[32] Vice President Dick Cheney was following Plato and Bickel's advice when his office leaked stories to *New York Times* reporter Judith Miller that claimed to substantiate Saddam Hussein's WMD program and then used the stories to justify the Iraq invasion. However tenuous, those who advocate wars of choice must first establish provocation both as a means to overcome public resistance and to impose a historical narrative.

Fukuyama maintains that a major shortcoming of the neo-conservative prin-ciple of preemptive war is that it requires the ability to predict the future. Like many of their fellows, experts in foreign policy are better at formulating the-ory than gazing into their crystal balls to ferret out the consequences of their actions. Vice President Cheney famously predicted that the Iraqis would greet U.S. troops as "liberators." When Defense Secretary Donald Rumsfeld said the Iraq War "could last six days, six weeks—I doubt six months" he was making an expert forecast.[33] The war lasted three months short of nine years or 1,650% longer than the Defense Secretary's longest estimate. When Deputy Secretary of Defense Paul Wolfowitz appeared before Congress and predicted that the Iraq War would cost approximately $60 billion but would most likely be self-financing once the oil began to flow, this former Dean of the prestigious Paul

H. Nitze School of Advanced International Studies at Johns Hopkins University was providing American taxpayers the benefit of his expert opinion.[34] The actual cost turned out to be approximately $3.5 trillion or 5,800% more than Wolfowitz estimated. The total number of American military casualties in Iraq as of February 11, 2012 was 4,486 dead and 33,184 wounded.[35] As rewards for their expert advice, Rumsfeld received the Medal of Freedom and Wolfowitz was promoted to the Presidency of the World Bank. Former Vice President Dick Cheney continues to provide the nation expert commentary on foreign policy issues.

Tonsor writes that unlike neo-conservatives, old-fashioned conservatives harbor "absolutely no hopes of a utopian political order. They live with sin and tragedy, not as a consequence of inadequate social engineering, but as a consequence of man's sin and disorder."[36] Ambitious wars of choice motivated by foreign policy theorists are almost always a bad idea. Despite good intentions, "nation building" represents the ultimate conceit in expert social engineering. The mistakes of the experts who practice the science or art of foreign policy resonate across the ages leaving future generations to deal with the political and economic consequences.

PUBLIC SECTOR EXPERTISE WRIT SMALL

In 2001, an 81-year-old woman in Rhode Island fell behind on paying her sewer bill totaling $150. Her house was sold at a tax sale for $836 and resold by investors for $125,000.[37] The National Consumer Law Center reports a large increase in tax lien foreclosures, especially among the elderly, with some municipalities charging up to 50% annual interest rates on the outstanding balance and penalties. In a case similar to the one in Rhode Island, a Baltimore homeowner was evicted from her home and her house sold at auction because she was unable to pay a $362 water bill that ballooned to $3,600 after interest, penalties and legal fees were added to the redemption charge.[38]

The National Consumer Law Center reports that many tax foreclosures involve people who are sick with Alzheimer's or other serious illness. If a Wall Street bank levied the same usurious rates, evicted elderly widows, and generally acted in the same manner, they would be pilloried by the media but because the perpetrator is government, the public has a higher tolerance for nasty and incompetent behavior. Time and again we bear witness to government programs that have been mismanaged or failed to deliver the quality of service at the price promised by public sector experts: public schools, pension programs, drug enforcement, anti-poverty programs, financial regulation, energy subsidies, road maintenance, farm subsidies, urban renewal programs, and the list goes on and on. Why has government become so involved in the economy and why do we have such a high tolerance for the incompetence of public sector experts?

Self-interest may be the organizing principle of markets but their efficient operation is critically dependent on trust. Adam Smith and John Stuart Mill both observed significant variations in social trust among people of different nations. Smith characterized the Dutch as "most faithful to their word" while Mill wrote that a major impediment to commerce in Europe "is the rarity of persons who are supposed fit to be trusted with the receipts and expenditures of large sums of money."[39] Mill may have lamented a shortage of honesty among 19th century European businessmen but most contemporary behavioral research reveals a surprisingly high degree of social trust among Western nations. Repeated research consistently finds that a significant percentage of players in anonymous prisoner's dilemma games will choose to trust their partners rather than defect to the economically rational Nash equilibrium.[40]

Who Wants to Be a Millionaire is a TV quiz show that is syndicated around the world and requires the contestant to answer a variety of questions. If the contestant is uncertain of his answer he has the option to exercise lifelines that allows him to "ask the audience." American contestants can generally trust the audience to help answer the question correctly regardless of his or her apparent abilities; data show that in the United States, the "ask the audience" lifeline results in the correct answer more than 90 percent of the time. When the show was introduced in Russia, the production team noticed that the audiences would often give the wrong answer in an effort to deliberately mislead both intelligent and less intelligent contestants alike.[41] Russian audiences were so inclined to give the wrong answer that contestants learned to be wary of trusting the "ask the audience" lifeline. Some social scientists attribute the difference in audience behavior to disparate cultural notions of "fairness" and Russian resentment of "undeserved wealth" but it also suggests fundamental differences in social trust that can have broader implications for the larger society.

Trust is evident in the most mundane rules and commercial transactions. When vacationing, we gas up the car at a service station and trust that the pumps are accurate and the fuel un-watered despite never having frequented the business nor intending to do so in the future. We eat at an adjoining restaurant and trust that the meal will meet minimum standards of hygiene and quality. While fishing on a remote river, we abide by catch/ release rules and dine on freeze dried beef stew despite a very small chance of being caught should we opt for a more tasty trout dinner. Why do people obey rules and exhibit such trusting behavior? Many contend that the fear of government sanction imposes minimum quality standards and that the threat of large fines or prison enforces obedience even when the probability of being prosecuted for violating the rules is very small.

Rules and traditions evolved from human interaction to form the basis for trust. Economic exchange occurs within a social structure that establishes the rewards and penalties for cooperation. Trust tends to be strongest among those most similar to one another, such as blood relatives, and diminishes as the family tree branches out. Evolutionary biologists characterize this process as "Hamilton's Rule" which posits that the degree of altruistic or trusting behavior is highest among family members and potentially in-breeding neighbors. The temptation to cheat becomes stronger when genetic and social ties among dissimilar parties are weaker. When informal sanctions such as social ostracism, loss of profit due to loss of reputation, and guilt associated with the violation of moral norms or religious principle fail to discourage cheating, society establishes formal mechanisms of trust enforcement such as police, regulators and the courts.

The government could theoretically post a regulator at every service station in order to guarantee that each gasoline sale meets quality standards but the cost would be prohibitively high. Without market-generated trust forming systems, it is likely that the transaction costs associated with formal enforcement of honest behavior would exceed the benefits for many types of economic exchange. Because formal trust enforcement results in high transaction costs, high trust societies spend less on trust enforcement and produce more output than those with low trust. Douglas North observed that the inability of some societies to create low-cost enforcement of trusting behaviors may be the "most important source of both historical stagnation and contemporary underdevelopment in the Third World."[42] Research finds that trusting societies grow faster and that some less developed countries are locked in a "Northian low-trust poverty trap."[43]

Countries of French legal origin, on average, exhibit lower levels of trust than common law countries and those of Scandinavian legal origin. This could suggest that the citizens of common law countries place more trust in their system because they are based on the slow accretion of bottom-up experience rather than top-down expert knowledge. The difference between the French and English legal systems developed over many centuries and was fashioned in response to very different levels of social disorder, with England being con-siderably more peaceful than France. The French and English legal traditions were subsequently transplanted through conquest and colonization to other parts of the world but there is no reason to believe that English versus French colonies began with significantly different levels of distrust. Some historians speculate that, compared to the English colonies, the more heavily regulated French colonies developed lower levels of trust because of a more intrusive state and that a self-perpetuating loop evolved with lower trust spurring additional demand for regulation despite regulators being obviously corrupt.[44]

Low-trust countries tend to have more regulation, which suggests that citi-zens and government presume to create trusting behaviors by substituting low cost informal sanctions with high cost formal regulatory enforcement, a presumption that is far from apparent. One reason informal sanctions can be more efficient is because they rely on more complete bottom-up knowledge rather than the incomplete knowledge of top-down regulatory experts. The French versus English model suggests that societies that rely more on formal trust enforcement may also be more prone to corruption and that citizens attempt to extract favors from the government, a behavior economists refer to as "rent seeking." Because formal enforcement is tied to statutory law, it does not adjust easily to the kind of technological change that has transformed much of the global economy over the last twenty years.

Formal trust enforcement in the U.S. is represented by a vast network of gov-ernment regulators and may be a necessary condition for economic progress in countries with large, demographically diverse populations; however, the record indicates that formal trust enforcement can sometimes be excessive. Excess is reflected in litigious behavior and expert regulatory failure, including the "rule of capture" which is the tendency for regulators to be captured by producers rather than serving the interests of consumers. Regulatory agencies are highly centralized, top-down organizations that tend to be staffed by like thinking persons who are often preoccupied with extending their authority. Like experts everywhere, regulators experience deficits in their knowledge. One example of knowledge deficit problem is the case of Bernie Madoff. Over a period of nine years, Harry Markopolos tried to convince the SEC to investigate Madoff. In Congressional testimony he blamed the "investigative ineptitude and financial illiteracy" of a SEC staff that is dominated by "securities lawyers."[45]

Informal rules which define the boundaries of trust are a key element of bottom-up knowledge in financial markets. Traders in the futures pit who attempt to renege on money losing trades are quickly ostracized. Commercial bank loan officers are said to place much more trust in experience derived knowledge associated with long-term "lending relationships" than the formal credit reports of rating agencies. The value of intrinsically worthless paper money originates from the collective trust in the integrity of the issuing government. In the absence of trust enforcing knowledge, the breadth and depth of financial transactions would be substantially reduced. Following a crisis, it may be much more difficult to restore public trust in intangible financial markets than in the markets for tangible commodities, manufactured goods and services.[46]

Alexander Hamilton recognized that public trust in American financial markets depended on informal reputation more than formal regulation. Many affluent citizens during the Revolutionary War invested in bonds while soldiers were often paid with promissory notes that plummeted in price under the Confederation and were subsequently sold to speculators at large discounts. After the war, some appealed to a sense of "fairness" that would redeem the debt at face value to the original holders. Hamilton understood that "security of transfer" required that government not interfere retroactively in financial transactions even if it meant rewarding greedy speculators and penalizing patriots. To quote Hamilton: "States, like individuals who observe their engagements are respected and trusted, while the reverse is the fate of those who pursue an opposite conduct."[47] Chernow argues that Hamilton's effort to instill reputational trust laid the foundation for America's future preeminence in finance.

Much of the subsequent formal trust enforcement in financial markets as represented by regulation, has been relatively modest in its reach and concise in its application. The National Banking Act of 1864 was 29 pages long followed by the Federal Reserve Act of 1913 at 32 pages and the Glass–Steagall Act at a relatively lengthy 37 pages. The Dodd–Frank Act of 2010, which presumes to protect the financial system against future crises, weighed in at 848 pages but the actual length is ridiculously misleading because of its open–ended structure. Unlike most laws that provide people with rules, Dodd–Frank is written for regulators giving them the open–ended authority to write additional provisions that they deem necessary.[48] For example, the Consumer Financial Protection Bureau created under Dodd–Frank published new mortgage "simplification" rules in the summer of 2012 that exceed 1,000 published pages and represent a compliance nightmare for smaller banks. The Consumer Financial Protection Bureau has the authority to dictate what kinds of financial products will be offered to which consumers and at what cost and has the authority to pursue institutions for acting in an "abusive" manner, a term without legal definition.[49]

The Volcker Rule was originally 11 pages long and was also enacted as part of Dodd–Frank in an effort to reduce systemic risk in banking by restricting proprietary trading. After the five agencies charged with enforcing the rule jointly submitted a 298 page proposal, one banker who had previously supported the Rule dismissed the revised proposal submitted by the regulators as "unintelligible." In testimony before Congress Sheila Bair, former head of the Federal Deposit Insurance Corporation said, "I fear the recently proposed regulation to implement the Volcker Rule is extraordinarily complex and tries too hard. Regulators should think hard about starting over again with a simple rule."[50] Volcker himself is quoted in the *New York Times* saying, "I'd write a much simpler bill. I'd love to see a four–page bill that bans proprietary trading and makes the board and chief executive responsible for compliance. And I'd have strong regulators. If the banks didn't comply with the spirit of the bill, they'd go after them."[51]

Not everything in Dodd–Frank is bad. It makes more information on derivatives available to regulators which is a good thing given the surprisingly large size of credit default swap exposure in 2008. But other important looming financial issues, such as bank capital adequacy, will be addressed internationally in Basel 3. Dodd–Frank did nothing to fix Fannie Mae and Freddie Mac, the two largest recipients of government sponsored bailouts. Their role in the secondary mortgage market is larger than ever. Perhaps most disappointing is that it did nothing to address the "too big to fail" problem, the biggest source of systemic risk in the financial system. Many bankers have been reluctant to speak out because they fear "regulatory retaliation" and a media backlash given the rock bottom public esteem in which banks are currently held. Many predict that the real legacy of Dodd-Frank will be a grinding decade or more of legal disputes and legislative lobbying that will ultimately result in a regulatory regime that is riddled with exceptions for the politically well connected and a banking system that is exposed to even greater systemic risk than that which existed in 2008.

Dodd-Frank was passed in response to the most severe financial crisis in modern American history in an attempt to restore trust in the financial system. Despite the good intentions of the authors, it is an extreme example of regulatory failure but is by no means an isolated case. Every year, the legislative and executive branches, along with bureaucrats at all levels of government, enact hundreds, if not thousands, of new regulations all of which have a cost, yet generate a frequently uncertain benefit. Experts interested in extending the government's reach will frequently minimize estimates of regulatory cost by defining them as little more than the time required to comply with the paperwork while simultaneously pumping-up the presumed benefits of regulation. Analysts who are pro-regulation sometimes include "private benefits" such as the presumed consumer savings on more energy efficient appliances and cars. But if consumers are indeed better off with more fuel efficient products, should they not be willing to purchase these items without being "nudged" by the government? Rejection of government enforced fuel efficient products means that consumers have applied a discount rate to future energy savings such that their present value is not worth the additional cost or that consumers do not trust government estimates of energy savings.

Regulators claim to exploit a new branch of economic science known as "behavioral economics" which demonstrates that economic actors sometimes make "irrational" decisions. If expert regulators characterize the consumer discount rate on energy savings as irrationally high, then they can use "economic science" to justify regulations consistent with a more "rational" or lower discount rate. A favorite refrain of behavioral economists is that if you offer a choice in which one option is seen as a default, most people choose the default option. Those automatically enrolled in a retirement plan are more likely to remain in the plan than those who choose plans for themselves. In most countries where people have to choose to be an organ donor, the majority of people are not donors but in countries where they have to actively say they do not choose to be a donor, most people are donors. Fine, both represent acceptable examples of how we can nudge people to improve the general welfare but do we really want regulators to impose "rational" discount rates or require that we purchase goods and services ranging from health insurance to corn ethanol?

The Renewable Fuel Standards bill passed in 2005 requires that 13.2 billion gallons of ethanol be blended into the gasoline supply in 2012 with 36 billion gallons required by 2022. Ethanol quotas are fulfilled almost entirely from corn ethanol such that in 2011 four out of every ten bushels of corn was diverted from food to fuel. In 2008, food riots erupted in two dozen of the world's poorest countries including Haiti, Bangladesh and Egypt, because of soaring grain prices partly caused by the artificial demand for corn ethanol. Then Senator Barack Obama, who suggested increasing the mandates while campaigning in Iowa, admitted on "Meet the Press" that "people getting something to eat" is a higher priority than biofuels.[52] In the midst of the worst drought in 50 years, corn prices in the summer of 2012 soared to record highs while the two billion people on the planet who live on less than one dollar per day once again faced rising food prices. Safety valves in the renewable fuels legislation grant President Obama and the EPA the authority to remove the mandates, a policy urged by a number of international groups, including the United Nations Food and Agricultural Organization and an alphabet soup of other groups including WTO, FAO, IFAD, OECD, UNCTAD, WFP and the IFPRI. Of course, 2012 is an election year and the agricultural lobby is a powerful political block. Apparently, "people getting something to eat" can wait until after November when much of the 2012 harvest will have already been distilled into ethanol.

Notwithstanding politics, there are honest differences over how the experts measure economic costs and benefits but the process has become increasingly politicized. Those who favor regulation tend to under-estimate the cost and over-estimate the benefits while the converse is true for opponents. For example, under President Bush the analysts at the EPA considered assigning a lower value to reducing the risk of death for the elderly since they had fewer years left to live. In contrast, President Obama's EPA contemplated raising the benefit of reducing the risk of death by cancer on the grounds that it is a more horrifying way to die relative to other less painful exits such as a heart attack.[53] If defining economic benefits and costs are purely a matter of political discretion why bother with the charade of reasoned analysis?

One suggestion to address the problem of politicized regulatory analysis is to establish a truly independent entity to develop consistent and reliable method- ologies for computing regulatory benefits/costs that would be modeled on the highly respected Congressional Budget Office. Another is to establish a group beyond political reach such as the one used to evaluate and close military bases. Still another would create a permanent advocate for regulatory rollback such as the "Office of the Repealer" in Kansas which is charged with the collection and collation of public complaints that are later used to make suggestions to the state legislature.[54] A study by the OECD found that poorly written laws, rather than subsequent rules authored by government bureaucracy, were the biggest problem with the American regulatory regime.[55] Given the vast number of lawyers who have infiltrated politics and government, the inability to author clear and concise legislation is yet another example of expert incompetence.

The power of vested interest cannot be minimized in any honest assessment of U.S. regulation. Companies in many industries have a significant invest- ment dedicated to regulatory compliance, which can act as a barrier to entry in the marketplace. Despite their grumbling over regulatory costs, many of these companies understand that deregulation and a departure of government from markets would open their industries to greater competition that would adversely impact their profits. Bovard argues that Archer Daniels Midland Corp. (ADM) is one of the best examples of taxpayer supported corporate welfare. Thanks to federal protection of the domestic sugar industry, ethanol subsi- dies, subsidized grain exports and other programs, ADM generated at least 43 percent of annual profits during the 1990s from products heavily subsidized or protected by the American government. Every $1 of profits earned by ADM's corn sweetener operation costs consumers $10 and every $1 of profits earned by its ethanol operation costs taxpayers $30.[56] Taxpayers would have been better off to pay ADM their profits directly and have them forgo production.

Government largesse to companies like ADM can take the form of direct sub- sidies but much of it is structured as tax incentives including tax credits, tax deductions and accelerated depreciation. Unlike dollar subsidies, tax subsidies are only indirectly related to budget line items and are prized by politicians for their gratuitous complexity. In fact, much of the complexity in the tax code is justified by "public policy" experts who devise tax incentives to promote desirable behavior and tax levies to discourage undesirable ones. Private com- panies in a variety of industries aggressively pursue a wide range of rent seeking behaviors under the guise of "public policy" that serves the public interest; and politicians use public policy tax strategies as "scientific" justification for distributing pork to their respective constituents.

Jim Cooper, a Democratic House member from Tennessee is quoted in *The Economist* as saying "People vote on things they have not read, do not have the time to read, and cannot read." [57] Like many others, he is concerned with the growing power of special interests. Never mind multi-billion dollar corporations like ADM. Representative Cooper says there is a pimento lobby that grows the small red peppers added to cheese spread and stuffed inside martini olives. The Congressman warns "you do not want to cross the pimento people."[58] The Center for Responsive Government found that 79% of the Congressmen who have left office since 1998 have worked as lobbyists for special interest groups like the "pimento people." [59]

When politicians and government experts promise to deliver spectacular results and consistently fail in their promise, it erodes public trust. If formal regulation is a substitute for informal sanctions, then the surge in regulation in recent years suggests that Americans have become much less trusting. Who can blame them?

CHAPTER 6

WHY THE DISMAL SCIENCE WILL NEVER PRODUCE AN ALBERT EINSTEIN

There is a story that Albert Michaelson, the first American Nobel Prize winner, originally studied economics but switched to physics because it was easier. If Michaelson was the source of the anecdote, it was likely tongue in cheek. Physics envy among economists as well as their affinity for constructing elaborate mathematical models is common knowledge. Before the financial crisis tarnished the discipline's image, the reputation of economics as real science was burnished by popular books like *A Beautiful Mind,* which was made into an Oscar winning movie. Russell Crowe's moving portrayal of John Nash and his struggle to overcome mental illness while being awarded the Nobel Prize in Economics is a story that resonates with audiences. Of course, Nash considers himself a mathematician, not an economist, and as Nassim Taleb likes to point out, the award is not really a "Nobel Prize" but The Bank of Sweden Prize in Economics which happens to be awarded at the Nobel ceremony in Stockholm. Despite all of the awards and acclaim, over the previous century the dismal science has failed to produce a single economist equal to the best of real science.

Certainly, no economists and few scientists match the stature of Albert Einstein. Feted by presidents and kings, Einstein was a towering scientific figure revered by almost everyone, including a Woodstock Nation that admired not just his formidable intellect but his fierce independence and outspoken advocacy for peace and nuclear disarmament. During the 1960s, the poster of Einstein in his signature afro sticking out his tongue could be found hanging in college dorm rooms across America. He seemed to thoroughly enjoy his celebrity and used it to promote causes close to his heart.

But life was not always so easy. His first attempt at a doctoral degree failed when his major professor became alarmed by Einstein's attack on the work of a colleague and asked him to withdraw his dissertation and request a refund of the 230 franc application fee. Unable to land a university job, Einstein took a position as a tutor at a small private academy twenty miles north of Zurich. His job consisted of tutoring a single rich English schoolboy for which he was paid the meager salary of 150 francs a month plus room and board while the academy charged the family of the student 4,000 francs per year. Impatient with authority and chafing at his exploitation, Einstein tried to get the boy's family to pay him directly cutting out the middleman, a strategy that did not endear him to the schoolmaster.

He left tutoring when he learned of a pending position at the Bern patent office. Concerned about losing the job to another person, he bumped into an acquain-tance on the street who assured him that he didn't have to worry about someone else applying for the patent office position because it was boring and of "the lowest rank." Undeterred, Einstein remarked to his wife that "certain people find everything boring."[1] In June 1902, Einstein assumed the position of a Technical Expert Class 3 of the Federal Office for Intellectual Property in Bern's new Postal and Telegraph Building near the famous clock tower built in 1191. He arrived at the patent office every morning at 8:00 AM, six days a week and during slow periods at the office, he would pursue his own research. In a letter to a friend the young patent inspector wrote: "I am frightfully busy, every day I spend eight hours at the office and at least one hour of private lessons, and then in addition I do some scientific work."[2] The 'additional work' produced by Einstein during his seven years at the patent office would represent one of the most prolific periods in the annals of modern science and would include the so-called "miracle year" of 1905 when he wrote four papers. He famously explained in a letter to a friend: "The fourth paper is only a rough draft at this point, and is an electrodynamics of moving bodies which employs a modifi-cation of the theory of space and time."[3]

Rather than bemoan his banishment from academia, Einstein wrote: "I enjoy my work at the patent office very much, because it is uncommonly diversified."[4]

Had Einstein won the assistant professorship he applied for, Isaacson specu-
lates that it would have not only denied him the opportunity to see the physical
ramifications of theoretical concepts, he might have felt pressured by senior
professors to tame his fertile imagination and pursue a more conventional
line of research. Instead of limiting his intellectual development as a scientist, Einstein referred to the patent office job as "that worldly cloister where I
hatched my most beautiful ideas." [5]

It is unlikely that Einstein's story could be repeated today. It is inconceivable
that it could happen in a discipline like economics. Imagine a GS 9 economist
who spent his twenties working for the government in a city with a population
equivalent to Bern, say Albuquerque New Mexico, later ascending to the pinnacle
of the profession. Debates in economics are seldom resolved. Instead, research
progresses in a kind of circular fashion so that every two or three decades, old
controversies are dusted off and recycled by a new generation of PhD students.

Rising stars in the field are identified not so much by the publication of path
breaking science but by a *de facto* committee of experts at a handful of prestigious universities who tend to anoint their former students. The John Bates
Clark Medal was awarded biennially from 1947-2009 to the American economist
under the age of forty who is judged to have made the most significant contribution to economic thought and knowledge. In 2010, they began awarding
the medal annually. Recipients of the award are not required to be American
citizens; they only need to have worked in the U.S. at some point in their
career. If the committee awarding the medal is a "good old boy's" club, then
the recipients constitute a "good young boy's" club since only three of the best
young economists in the last 65 years were judged to be women and all three
were awarded the medal since 2007. [6]

MIT and Harvard produced 50% of medal winners with nearly 90% produced
by a half dozen universities. On average, about 40% of winners will be awarded
the Bank of Sweden Prize in Economics 22 years later and in at least one instance
the pedigree of the Medal winners runs deeper than simple institutional affiliation. Lawrence Summers won it in 1993 and his uncles Paul Samuelson and
Kenneth Arrow received their medals in 1947 and 1957, respectively. Samuelson
and Arrow would go on to win the Nobel Prize. Both were brilliant economists,
as is Summers and all of the other Clark medal awardees, but some view the
close-knit network of American economists as fundamentally unhealthy.

One study characterized the concentration of authors in the top economics journals with PhDs from the same institutions as "startlingly high" raising concerns about "inbreeding" of young economists. The English speaking countries of the U.S., Canada and the UK publish 93.9% of citation weighted articles, while faculty of MIT, University of Chicago and Harvard publish more articles in the prestige journals than all of the economists in the rest of the world combined.[7] Another paper concluded that "geographic and institutional concentration of editors and authors may be unhealthy for innovative research in economics." For a discipline that champions free and accessible markets, the researchers question whether the concentration of "editors and authors of economic journals is a case of institutional oligopoly."[8]

It is difficult to compare the institutional concentration of research in economics with real science because the latter does not regard it as a problem. Within disciplines like chemistry, physics, biology, etc., there tend to be greater specialization resulting in journals devoted to very narrow sub-disciplines. Economics journals are also somewhat specialized but economists, especially those associated with elite schools, are much more likely to publish across sub-disciplines while scientists tend to remain within the narrow bounds of their specialty. Perhaps the biggest difference between economics and real science, is that published research in the latter tends to be much more international in scope reflecting a collective brain that is more geographically diversified.

The institutional concentration of editors and authors in top economics journals is accompanied by what many consider to be a "too cozy" relationship with the Federal Reserve. Medical journals have been criticized for a similarly close affiliation with the pharmaceutical industry; the difference is that there are several competing drug companies and only one central bank. A review of the seven top economic journals found that 84 of the 190 editorial board members were affiliated with the Federal Reserve in some fashion. A Fed affiliation carries prestige, invitations to conferences and offers of visiting research positions at the central bank. Milton Friedman thought that "having something like 500 economists is extremely unhealthy [and]...not conducive to independent, objective research. You and I know that there has been censorship of the material published. Equally important, the location of the economists in the Federal Reserve has had a significant influence on the kind of research they do, biasing that research toward non-controversial technical papers on method as opposed to substantive papers on policy and results."[9] The *structure* of the economic research 'industry' may not prove the discipline's *conduct* is extractive but similar concentrations of output in private industry have been sufficient to provoke restraint of trade investigations by antitrust authorities.

For much of the latter half of the 20th century the ideological poles in the dismal science were represented by two brilliant economists of unimpeachable integrity: Milton Friedman on the right and Paul Samuelson on the left. Both won the John Bates Clark Medal as well as the Nobel Prize and both authored popular columns in *Newsweek* magazine in the pre-Internet era. Despite ideological differences, their *Newsweek* articles were first and foremost about ideas rather than partisan politics. Friedman was a tireless defender of free markets who was reluctant to concede any role for government while Samuelson was much more of an interventionist. In the 1961 edition of his textbook, Samuelson made the Orwellian prediction that the national income of the Soviet Union would overtake U.S. national income by 1984. Subsequent editions moved the date back to 2002 and 2012.[10] Neither Friedman nor Samuelson seemed phased by popular celebrity and both enjoyed a good joke. Samuelson remarked that "economists are like dermatologists, they don't help anyone but then again they don't hurt anyone." Professor Samuelson might have been correct in a more innocent era when economists spent their time teaching and writing papers that were read by other academics and captive PhD students in pursuit of a degree, but many of today's macro-economists actively pursue jobs as purveyors of expert advice and move freely, often with impunity, from campus to Washington to Wall Street and then back to campus where they start the process all over again.

Einstein observed: "Politics is for the moment, an equation for the eternity." Early in his career the ambitious young economist must self-identify as a Democrat or Republican and generate equations that are consistent with his political affiliation, if not for eternity then at least for the next election cycle. There is a symbiotic relationship between competing economists who are secure in the knowledge that every partisan position necessitates an opposing view and that the next potential appointment is no more than four years away. Bad policy decisions may be driven by the politicians but whether institutionally enshrined by Democrats or Republicans, they eventually become co-owned so that accommodation becomes the more convenient governing strategy. Economists, like everyone else, "go along to get along."

To stay in the game it is imperative not to linger in any position for too long. Like a shark, the rotating economist must be in constant motion cultivating an ever growing circle of influence. The Think Tank is a relatively new harbor for the economic expert who finds himself between real jobs or wanting to take an extended breather. Economists employed by the "institute" are expected to generate research and write op-ed columns that support its mission. If the institute is funded by donors in high marginal tax brackets, the economic expert might create a mathematical function that demonstrates how a tax cut will actually generate more tax revenue closing fiscal deficits. It helps to name it something catchy like "the Laugher Curve." If a "progressive" policy institute signs the checks, our rotating economist might write a research paper demonstrating how a rebate to the middle-class accompanied by a "Kenyesian multiplier" of 2, 3, 4, 5 or 10, will close the gap between actual and potential income.

Larry Summers is good example of the rotating economic expert. Summers left Harvard in 1991 to become chief economist for the World Bank and in 1995, was recruited into the Clinton Administration as Deputy Secretary of the Treasury under his long-time political mentor Robert Rubin. In 1999, he succeeded Rubin as Secretary of the Treasury when Rubin joined Citigroup. Summers was back at Harvard in 2001 where he became the 27th President of the University. Following a bumpy tenure as President and a no confidence vote by the faculty in 2006, Summers returned to the Harvard faculty and became a part-time managing director at the investment firm D.E. Shaw & Co. He left in 2008 receiving $5.2 million in compensation for the two year, part-time stint. Professor Summers would serve briefly as the chair of The National Economic Council in the Obama Administration before departing in 2010.

In 1998, while Deputy Secretary of the Treasury, Summers responded to a Congressional Committee regarding a concept release issued by the Commodity Futures Trading Commission (CFTC) soliciting input to determine "how best to maintain adequate regulatory safeguards without impairing the ability of the OTC derivatives market to grow." He testified against more oversight: "the parties to these kinds of contracts are largely sophisticated financial institutions that would appear to be eminently capable of protecting themselves from fraud and counter-party insolvencies."[11] Treasury Secretary Robert Rubin and Federal Reserve Chairman Alan Greenspan agreed that greater oversight by the CFTC was unnecessary. A decade later, credit default swaps written by AIG would play a prominent role in the near collapse of the world financial system. Summers, Rubin and Greenspan along with other economic experts, the Congress and several Presidents, were instrumental in the design of a financial system that institutionalized systemic risk rendering some banks "too big to fail." Their collective expertise would worsen the Great Recession and expand the size of the bank bailouts.

Einstein frequently spoke against social injustice and on behalf of peace and racial equality. He was a member of the Princeton chapter of the NAACP and co-chaired *The American Crusade to End Lynching* with Paul Robeson. An avid supporter of nuclear disarmament, Einstein famously remarked: "I do not know how the Third World War will be fought, but I can tell you what they will use in the Fourth – rocks!" In a speech with anti-Semitic overtones, Congressman John E. Rankin from Mississippi accused him of being a foreign-born agitator who "has been engaged in communist activities."[12] Despite lending his celebrity to a variety of causes, Einstein retained the deep distrust of politics that was common among Europeans who survived the carnage of the early 20th century. He was an iconoclast quite willing to criticize other members of his profession when he felt it was justified.

In economics, criticism of fellow economists tends to follow partisan lines. It is common for real scientists to resign in protest or over issues of scientific integrity. In 2011, Norwegian Nobel physicist Ivar Giaever resigned as a fellow from the American Physical Society because of policy statement wording and in 2012, eminent aerospace scientist Roddam Narasimha resigned as a member of the Indian Space Commission in protest over the treatment of four fellow scientists. American economists in important policy positions almost never resign over issues of "economic integrity." Despite the thousands of economists employed in industry and government, most academic economists remain largely detached from the practice of "economic science" outside of Washington, the Federal Reserve and academic circles. In contrast, application to the larger world, or what Einstein referred to as his "worldly cloister," is one of the hallmarks of real science. Non-economists wonder what good are all of the self-congratulatory prizes if economists cannot help us recognize lurking catastrophes and may even contribute to their severity. Economists at the Federal Reserve, Treasury and throughout the policy bureaucracy had ample opportunity to raise alarm bells on housing and banking. The vast majority either failed to understand the structural dynamics of these markets or chose to remain silent for professional reasons.

WHEN A HOUSE IS MORE (OR LESS) THAN A HOME

Parsing the causes of the financial crisis has been something of a cottage industry among business writers. Suggested causes include easy money by the Fed, lax oversight of over-the-counter derivatives, inadequate bank capital, a securitized real estate market run amok, incompetence of bond rating agencies, lack of due diligence in mortgage originations and outright fraud by borrowers and lenders. The list is long, but markets would have likely adjusted to all of these problems had there not been core weakness caused by the cumulative effects of misguided housing policy and a failure of the experts to understand systemic risk in banking.

The modern mortgage has its roots in Roman law. The earliest legal instrument used in real estate loans was the *fiducia* taken from the Latin word for trust. Despite the translation, Roman lenders were not particularly trustful since legal title as well as possession remained with the lender. Once the loan was paid off and the terms of the *fiducia* were met, ownership would be re-conveyed back to the borrower. With the decline of Roman influence, the *fiducia* was displaced by the Germanic *gage* system under which a borrower would make a deposit of property such as livestock, as a pledge against the fulfillment of a loan. In the event of default, the lender could not press for relief beyond the value of the livestock or other asset pledged as security in the *gage*. The German *gage* system was introduced into England by the French after William the Conqueror's invasion in 1066. Unlike a *gage* of livestock or other chattel, real estate could not be physically delivered to the lender so it was called a "dead *gage*." Because the French word for dead is *mort*, a dead gage became a *mort gage* or mortgage.

In early America, home financing was not a pressing issue. Most city dwellers rented while farmers would build their houses out of logs, stones or lumber that they cut themselves or bought at a relatively low price from the local saw mill. Free land as a consequence of homestead laws encouraged settlers to continually push back the western frontiers. It was not until after the Civil War that the need for home and farm financing became apparent and mortgage bankers began originating loans on behalf of eastern investors for a population that was moving ever westward. The financial interests of the East versus the agricultural concerns in the West created a political divide that would persist well into the 20th century. It would be famously revealed at the 1896 Democratic convention in Chicago where populist William Jennings Bryan delivered his *Cross of Gold* speech pleading debtor relief from the hard money policy of the Eastern financial establishment. This division would also motivate states in the Midwest and Great Plains to enact laws limiting branching by out-of-state banks, laws that were clearly directed at money center banks that were suspected of "upstreaming" deposits away from rural areas to the big cities where they earned a higher return. Not until 1994 were state restrictions on interstate bank branching struck down.

The typical home or farm loan of the late 19th century was a callable, interest only, short-term loan of five years that required a 40 or 50 percent down payment. At the end of five years the loan would be rolled over or, if the farmer made sufficient profits on his crops and livestock, paid down when it was refinanced. Mortgage bankers dominated the small farm mortgage market during the post Civil War era because large numbers of Savings and Loans did not come into existence until late in the 19th century and federally chartered banks were prohibited from making real estate loans until the Federal Reserve Act of 1913 changed the law.[13]

During the first 30 years of the 20th century the number of Building and Loan Associations operated by managers like George Stevens in the movie *It's a Wonderful Life*, more than doubled from 5,000 to over 11,000 while total assets increased by 1500%. Surveys of old financial institution records suggest that approximately 75% of all home loans were short term, interest only loans.[14] The short term loans allowed the lender to control interest rate risk since any rate increase would be reflected in the new mortgage when the loan was rolled over. However, default rates on non-amortizing loans were significantly higher than amortized loans even before the collapse of the market and the onset of the Great Depression.

Easy money during the 1920s contributed to a real estate bubble that resulted in many loans that would be characterized as "sub-prime" in the mortgage lending lexicon of the present day. When the bubble deflated, real estate prices fell 50% from their 1928 peak resulting in a rash of defaults and foreclosures very similar to those following the 2008 financial crisis. From 1931 to 1933, S&L deposits shrank by one third. In an attempt to address the crisis and shore up

S&Ls, government created the Reconstruction Finance Corporation, The Federal Home Loan Bank System and The Homeowners Loan Corporation. Federal money was funneled to the Savings and Loan industry which then lent it to homeowners to finance and refinance their mortgages. The Federal Saving and Loan Insurance Corporation was created to insure S&L deposits and the Federal Housing Administration insured mortgages up to 80% of value by charging the borrower a fee. The Federal National Mortgage Association, later nicknamed Fannie Mae, was created in 1938 to purchase and sell FHA insured mortgages.[15]

As a consequence of federal housing policy, a 1920s market that was dominated by short term, non-amortizing loans was, by the late 1940s, transformed into one in which 94% of all home loans were amortized to include payment of interest and principal with the average maturity over 9 years. Lenders replaced non-amortizing, short-term loans characterized by high default risk and low interest rate risk with long-term amortizing loans that carried low default risk but higher interest rate risk.

A revived S&L industry prospered during the early post WWII years by lending money to people anxious to get a mortgage on their share of the American dream. In contrast to the median sized house of today, it was a relatively small dream typically located on a quarter acre lot in one of the vast new subdivisions that were springing up across the country. To fulfill this function, the experts had created a highly regulated S&L industry that was focused on making long-term home loans funded by short-term deposit liabilities. S&Ls were granted favorable tax status while Regulation Q enforced a 5.25% maximum interest rate on deposits. The experts failed to anticipate that an industry dedicated to such a narrow slice of the lending business and predicated on low, stable interest rates would find itself in trouble if debt markets became more volatile and the cost of deposit liabilities exceeded the legal maximum set by Regulation Q. As the industry bled deposits in the late 1970s and early 1980s, financial institution "disintermediation" would culminate in the S&L crisis and another round of regulations and taxpayer financed bailouts.

But we are getting ahead of the story. In 1968, the Johnson Administration thought it would be a good idea if Fannie Mae (FNMA), created during the 1930s to purchase FHA guaranteed mortgages, was privatized. A sister institution known as Freddie Mac was created in 1970. Fannie and Freddie are known as Government Sponsored Enterprises (GSE) that bought mortgages which they pooled and resold as mortgage backed securities in a process known as "securitization." Most people would later assume that there was an implied government guarantee behind *all* of the mortgage backed securities sponsored by Fannie and Freddie. Despite calls for the government to formally disavow any guarantee, it was never acted on.

The disavowal never happened partly because the personal benefits of a taxpayer implied guarantee became very apparent to economic experts, politicians and crony capitalists associated with Fannie and Freddie. The two GSEs provided another stop for rotating economic experts and since they were ostensibly "private," they could justify salaries and consulting fees competitive with Wall Street investment banks. Best of all, unless Fannie and Freddie went totally off the reservation (which they did), the implied guarantee gave them a measure of stability not found among private sector financial firms. During the boom years of the 1990s, investors like Warren Buffet reaped huge profits from Fannie shares.

For politicians in Congress and the White House, the GSEs were a money machine that donated countless millions to the campaigns of incumbents in both parties, especially Congressmen serving on key committees. Temporarily out of office and in need of money? Not to worry, between 1999 and 2007, Freddie reportedly paid Newt Gingrich $1.6 million for his expertise as a "historian." Gingrich traveled to Atlanta in 1995 to help open a Fannie Mae office promoting home ownership for low-income and moderate-income families. His press release stated: "Fannie Mae is an excellent example of a former government institution fulfilling its mandate while functioning in the market economy."[16] Fannie and Freddie awarded grants to a small army of economic experts who published complimentary "research" on the risk mitigating benefits of mortgage securitization and other "financial innovations."

It would be disingenuous to blame the housing crisis exclusively on the system of mortgage securitization when other housing policies contributed to the debacle. The Tax Reform Act of 1986 took away the tax deductibility of consumer interest but another "financial innovation," known as the home equity line of credit, allowed home owners to convert consumer debt into mortgage debt and deduct the interest on their tax returns. Many households began financing vacations and short-lived durable goods with home equity loans that are second mortgages against equity that would disappear when housing prices plunged. Before the collapse, a number of economists wrote scholarly papers on how the home equity loan "stabilized consumption," vanquished the business cycle and led to a "great moderation" in the American economy. After the bubble deflated, proponents of the "great moderation" hypothesis quickly disappeared much like the experts on Japanese business practices did a decade earlier.

Easy money, courtesy of Allen Greenspan and the Fed, ensured low mortgage rates while the implied government guarantee on Fannie and Freddie bonds provided an ideal "low risk" investment vehicle for countries running a trade surplus with the U.S. and looking to recycle dollars. Only Treasury bonds provided greater liquidity than the securitized mortgage market. A circular feedback loop occurred in which housing prices were buoyed by a consumer economy that was largely supported by borrowing against hypothetical home equity. By the late 1990s, one would think it was time to pump the breaks and take a chill pill; instead, the experts goosed the bubble even more. Before 1997, the only way to avoid paying capital gains taxes on the sale of a house was to plow the money back into another house within two years. Sellers 55 or older could take a once-in-a-lifetime tax exemption of up to $125,000. For married couples, The 1997 Taxpayer Relief Act eliminated the once in a lifetime rule and increased the tax free exemption to $500,000 every time you sell a house that was a principle residence for 2 of the 5 years preceding the sale. Some wealthier people with two homes sold their primary residence and moved into their second home for two years to establish principle residence, then sold it and repeated the process. Others cashed in and put the money into the 1990s dot.com stock market but many people "doubled down" on housing because it could be heavily leveraged and if capital gains stayed under $500,000 it was a better tax shelter than an IRA that deferred taxes.

The mortgage deduction and capital gains exemption encouraged turnover and increased demand for more expensive houses as a means to fully exploit the tax advantages. The potential for leveraging tax free returns fed "housing lust" and suckered many people into buying McMansions that they could not afford. From 1970 to 2007, the median sized owner occupied house increased from 1,535 to 2,277 square feet. The average American occupies almost 1,000 square feet of living space which is twice the amount enjoyed by the average person in France, Germany or Great Britain; but square feet does not factor in the growth in other amenities that included two and three car garages, granite counter tops in kitchens with restaurant quality appliances, spas, Jacuzzis, home theaters, etc.

People of modest income enjoy housing's tax benefits but the lion's share accrues to households in higher income brackets. Seldom discussed is the fact that rental income is taxed while the imputed rent from owner occupied housing goes untaxed. In 1991, the median household income of renters was 75% of the median household income of homeowners, but by 2007, it had declined to 50%. The tax benefits from owner occupied housing are regressive and go disproportionately to those with incomes over $100,000. At the peak of the bubble in 2007, tax savings worth nearly $200 billion were shared by homeowners. Households earning more than $250,000 per year received ten times as much in tax subsidies as households with incomes between $40,000 and $75,000.[17]

Both political parties have long championed the benefits of home ownership, often blindly. Former HUD Secretary, Republican Presidential candidate and NFL quarterback Jack Kemp, promoted home ownership via his HOPE program as a fix-it for many of the problems that plague urban America, going so far as to suggest that residents should buy public housing. But just because rich and middle class people own nice homes in low crime neighborhoods and send their kids to high quality local schools, it does not automatically follow that owning your own home will make you richer, your neighborhood safer or the local schools better. One study looked at 140,000 home sale transactions in the city of Memphis for a fifteen year period and found large differences in price appreciation across neighborhoods. Memphis is a relatively poor city with a large African-American population. Urban neighborhoods with the most affordable homes were more often in transition with a higher proportion of rental property. Houses in these transitional neighborhoods experienced significantly lower price appreciation than their suburban counterparts. For residents in many of these neighborhoods, renting rather than buying is typically the better economic option.[18]

Sophisticated credential cartels like The National Association of Realtors use the language of social responsibility when advocating policies that expand home ownership to low income households and generate more commissions for their brokers. Along with other self-interested lobbyists that advocate for "the less fortunate," they helped convince the 1992 Congress that everyone should participate in the home "ownership society." Congress enacted an affordable housing "mission" for Fannie and Freddie and also extended the reach of the Community Reinvestment Act (CRA) to include mortgage lending. The CRA which was enacted during the Carter Administration originally required banks to make an *effort* to serve the entire community, not just the affluent and middle class. Regulators enforced CRA by withholding approval for mergers, expansions, etc., if members of the community complained that the bank was not fulfilling its CRA obligation. If a bank was anticipating a merger, it would often make a large contribution to a community group such as ACORN as a strategy to diffuse the complaint mechanism and expedite approval, which is one reason many bankers considered CRA a form of legalized extortion.

In 1995, the CRA rules were amended to *require* banks to actually make the loans rather than simply make an *effort*. The new regulations dictated that banks be "flexible and innovative" in their mortgage underwriting, code words suggesting that they should qualify lower credit quality applications. Lower quality loans had limited risk if the banks could dump most of them on Fannie and Freddie. Ellen Seidman, director of the federal Office of Thrift Supervision, said in a speech before the Greenlining Institute on Oct. 2, 2001, "Our record home ownership rate [increasing from 64.2% in 1994 to 68% in 2001], I'm convinced, would not have been reached without CRA and its close relative, the Fannie/Freddie requirements."[19]

Initially, the regulations required that 30 percent of Fannie and Freddie mortgage purchases had to be "affordable" housing but by 2007, it had increased to 55 percent with a sub-limit of 25 percent allocated to low or very low income buyers. Between 1993 and 2007, over $3.5 trillion in single-family CRA loans were originated. About half of these went to Fannie and Freddie to meet their affordable mortgage requirements, about 10% were insured by the FHA, another 10% were sold as private mortgage backed securities while most of the rest resided on the balance sheets of either too big to fail banks like Bank of America, Citigroup, JP Morgan Chase and Wells Fargo or banks that were eventually acquired by the big four. By the middle of 2008, there were 27 million subprime and Alt-A loans in the U.S. financial system or about 50% of all mortgages that were largely the result of CRA requirements.[20] The irony in all of the policy smoke and mirrors is that the more money thrown at housing, the less affordable it became. Rather than doing them a favor, many low income people who bought houses financed by the CRA affordable mortgage program, would likely be better off today had they continued to rent.

U.S. housing policy diverted trillions of dollars into the housing stock at a time when our industrial and public infrastructure was crumbling. It also side tracked the lives of young people who delayed or dropped out of college to take relatively high paying construction or other bubble related jobs. Housing policy transformed the American Dream into a tax shelter that disproportionately benefited those at the top of the "meritocracy." And it was misguided housing policy, easy credit accommodated by the Fed, and the implied guarantee of Fannie and Freddie that were responsible for housing's meteoric rise and catastrophic collapse. When the dust settled, the experts proposed a new round of policies to address the crisis that they and the politicians created; Democrats blamed the bankers while the Republicans said little, apparently fearful that they might have to admit complicity.

BANK ON IT

When misguided housing policy collided with ill conceived bank regulation, it created a perfect economic storm. The history of banking in the U.S. is a prolonged period of prosperity fed by easy credit culminating in the inevitable bust. For sheer financial devastation, none of the panics of recent history matched the Great Depression. From 1929 to 1933, half of the banks in the U.S. failed, decreasing their numbers from 30,000 to approximately 15,000 institutions. The financial panic was accompanied by an economic contraction that left 25% of workers unemployed and so traumatized the nation that the government created a regulatory regime that placed bank safety above all other considerations. In addition to the reforms in mortgage lending discussed in the previous section, the 1933 Glass-Steagall Act restricted commercial banks from engaging in investment banking. Reforms also created the Federal Deposit Insurance Corporation in an attempt to restore trust among the public and forestall the cascading effect of bank runs.

The term "dual banking system" refers to the multiple layers of state and federal agencies that include state examiners, the FDIC, the Federal Reserve and the Comptroller of the Currency, all of whom employ large numbers of people to supervise banks. Despite the substantial resources devoted to bank supervision at the state and federal levels, regulators were unable to prevent the 2008 financial meltdown. In order to appreciate how regulated the banking industry has been, one need only examine the historical failure rate of banks relative to other industries. The 1950s averaged only 2.8 bank failures annually for a decade long average of less than 1 failure per year for every 5,000 banks. The ratio increased to 1 failure for every 3,400 banks during the 1960s. Virtually any other industry with over 15,000 companies will experience more failures if for no other reasons than fraud, laziness or random stupidity. When one considered the job security and the "banker's hours" represented by a 9:00 to 3:30 day, being employed in a highly regulated industry like banking was pretty good work—if you could get it.

It is a truism in banking that the rules written to fix the last crisis usually contribute to the upcoming one. During the 1930s, S&L regulators replaced the short term, interest only loan carrying high default risk with a long term, fully amortized loan funded with short term liabilities and carrying high interest rate risk. It took fifty years but when the S&L crisis of the 1980s finally arrived, the interest rate risk associated with borrowing short and lending long in a rising rate environment would shrink the industry by 80%.

In the early 1980s, bank experts embarked on a twenty-year odyssey of deregulation, an epic journey that many critics blame for the 2008 financial crisis. Yet, it would be a mistake to presume that the banking structure that has served the nation since the Great Depression could have continued unchanged. Despite "deregulation," banking remained a highly regulated industry. With a few exceptions, deregulation occurred around the edges and was largely imposed by market imperatives. The 1930s law that placed a ceiling on the interest rate that S&Ls and banks could pay for deposit liabilities had already been nullified by the market; the 1980 law phasing out Regulation Q simply acknowledged this reality.

It was commonly believed that the regulatory structure, legally enshrined by the trauma of the Great Depression, had rendered banks increasingly inefficient and ill-equipped to compete in a global financial system that operated on a 24/7 clock instead of "banker's hours." The mainframe computer had revolutionized the back office operations of financial firms, displacing an army of clerical staff once needed to sort checks, maintain paper files and other routine office work. The boom in information technology would replace many tellers with ATM machines and cash/checks with electronic payments. Against the backdrop of a brave new banking world, rules that established artificial state boundaries in a self-interested attempt to maintain regional credit markets that largely benefited local banks and their more affluent customers, seemed inefficient and out of step with the times. Few knowledgeable observers opposed the 1994 law known as Riegle-Neal, which allowed unlimited inter-state bank branching.

In late 2011, an Occupy Wall Street protester being interviewed on a network TV broadcast identified the 1999 Gram-Leach-Bliley Act that repealed Glass-Steagall Act separating investment and commercial banking as the major culprit in the crisis. Whether the young occupier was expressing his own opinion or reiterating Occupy talking points is not known; but the Glass-Steagall sound bite meshed well with the anti-Wall Street narrative. The difficulty with that line of reasoning is that Bear Stearns and Lehman Brothers, the investment banks that ignited the meltdown, were largely unaffected by the Gram-Leach-Bliley Act, frequently referred to as the law that allowed "one stop financial shopping."

Since the early 1970s, the share of assets controlled by the five largest banks in the U.S. has increased from 17% to 52%. Gram-Leach-Bliley motivated banks to further emphasize fee income, often called off-balance sheet income, as an alternative to interest income and the interest rate risk that has proved so treacherous to lending institutions over numerous business cycles. Unlike traditional lending that shows very little evidence of scale economies, some fee income activities require banks to grow in order to achieve the cost advantages. Along with Gram-Leach-Bliley, Riegle-Neal also encouraged larger size through merger and consolidation. A number of economists wrote scholarly papers extolling the risk mitigating benefits of geographic diversification as a means for banks to decrease exposure to "macroeconomic risk." Of course, growth as a method to achieve "too big to fail" status may reduce the risk of the individual bank but it increases systemic risk for the larger economy.

Both the Clinton and Bush Administrations dropped the ball on the oversight of over-the-counter derivatives, especially credit default swaps. Still, without the misguided housing policy and absent the implied guarantee awarded Fannie and Freddie, the problems in securitized real estate would have been much less severe. The Securities and Exchange Commission proved to be largely ineffectual in rooting out swindlers like Bernie Madoff but that has always been the case. Finally, Alan Greenspan and the Fed's easy money policy accommodated the bubble so that by the time Ben Bernanke took away the proverbial punch bowl, the American economy was already headed for a DUI. Again, excessive stimulus by the Fed is nothing new.

Historically, a commercial bank fails for one of two reasons: illiquidity or insolvency. The classic bank run is a liquidity failure. If depositors all want to withdraw their money at the same time, the bank will first try to satisfy withdrawals from vault cash; but if the outflow is severe enough, the bank will eventually need to sell assets with the most liquid assets sold first. In an attempt to mitigate liquidity risk, banks buy FDIC insurance that insures depositors against losses. Since fear of losing deposits is the primary reason for a bank run, FDIC insurance against deposit losses less than $250,000 goes a long way toward preventing the cascading psychology that motivates bank runs. Another mechanism to forestall a bank run is that the Federal Reserve is empowered to act as "a lender of last resort" to commercial banks. This should not be confused with "lender of last resort to sovereign nations" as is often the case in discussions of the euro crisis.

The second cause of failure is insolvency, the condition that exists when the market value of bank liabilities is greater than the market value of its assets and stockholder equity is negative. Insolvency tends to occur because bank operations use a relatively large proportion of borrowed money relative to the funds supplied by stockholders. On average, banks report that about 90% of assets are financed by borrowing with only 10% supplied by stockholders; this means that if each dollar of bank assets decline by more than 10 cents, then the bank would be insolvent. Banks like to use debt because it increases the return on equity but insolvency risk is greater than reported because regulators allow a flexible definition of equity and too big to fail institutions are far more complex than anyone thought. Because of insolvency risk, capital adequacy has been the main preoccupation of bank regulators for the last 30 years.

Central banks representing all of the developed countries gathered in Basel Switzerland in 1988 to adopt new rules on capital adequacy. Labeled the Basel Accord, the rules define capital requirements uniformly across all nations, apply risk weights to all assets and off-balance sheet exposures and set minimum levels of capital for international banks. The objective was to relate a bank's capital requirements to asset risk by assigning higher weights (more capital) to more risky asset classes. In theory, the system of risk-based-capital standard (RBC) appeared "reasonable" as do many expert systems but it proved much more problematic in practice. A major "common shock" like the housing crisis in the U.S. or the sovereign debt crisis in Europe resulted in a significant decline in the value of mortgage backed securities and sovereign debt that was held as assets on bank balance sheets and increased the risk of insolvency. The Basel Accord defines mortgage-backed securities as a low risk asset with minimal capital required while sovereign debt like U.S. Treasury bonds or Greek bonds have a zero weighting because they are "risk free" in the argot of financial economics.

Presumably, the experts used state of the art statistical methods to analyze the historical price behavior of various asset classes before arriving at their risk weightings. Since the modern history of housing prices is one of fairly consistent price increases, the capital weighting for home loans was low and securitized real estate was even lower because it was considered more diversified than other debt, such as corporate bonds. When regulators pressured banks to increase capital, many banks simply moved assets from high risk categories to low risk categories. In retrospect, the experts had it backwards since many low risk assets turned out to be high risk and vise versa. Rather than an industry of diverse banks specializing in a variety of different lending activities, the Basel Accords contributed to an international homogenization of bank operations significantly increasing systemic risk. Some large banks got around capital requirements by pooling risky assets into AAA securities that had lower risk weights and then placing these securities in "special purpose vehicles" that carried off-balance sheet credit guarantees. The securities in the special purpose vehicles carried the same risk but required zero capital.

Despite all evidence to the contrary, the bailouts and subsequent actions by the Fed and the Treasury impart the following message: given that "too big to fail banks have outgrown market monitoring, regulatory monitoring is an acceptable substitute." The fundamental contradiction of this message is that "creative destruction" is incompatible with "too big to fail." If a bank is too big to be monitored by the market then it is too big, period. It should be miniaturized; if it can't be miniaturized, then it should be nationalized. Anything in between is an inferior "second best solution." Regulators can aid banks in the event of a liquidity crisis but investors assume insolvency risk.

HUBRIS IN ECONOMICS AND FINANCE

One of my graduate school professors was a bluff, ruddy faced Irishman who liked to puff on a cigar while presiding over his weekly seminar. One afternoon he read a rejection letter from an academic journal where he had submitted a paper, a performance intended to convey to young would-be authors the

necessity of a thick skin. The referee characterized the premise of the professor's paper as "hubris." After reading the word he looked at the class over the
top of his glasses and said, "I think that's just a polite word for bullshit."

As long as hubris remains embedded in the pages of scholarly papers it is harm-
less enough but, when translated into action, it can be dangerous. During the
first Gulf War known as Desert Storm, George Bush Senior built a coalition of
forces that represented a broad cross-section of nations determined to forcibly
remove Saddam Hussein from Kuwait. In charge of the campaign was Colin
Powell, Chairman of the Joint Chiefs of Staff, a military leader who was a firsthand witness to the hubris that afflicted the American strategy in Vietnam.
While some pushed for a quick response to Iraq's invasion of Kuwait, the General
would not be rushed. His plan of action became known as the Powell Doctrine:

"The Doctrine expresses that military action should be used only as a last resort
and only if there is a clear risk to national security by the intended target; the
force, when used, should be overwhelming and disproportionate to the force
used by the enemy; there must be strong support for the campaign by the general public; and there must be a clear exit strategy from the conflict in which
the military is engaged."[21]

The Powell Doctrine is a reasoned response to the failure of military experts in
Vietnam and would foretell future failure in Iraq. Experience suggests that in
many instances the best response to ignorance is to over-compensate, especially
when the downside risk is measured in human life. Big picture experts may be
more inclined to take risk because they get the credit when their choices are
correct and others bear most of the cost when they are wrong. If the short run
outcome of the first and second Gulf Wars favored General Powell's approach,
over-compensation by policy experts in other areas can create problems further down the road.

It is no secret that the Federal Reserve failed to anticipate the grave danger
posed by the housing bubble. In 2004, then-Federal Reserve Chairman Alan
Greenspan said that "a national severe price distortion [is] most unlikely."[22] A
year later, Chairman Ben Bernanke said that the boom "largely reflect strong
economic fundamentals."[23] No doubt, the Fed Chairman will someday give a
detailed account of his thoughts following the collapse of Lehman Brothers in
September of 2008. Professor Bernanke spent much of his career studying the
mistakes surrounding the Great Depression and if not "déjà vu all over again"

as Yogi Berra would say, then at a minimum he had to suspect the economy was confronting a Japanese style crisis that included the very real possibility of deflation and an extended period of low growth. Cognizant of political limitations, the Chairman chose to emulate Colin Powell with the "Bernanke Doctrine." Bernanke's support for the Troubled Asset Relief Program and quantitative easing one, two and three included the purchase of hundreds of billions of dollars in mortgage backed securities that dramatically expanded the Central Banks balance sheet and attests to his willingness to apply overwhelming force to resuscitate an economy that had flat-lined.

There is a contingent of academic economists who maintain that the Fed under-responded, a view that fails to factor in political realities and the threat posed to central bank autonomy by an even more aggressive stimulus. For those who believe it was excessive, we will never know whether the economic "shock and awe" was justified because no one knows the circumstances that might have prevailed if it had been more measured. Whatever side one takes, the Bernanke Doctrine could be interpreted as an admission of expert ignorance. It accepts the negative consequences of overcompensation when the potential costs of doing too little loom unacceptably large.

The Bernanke Doctrine is instructive because economists are seldom willing to concede ignorance. Walter Heller, the head of John F. Kennedy's Council of Economic Advisors spoke of "fine tuning the economy" with short-run fiscal adjustments as if his technical understanding of the macro-economy was equivalent to a master mechanic's working knowledge of an automobile engine. Following the 2008 financial meltdown, many more economists were willing to admit that the complexity of the financial system exceeded their intellectual grasp.

Federal Reserve economists Fisher and Rosenblum wrote: "the phrase 'too big to fail' is misleading. It really means too complex to manage. Not just for top bank executives, but too complex as well for creditors and shareholders to exert market discipline." The big banks are also too complex for "bank supervisors to exert regulatory discipline when internal management discipline and market discipline are lacking." The phrase "too big to fail" is a misnomer because financial "institutions holding one third of U.S. banking system assets did essentially fail in 20008-2009, surviving only with extraordinary government assistance. They were quasi-nationalized—bailed out in everyday parlance."[24]

The Volcker Rule is part of the Dodd-Frank Act and is intended to limit risk by restricting "too big to fail" (TBTF) banks from *speculating* in financial derivatives, a policy consistent with economic theory which predicts that no one has sufficient skill to consistently beat the market. It appears that not only are TBTF banks not smart enough to consistently win *speculative* bets, in the spring of 2012 JP Morgan Chase did not possess the technical expertise necessary to *hedge* financial risk, a task that theoretically much easier. In a two week period, a strategy designed to hedge the bank's exposure to the European crisis lost billions of dollars and erased almost 10% of market equity in a single day.[25] Without the TBTF guarantee, even more market equity might have been lost. The experts at JP Morgan Chase should be free to lose all of the money their shareholders will tolerate but it's time to end the taxpayer safety net.

In addition to government regulators, the system of financial oversight employs a variety of third-party monitors such as certified public accountants, real estate appraisers, credit rating agencies, etc. Ostensibly independent, they provide a service but the extent of their work would be substantially curtailed in the absence of legal mandates requiring it. Bad real estate appraisals were identified as a contributing factor in the 1980s S&L debacle and all of the subsequent regulation did not prevent bad appraisals from contributing to the 2008 crisis. After the dot.com bubble of the 1990s, the accounting profession was targeted with new rules that placed the public accounting standards board under the jurisdiction of the SEC, yet creative accounting played a role in bank failures, such as Lehman Brothers, which took liberties in the reporting of repurchase agreement transactions. Like real estate appraisers, rating agencies provided overly optimistic ratings and some may have engaged in conflict of interest.

The rating agencies were not content with their rating monopoly; they also wanted to cash in on the deal-making. The California Public Employees Retirement System (Calpers) has sued the rating agencies for losses on structured products that were assigned AAA ratings. Calpers criticized what it contends are conflicts of interest by the rating agencies, which are paid by the companies issuing the securities. In the case of the structured products sold to Calpers, the agencies went one step further and received lucrative fees ranging from $300,000 to $1 million for each deal they assisted in putting together. In 2007, ten days after Moody's had downgraded some securitized packages, Moody's issued a report titled "Structured Investment Vehicles: An

Oasis of Calm in the Subprime Maelstrom" promoting some structured prod-ucts while downgrading others.[26]

Given the gratuitous complexity embodied in some structured products, the hubris displayed by the rating agencies is almost breathtaking. The following sequence of steps used to create a structured Collateralized Debt Obligation (CDO) gives some indication of their complexity. Residential mortgages are combined into pools known as residential mortgage backed securities (RMBS). The RMBS are subdivided into "tranches" that are sold as separate classes of securities with the most senior class given an AAA rating. Some of the tranches from one pool were combined with tranches from another pool to form Collateralized Mortgage Obligations (CMO) and some were combined with tranches based on pools from commercial mortgages, auto loans, student loans, small business loans and even corporate loans called Collateralized Loan Obligations (CLO). These new heterogeneous pools were called Collateralized Debt Obligations or CDOs. But wait, it gets even more "innovative." Some CDOs were combined with other CDOs resulting in what Scott and Taylor call a CDO2. If a CDO2 held 100 CDOs each holding 100 RMBS comprising only 2,000 mortgages, then our expert rating analyst would need information on 20 million different loans to accurately evaluate risk and return—financial innovation, indeed![27]

The 1980s, 1990s and 2000s were heady decades for "financial economics," the branch of the dismal science concerned with the study of financial mar-kets. Financial innovation ushered in a brave new world that was credited with transferring risk from Main Street to Wall Street, moderating interest rates and temporarily reducing volatility in the real economy. While their brethren in main stream economics debated arcane issues more suited to a 12th century monastery, financial economists regarded themselves as practical men and women who applied their skills to the serious business of making money.

"Financial engineering" became a popular phrase used to describe the techni-cal precision and mathematical sophistication of this emerging science. After all, financial economists had used partial differential equations to formulate option prices in a manner conceptually similar to how it is used in physics to solve problems dealing with the propagation of heat, sound and fluids flow. It was only fitting that the 1990 Nobel Prize in Economics would be awarded to William Sharpe, Harry Markowitz and Merton Miller who are regarded as the architects of modern portfolio theory. This would be followed by a 1997 Nobel given to Robert Merton and Myron Scholes for their work in derivatives pricing. Long relegated to second class intellectual status, the awards were perceived as vindication for a branch of the dismal science that had finally arrived.

Cracks in the intellectual edifice of the new science became apparent with the spectacular failure of Long-Term Capital Management (LTCM), a U.S. hedge fund. Formed in 1994, Nobel laureates Merton and Scholes were principals in LTCM; their financial expertise along with others would be utilized to post annualized returns of over 40% in the early years before losing $4.6 billion in four months of 1998. The Federal Reserve organized a bailout of LTCM among Wall Street investment banks that some believe forestalled a wider financial panic. Notably, Bear Stearns declined to participate but that is another story.

The more stodgy critics worried that the bailout of LTCM fostered a moral hazard problem that would encourage other financial firms like 1990s Wall Street darling Fannie Mae to grow too fast and assume too much risk, but they tended to be dismissed as old school types out of step with the go-go atmosphere of the decade. If the private sector had been required to cope with the creative destruction precipitated by LTCM, it might have humbled some of Wall Street's rocket scientists and acted as a stop sign on the road to the sub-prime mess. Instead, it was little more than a speed bump.

By the new millennium, many financial firms were actively recruiting new PhDs in physics and mathematics who would build computer models to rate risk, price derivatives and formulate portfolio strategy. Like the majority of new PhDs in technical fields, many were foreign students who often possessed little knowledge of U.S. business practice or institutions; but it really didn't matter because the principals in the firms where they labored were selling "science" and the more esoteric and arcane the model, the bigger impression it would make on customers. Of course, an elegant model designed by a lowly PhD in pursuit of a green card is less than worthless if everyone in the chain from the lowly mortgage broker to the CEO of Bear Stearns falls down on the job.

Nassim Taleb, author of *The Black Swan*, is an out-spoken critic of financial economics.[28] Much of Taleb's criticism focuses on technical issues surrounding the distributional properties of security returns. Despite frequent reliance on statistical assumptions that assume a normal distribution, most returns deviate significantly from the bell curve. The shorter the return interval—say daily versus monthly returns—the greater the deviation. Taleb argues that the presumption of normality and the emphasis on long horizon performance by the purveyors of investment advice cause many market participants to under estimate financial market risk and the potential for Black Swan events. Despite addressing a relatively technical subject, *The Black Swan* found a wide popular audience.

Some go so far as to suggest that propositions in financial economics, such as option pricing theory, may be "performative" in nature.[29] This means that the use of a widely accepted model, like the one used in option pricing during the 1970s, may over time actually cause financial markets to price options more consistent with the theory. Conversely, some evidence indicates that classic option pricing theory became "less true" after the 1987 stock market crash and that practical applications of the theory to "portfolio insurance" may have exacerbated the collapse. This type of response is characterized as "counter-performativity" or the use of a theory or model causing economic processes that are *less* like their depiction by economics.

Much research suggests that finance follows rather than leads real economic activity. Instead of an end in itself, its purpose is to grease the wheels of commerce in the production of real goods and services. The real economy can function at a reasonably high level with a financial system that is less than perfectly efficient, especially if efficiency contributes to systemic risk. By 2008, the financial sector had grown too large with too many financial grease monkeys greasing wheels that didn't need it, while many investors were lulled into high risk investments on the basis of largely unjustified intellectual prowess. No other industry is compensated as well as Wall Street or more populated by the graduates of elite universities. And when things go wrong, no other industry can depend on a trillion dollar government bailout and four years of essentially zero interest rates courtesy of the Fed. The most curious defense of "financial science" comes from academics who claim that criticism is unde-served because most of the bailout money has been repaid. Essentially this view maintains that "our mathematical models work great, until they don't, in which case we need a higher power to temporarily save us"—a defense that renders financial economics more like "intelligent design" than real science.

The biggest banks are too complex for regulators to supervise and managers to operate without resorting to public bailouts. Man-made complexity allows

CPAs and lawyers to build financial castles in the air that neither they nor outside investors are able to fully understand. Expert appraisers tend to make mistakes in real estate valuations during periods of economic turbulence precisely when accurate estimates are most needed and much the same can be said for credit rating agencies that did a woeful job evaluating the risk of complex debt instruments leading up to the 2008 crisis.

More top-down government regulators and third party experts will only add to the complexity. Instead, policy makers should begin a concerted effort to restore market monitoring in the banking system. If a bank is too big to be monitored by the market because of the systemic threat posed by failure, then it should be downsized. In time, Fannie and Freddie should finally be dismantled and replaced with competing securitizers without benefit of the government guarantee. Assorted housing subsidies, including the mortgage interest deduction and capital gain exemption, should be scaled back. The required use of third party regulators such as real estate appraisers and rating agencies should be reconsidered and eliminated in instances where their services are largely perfunctory.

The complexity created by the plague of economic and financial experts is beyond their intellectual capacity to resolve. Asking people to continue to believe in their expertise is like asking children to continue to believe in Santa Claus after they saw mommy and daddy place the presents under the Christmas tree.

JOHN BATE CLARK MEDAL WINNERS

1947 Paul A. Samuelson Harvard

1949 Kenneth E. Boulding Oxford

1951 Milton Friedman Columbia

1953 No Award

1955 James Tobin Harvard

1957 Kenneth J. Arrow Columbia

1959 Lawrence R. Klein MIT

1961 Robert M. Solow Harvard

1963 Hendrik S. Houthakker University of Amsterdam

1965 Zvi Griliches Chicago

1967 Gary S. Becker Princeton

1969 Marc Leon Nerlove John Hopkins

1971 Dale W. Jorgenson Harvard

1973 Franklin M. Fisher Harvard

1975 Daniel McFadden Minnesota

1977 Martin S. Feldstein Oxford

1979 Joseph E. Stiglitz MIT

1981 A. Michael Spence Harvard

1983 James J. Heckman Princeton

1985 Jerry A. Hausman Oxford

1987 Sanford J. Grossman Chicago

1989 David M. Kreps Stanford

1991 Paul R. Krugman MIT

1993 Lawrence H. Summers Harvard

1995 David Card Princeton

1997 Kevin M. Murphy Chicago

1999 Andrei Shleifer MIT

2001 Mathew Rabin MIT

2003 Steven Levitt MIT

2005 Daron Acemoglu London

2007 Susan C. Athey Stanford

2009 Emmanuel Saez MIT

2010 Esther Duflo MIT

2011 Jonathon Levin MIT

2012 Amy Finkelstein MIT

> **MIT** =9, **Harvard**=7 **Chicago** =3
> **Oxford**= 3 **Princeton**=3 **Columbia**=2
> **Stanford**=2 **London, Minnesota,**
> **Johns Hopkins, Amsterdam** (1)

CHAPTER 7

CAULIFLOWER IS NOTHING BUT CABBAGE WITH A COLLEGE EDUCATION

Some experts are self-taught while others learn from mentors in highly structured apprentice programs. Many boast graduate or professional school training, but the formal post-secondary education of most experts begins with the acquisition of a four-year university degree. Millions of Americans know all too well that transforming cabbage into cauliflower, as described by Mark Twain, has become a much more expensive process. In an effort to place the rising cost of college in perspective, an analyst testifying before the Senate Finance Committee in 2007 estimated that if milk and gasoline had risen at the same rate as tuition over the previous 30 years, a gallon of milk would sell for $15 and a gallon of gas for $9.10. To make matters worse, the inflated price of a college education is accompanied by the perception that the experts who preside over the system have watered down the quality of their product. Following the 2008 financial crisis, persistently high unemployment among recent college graduates caused many people to question whether or not a bachelor's degree was still a ticket to a middle-class life.

Unemployed college graduates were prominent participants in the 2011 Occupy demonstrations that began in New York and spread to other cities around the world. Part of the media coverage focused on the rapidly increasing debt burden that some students incur during their college careers. Student loans in 2011 averaged approximately $25,000 with the aggregate loan balance used to finance college estimated in excess of $1 trillion and growing. Parents and students pay tuition but public higher education receives direct subsidies from state and local government while the federal government funnels billions of dollars to universities via competitive research grants.

In addition to direct payments, tax subsidies include the Helping Outstanding Pupils Educationally tax credit, the Lifetime Learning tax credit, the tax treatment of education individual retirement accounts, state prepaid tuition plans, the deductibility of student loan interest and the tax-free discharge of student loan indebtedness. Universities receive tax-free status on income earned from activities related to their educational function, tax-free investment income, the right to issue tax-exempt bonds to finance activities related to the educational function, and the ability of donors to deduct gifts to universities made during life or at death. There is also a government subsidy associated with guaranteed student loans and the property taxes lost to local government on not-for-profit college real estate. When direct funding by government is combined with the tax subsidies, student tuition payments and the opportunity cost of lost wages attributable to a four-year degree that is gradually lengthening to six years, the total tab for turning cabbage into cauliflower is staggering; but there are considerable differences in how the money is allocated across regions and institutions.

Coinciding with concern over rising tuition, increasing debt and persistently high unemployment among recent college graduates, is the declining quality of undergraduate programs. A controversial report titled *Academically Adrift: Limited Learning on College Campuses* parses the results of more than 3,000 full-time traditional-age students on 29 campuses who took the Collegiate Learning Assessment, a standardized test that measures critical thinking, analytic reasoning and writing skills. The report more or less confirmed what everyone suspected, which is that the college credential has been substantially devalued. Performance varied by type of institution and academic major; however, about half of students showed no significant learning after two years of college; and after four years, more than one third showed little change. Today's students study less, read less and write less but receive higher grades than their predecessors a few decades earlier.[1]

Full time college students during the 1960s spent roughly forty hours per week in combined study and class time. Average study time fell from twenty-five hours per week in the early 1960s to twenty hours in the 1980s all the way

176

down to thirteen hours in 2003. In 1961, sixty-seven percent of college students reported spending more than 20 hours per week studying compared to only twenty percent of students today. The average college student spends only twenty-seven hours per week of class and study time combined, less than the average high school student.[2] If the college credential has indeed been devalued as argued in *Academically Adrift*, then the quality adjusted cost of higher education has been increasing faster than suggested by tuition increases. It also partly explains why parents are willing to endure "the arms race" to get their kid into an elite college that they hope will differentiate them from the masses of under-achieving students.

Explanations for the devaluation of undergraduate education in the face of escalating tuition should start with the experts responsible: administrators and faculty. Not so long ago, top university administrators were selected from the faculty but even mid-level managers were often professors who returned to teaching after a brief administrative stint. Many of these temporary administrators proved to be effective managers who helped build a higher education system that was the envy of the world. Like a politician who serves a single term, the temporary administrator may be more inclined to make decisions that are in the best interests of students and the institution rather than their career. Campus unrest and anti-war demonstrations during the Vietnam era led to frequent clashes that culminated in the Kent State tragedy. Some critics blamed school administrators for a permissive campus environment which provided additional impetus to the post-Vietnam professionalization of college administration.

The creation of a new class of full-time expert administrators contributed to a corresponding "agency problem" similar to corporate America's but in some respects more difficult to resolve since those paying for higher education include taxpayers, students, parents and private donors. With the exception of staff devoted to student services, most higher education administrators have little interaction with students. Curriculum and instruction are appropriately considered the purview of the faculty, particularly among the better colleges with a strong tradition of faculty governance. However, in the less prestigious private and regional public universities where faculty autonomy has less of a tradition, administrators can exert significant influence on curriculum through budget and other processes. The relative power of administrative staff has also increased because of the large increase in part-time instructors who have little say in either curriculum or administrative matters.

Over the last three decades, non-faculty staff has been the fastest growing category of professional employment in higher education. Some of the increase has been in traditional administrative functions like human resources and maintenance; but the majority of new hires are employed in "student services" such as admissions, career placement, counseling and athletics. Even some small regional state universities without extensive graduate and service programs, can devote more than half of the total salary pie to non-instructional employees. According to the Department of Education, in 2009 public degree granting institutions spent only 28 percent of annual operating budgets on classroom instruction. From 1975 to 2005, full time faculty increased by 51%, executive administrators by 85% and other professional administrators by a whopping 240%.[3] In response to increasing public criticism that questions the payoff from a college degree, many universities hired Chief Marketing Officers at salaries "ranging from \$200,000-\$400,000 annually," a reaction that suggests universities regard the fundamental issue in higher education finance as a public relations problem rather than runaway costs as a consequence of mission drift.[4] It is the kind of response one would expect from private companies rather than a "not-for-profit" industry that receives hundreds of billions of dollars in taxpayer support.

The decline in academic standards and large increases in college tuition correlate closely with the increase in non-faculty employment. The growing number of "educrats" employed in higher education has long had its counterpart in K thru 12 public school systems. In some cities, patronage jobs in the education bureaucracy are used by politicians to reward political friends, a *quid pro quo* once confined to the departments of sanitation, motor vehicles and the like. Similar behavior has crept into higher education. For many years, the University of Medicine and Dentistry of New Jersey was known as a "political patronage pit" whose administrators regularly provided jobs to New Jersey politicos and the relatives of trustees using a rating system of one, two or three on job applications to indicate the political patron's degree of influence.[5] In Alabama, the community college system awarded contracts and jobs to forty-three members of the state legislature or their close relatives. The chancellor of the system, himself a former Alabama state legislator, saw nothing wrong with using the state's higher education system to cultivate "allies" among legislatures. [6]

"Higher education administration" is now a doctoral degree program that presumes to train experts in college management. University presidents and top administrators with non-academic backgrounds are increasingly selected from applicant pools constructed by professional consultants who specialize as higher education head hunters. For the biggest universities, administrative salaries have skyrocketed not unlike those of BSC football coaches. From 2000 to 2010, the average college president's pay at the 50 wealthiest universities increased by 75%; in contrast, professor's salaries grew by 14%. Over the same decade, inflation increased by 31% compared to a 65% rise in tuition costs. [7] Not surprisingly, the large increase in non-faculty employment has altered campus culture. One manifestation of the agency problem is that administrators no longer act on behalf of taxpayers despite the billions of dollars in direct payments and tax subsidies. Instead, they have de-emphasized the "public good" component of higher education in favor of what is sometimes referred to as the "customer model" or private good. The customer model focuses on the college experience which can include state of the art exercise facilities, performing arts centers, aquatic centers and sports teams that play in stadiums that are the envy of the NBA and NFL franchises. Instead of a traditional college dormitory, many students occupy "suites" that include private bathrooms, kitchenettes and full Internet and cable TV access. International travel as part of the educational experience has become *de rigeur* at some colleges and, while the appeal is obvious, it has increased college costs with often mixed educational results. Much of the traditional print library budget has been diverted to fund networked systems and on-line holdings, many of which can be accessed remotely and are undoubtedly more efficient but they also encourage students to remain cocooned in their "student suite" with all of its diversions rather than slogging to the library.

Students and parents support the customer model since those attending the larger state universities with the most elaborate amenities tend to be the greatest beneficiaries of taxpayer subsidies. Not unlike housing policy, government subsidies to higher education tend to be regressive, benefiting higher income households. Because low income students receive grants and financial aid, the burden of rising tuition has fallen disproportionately on the middle-class. If students and their parents were paying the full cost of their education, then the customer model is an appropriate one but the large taxpayer subsidy sug-gests that the general public has a shared interest in the cabbage-to-cauliflower transformation. Society's interest is reflected in the expectation that the system produces graduates who understand the common culture sufficient to perform as good citizens and that they develop the skills necessary to compete in the global marketplace. [8]

Predictably, the customer model encourages students to approach their college education less as a learning opportunity and more as a credential necessary to gain access to a more remunerative career. "The payoff for a particular cre-dential is the same no matter how it was acquired, so it is rational behavior to try to strike a good bargain, to work at getting a diploma, like a car, at a substantial discount. The effect on education is to emphasize form over con-tent." [9] In general, the customer model provides little incentive for professional administrators to emphasize undergraduate academic rigor when their own performance is increasingly measured by the number of buildings constructed, increases in enrollment, student retention, endowment growth and the ranking of the university's sports teams. When the issue of academic quality arises, it is invariably associated with higher status graduate programs and the amount of competitive grant money raised by research faculty.

Administrators may invoke the customer model but it is the faculty who are ultimately responsible for much of the quality decline. One manifestation of declining quality is grade inflation, which tends to be a much more pernicious problem at less selective universities. Because of the high admission standards, elite colleges exhibit relatively small differences among student abilities when compared to the much larger variation in the academic skills of students attend-ing colleges with open admissions. Consequently, grades are a more important indicator of student achievement among graduates of less selective colleges.

Everything else being equal, an employer can hire the graduate of a less selec-tive university with a high grade point average (GPA) or the graduate of a highly selective university who also has a high GPA but has been pre-screened by a rigorous admission process. Because grade inflation makes it more difficult to identify the most qualified students, employers can mitigate the risk by hir-ing exclusively from highly selective universities. The employer may still hire an occasional lemon even from a prestigious university but the risk is reduced because of pre-screening. [10]

Grade inflation imposes a cost on high achieving students since it is more diffi-cult to distinguish them from their less qualified peers such that some superior students may reject even a full scholarship at a less selective university if they believe the savings does not off-set the selection bias imposed by grade inflation. Because grades are a less reliable indicator of qualifications, some employ-ment counselors report resurgence in the "good ole boy" network, which is bad news for women and minorities. When grade inflation causes employers to hire based on university status instead of grades, the best students at less selective colleges are penalized and elite schools are granted the market power to charge ever higher tuition. Admission boards for graduate and professional schools are also more likely to rely on standardized graduate entrance exams if GPA is a less reliable indicator of student ability.

Grade inflation has been greater at private colleges than public universities and is more apparent in the humanities than the sciences. It increased during the Vietnam Era, stabilized from the mid-1970s to the mid-1980s, and then accel-erated over the last two decades. It also coincides with the ascendancy of the customer model that reinforced credentialism in the workplace. Parents may be less likely to complain about taking out a second mortgage on the house to pay for tuition increases if junior graduates with honors; of course, if the average student graduates *cum laude* then the recognition bestows no "honor."

Certainly, the increasing numbers of college students who are unprepared for col-lege level work and subtle pressure by administrators to increase retention rates to help pay for the "bells and whistles" have made it more difficult for professors to maintain academic standards. Politicians in some states have introduced fund-ing formulae that reward high retention while the average academic preparation of high school graduates has declined making it more difficult to teach courses that require a background in mathematics or significant reading and writing. The student loan situation has an obvious corollary with the sub-prime mort-gage crisis. The experts have devised policies that in some instances encourage students who are unprepared for college to take on student loans just as some people not economically prepared for home ownership were enticed to assume mortgage debt. Of course, you can walk away from a mortgage but student loans cannot be discharged in bankruptcy—a difference that can result in a lifetime of indentured servitude. Many students graduate with a degree of questionable value and a large student loan balance but many others drop out and still have to repay student loans, having failed to acquire even a watered-down credential.

"Higher education access" for "at risk students" are politically correct mantras but there is little doubt that a large number of colleges are primarily interested in maximizing tuition revenue which is the major reason so many marginal students are admitted to four-year colleges despite limited chances of success. A career counselor writing in the *Chronicle of Higher Education* addressed the issue: "Among high-school students who graduated in the bottom 40 percent of their classes, and whose first institutions were four-year colleges, two-thirds had not earned diplomas eight and a half years later...Yet four-year colleges admit and take money from hundreds of thousands of such students each year!"[11] A study that tracked an entire Boston public school graduating class found that of 2,964 graduates, 1,904 or 64.2% went on to college with most attending three local community colleges and three nearby four-year colleges— Northeastern Northeastern, Quincy College and UMass Amherst. Seven years later only 35.3% had earned a bachelors degree, an associate's degree or a one-year certificate. The graduation rate was only 12% for students attending community college.[12]

There are two major reasons for low retention and the modest graduation rates among the vast majority of students who attend less selective colleges. First, because tuition has been rising at almost twice the rate of inflation, students are required to work more hours than in the past. Since most students who work are employed in minimum wage jobs, such as food service, retailing, etc., wages fail to keep pace with tuition increases; so, students work more hours and devote less time to attending class and studying. Secondly, despite test scores proclaiming that competency in math and reading among high school students has stabilized, there are many more students who are not as academically well prepared than in years past. Higher education experts have created a shadow curriculum of remedial courses in an attempt to raise retention but evidence suggests that it is just another revenue center with little impact on student performance. One study examined the 453,000 students who took the basic skills test required of students entering two and four-year Texas colleges in the 1990s. The analysis focused on the 93,000 students who either barely passed or barely failed the test; students who barely failed took remedial courses and those who barely passed took college level courses. There was essentially no difference in the subsequent college achievement of the two groups nor did remediation have any effect on income seven years after starting college.[13]

Having failed to raise achievement and retention by remediation, some administrators and higher education experts blame the low graduation rates on the poor teaching skills of college faculty. Teaching in public schools is a tough job and few professors on college campuses would question the competency of education professors who are responsible for training K-12 instructors in education pedagogy. However, colleges of education are not particularly well respected compared to those housing more rigorous academic disciplines. Thomas Sowell claims that 120th Street adjacent to Columbia Teachers College is said to be "the widest street in the world because it separates that institution from the rest of Columbia University."[14] Whether such criticism is deserved or not, as long as pedagogical experts ply their trade within their multi-billion dollar franchise of teacher certification, other university faculty were willing to let them do their thing. But many pedagogical experts are not content with their public school monopoly; they recognize low university retention as an opportunity to extend their expertise and work the same magic on higher education they worked (or failed to work) on K-12. Certainly, there are many bad teachers on campus, including many in colleges of education, but it is unlikely that an expert in teaching pedagogy knows how to teach organic chemistry better than an experienced chemistry professor.

Low retention along with the customer model spurred demands for "assessment" and "accountability" of faculty leading many colleges to introduce standardized student evaluations of professors. Student evaluations can be useful but research indicates that their misuse contributes to grade inflation. Valen Johnson analyzed a unique data set and reviewed dozens of studies. He presents convincing evidence that professors who assign higher grades are rewarded with higher student evaluations despite their being a poor measure of teaching effectiveness.[15] Grading inequity across disciplines also diverts students and resources away from academically challenging STEM (science, technology, engineering, mathematics) fields that award lower grades but provide greater economic opportunity for graduates. Despite higher compensation and more abundant jobs, U.S. businesses have little choice but to fill many of the job openings in these areas with immigrants. To the degree that tougher grading diverts students from STEM fields, grade inflation increases science illiteracy, erodes our comparative trade advantage in technical industries and makes it more difficult for voters to arrive at informed opinions on complex issues like stem cell research and climate change while rendering juries more susceptible to "junk science."

The decline in the quality of undergraduate education may also reflect the incentive system. Professors who publish extensively in the more prestigious journals enjoy higher salaries, greater status and teach more interesting graduate courses. Within the same department there exists a status continuum not unlike the military. Graduate teaching assistants occupy the lowest rung on the ladder followed by non-tenure track part-timers, then tenure track assistant professors, associate professors, full professors and those who occupy endowed chairs. Much of the freshman/sophomore general studies programs are taught by graduate students primarily concerned with finishing their dissertation and part-timers many of whom hold other jobs. Full-time, non-tenure track instructors are not expected to publish so their continued employment often depends on good student evaluations. Senior faculty expect adjuncts to act as gatekeepers and "screen" underperforming students from entering their major by assigning appropriate grades while Deans and department heads frequently encourage part-timers teaching introductory courses to recruit majors by making the class more "engaging," code-speak sometimes meaning dumbing it down. Because there is an abundance of qualified applicants waiting to take the part-timer's place, they often enter into tacit agreement with students to scale back academic expectations and award higher grades in exchange for good evaluations. It is not surprising that the authors of *Academically Adrift* found little learning for half of all college students after two years given the low priority assigned to general studies and the system of faculty incentives.

The business of student evaluations is a multi-million dollar industry that continues to insist that professors receive higher student evaluations because students are "learning more" not because they assign higher grades. Johnson argues that the use of flawed evaluations persists because many decision makers benefit from the grading inequity and expert administrators are eager to demonstrate to politicians and accreditation bodies that teaching performance is being "assessed" even if the assessment is defective.[16] It is a kind of "through the looking glass" reasoning that one frequently encounters in American education. Virtually everyone employed in higher education is complicit in grade inflation. Rather than beacons of truth, colleges and universities have joined *the cheating culture*.[17] False praise may temporarily enhance student self-esteem but it does nothing to prepare them for a competitive global economy.

With over 347,000 graduates in 2008-2009, business administration awards far more degrees than any other major and represent an attractive cash cow to universities. Faculty salaries in business are higher than many other degree

184

programs but overhead costs, such as laboratory facilities, are small or non-existent. Consistent with the findings of *Academically Adrift*, business is often a "default major" that attracts lackluster students without an interest in a specific academic subject but wanting to minimize requirements in foreign language, mathematics, reading, writing and laboratory science. Perhaps more than any other major, colleges of business have exploited the customer model by catering to students in pursuit of a credential. Not only have the experts in higher education misled students by awarding them grades that are undeserved, they actively promote the increasingly false notion that a college degree in any discipline will lead to a lucrative job. The promotion of credentialism along with differential grading across disciplines is one reason U.S. universities have seen a surge in less academically demanding majors while the number of graduates in more difficult science, technology, engineering and mathematics (STEM) has stayed the same or even declined.

Degrees Awarded by Major: 1986 Versus 2009

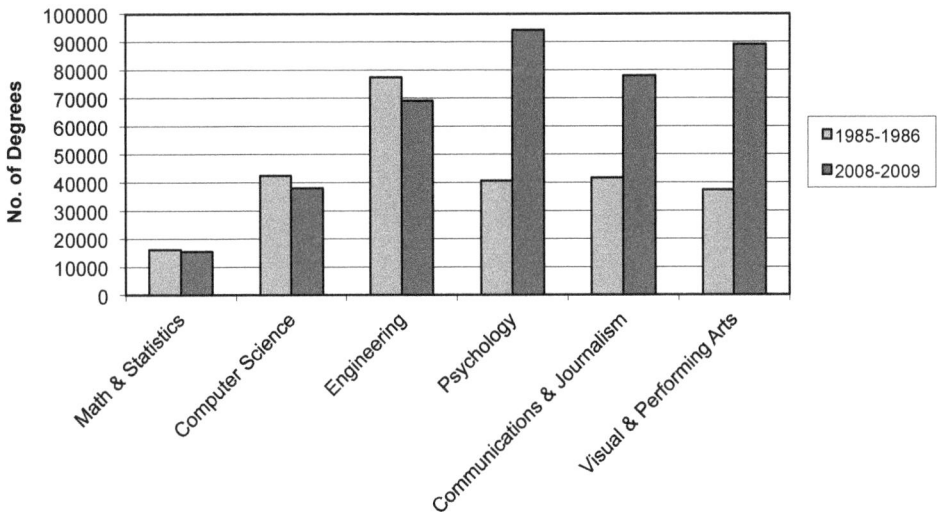

The data for the graph above is taken from the Digest of Education Statistics 2010 and shows changes between 1986 versus 2009 in the number of degrees awarded for a sample of majors. The findings are typical of the growth in non-technical fields versus stagnation or decline in technical fields such as engineering, math and computer science. Certainly, psychology, communications and journalism, and visual and performing arts are valuable majors; but students should be cautioned that it may be more difficult to repay large student loan balances given the more abundant graduates, limited job opportunities and lower average salaries in these fields—information that colleges seldom disseminate to students. It is not uncommon for students to confess that they chose a less challenging major because they do not want to risk jeopardizing their scholarship or grant by taking tough courses that could lower their GPA.

Students are encouraged by the university to declare a major as soon as possible, often before they have been exposed to a variety of fields or the intellectual excitement some highly skilled teachers bring to the classroom. Because the incentive system tends to remove senior professors from undergraduate instruction, many undergraduates may not encounter a tenured professor until they take junior and senior classes in their major if they encounter one at all. Some senior professors avoid teaching freshman/sophomore classes precisely because the general studies curriculum has been watered down and rendered so "interdisciplinary" that many feel they have little to contribute in the introductory course.

On most campuses, higher education experts replaced a general education curriculum characterized as Eurocentric, misogynistic and discipline specific with one that is steeped in the ethos of "multicultural diversity." These new general studies programs claim to promote "critical thinking" rather than "content knowledge" but tend to be less academically challenging than the more traditional curriculum. A 1996 report issued by the National Association of Scholars titled *The Dissolution of General Education: 1914-1993* found that the general education component of a college degree meant to broadly familiarize students with major elements of the common culture has substantially reduced requirements in mathematics, foreign language and laboratory science. The report concludes that general education has become "devalued as an institutional objective."[18] A subsequent 2004 study titled *The Hollow Core* surveyed 50 elite schools and found that only seven required American history, only six required literature, none required an economics course and a majority didn't require a college level math course.[19] Perhaps most disturbing are the findings of *Losing America's Memory: Historical Illiteracy in the 21st Century* which revealed that 81% of seniors from the top 55 U.S. colleges and universities failed a high school level history exam and that none of the institutions surveyed required a course in American history. Three-quarters required no history at all.[20] Without historical context, "critical thinking" in many general studies courses is often little more than a vacuous critique of Western oppression. Politicized and frequently devoid of rigorous content, general education programs have contributed to grade inflation while doing little to educate students in the common culture or prepare them for demanding majors.

Perhaps because they identify more closely with management, cultural experts on the right invariably blame faculty for how the multicultural movement has politicized college campuses but administrators share responsibility, too. After three players on the Duke University lacrosse team were falsely accused of raping an African American exotic dancer, campus activists dismissed the presumption of innocence and demanded summary punishment of the players before due process. The Duke University president and many top administrators continued to support the claims of campus activists even after the evidence in the case began to unravel.[21] In two unrelated cases at the University of Iowa, professors accused of sexual harassment committed suicide before their cases were fully adjudicated, possibly because they saw how eager the administration was to declare their guilt.[22]

Like expert corporate executives who co-opt the rhetoric of social responsibility as a means of diverting attention from poor economic performance, unaccomplished college administrators burnish their diversity credentials as a way to divert attention from rising tuition and eroding standards while currying favor with a small but vocal group of campus activists. Diversity awards are proudly displayed on the paneled walls of plush presidential offices and prominently listed on resumes. Nothing can end an administrative career more abruptly than a hint of "controversy" or conduct that demonstrates less than 100 percent commitment to the multicultural agenda. Not unlike corporate America, head-hunters avoid potentially controversial administrators in favor of those who have mastered the multicultural rhetoric. Because politically conservative faculty keep to themselves and are less likely to hold jobs in administration or teach in fields directly concerned with multicultural issues, highly vocal faculty and administrators on the political left are seldom challenged by a loyal opposition.

Windschuttle traces the transformation of undergraduate general education programs to a few prestigious American universities in the 1970s. Initially, there was little controversy since most followers were confined to a few narrow specialties; however, by the mid-1980's a large number of schools had succumbed to the influence of these supposedly forward thinking programs and joined the ranks of the "new humanities." [23] Not everyone acquiesced to the new agenda and a few opponents managed eloquent rebuttals. One prominent critic was the late Allan Bloom who argued that universities abandoned objective standards in the study of individuals and human society in favor of a highly politicized radical theory that is hostile to traditional Western values. [24] Kimball and others have expressed similar concerns in regard to the politicizing of university curricula. [25]

Windschuttle argues that a shortcoming of Bloom's and Kimball's critiques is that their concept of preserving the Western canon was not extended to the intellectual disciplines within which most of the Great Books were written. According to Windschuttle, the basis of Western learning has been the organization of knowledge into distinct fields, which were founded in ancient Greece and gained momentum from the work of Aristotle. Organizing knowledge by "discipline" imposes a systematic research method which produces an accretion of consistent findings that allow effective teaching and permit a large and growing body of knowledge to be transmitted from one generation to the next.

Supporters of the new general studies programs are particularly hostile to traditional disciplines, especially in the humanities and social sciences, and tend to advocate a cross-disciplinary approach to all fields of study. The new approach favors interdisciplinary fields that are organized as "cultural studies, textual studies, gender studies, media studies and peace studies." The new taxonomy not only complicates how accumulated knowledge will be integrated with future knowledge, it allows and even encourages professors to expound on subjects outside their area of specialization. In an attempt to differentiate their programs, many universities have designed a highly idiosyncratic general education core that imposes added costs on students trying to transfer credit hours from other colleges. Businesses characterize this strategy as building in "switching costs," the purpose of which is to increase monopoly power by making it more costly for a customer to switch to a competitor. In the terminology of economics, the demand for a university's junior and senior level courses is much more "inelastic" than the freshman and sophomore general studies courses and one of the reasons why some universities charge more for upper division courses is because they can.

After completing a grade inflated and frequently unchallenging general studies program, many students are unprepared for the more demanding major courses that begin their junior year. Most students accept responsibility and perform admirably but others react with shocked indignation to their first low grade in college and waste little time changing to one of the less challenging majors many of which exist precisely for this purpose. Too often colleges accept tuition payments along with the government subsidies and dispense a diploma for requiring the student to do little more than show up. How did the experts lead us to this juncture and what are the forces that continue to shape the system? As in politics, the mother's milk of higher education is money. It's time to follow the money.

MONEY IN HIGHER EDUCATION

Maintenance of the *status quo* is a top priority of colleges and universities. The experts never tire of reminding us that the U.S. system of higher education is "the envy of the world" and that universities are major driving forces in the economy. The comments are frequently intended as a veiled warning that any change in the method of funding would jeopardize the benefits that are presumed to flow from the current system.

Financial support to higher education by state and local governments has increased substantially over the past twenty-five years. From 1986 to 2008, state and local government support for general operating expenses of public and independent higher education institutions increased from $31.4 to $88.8 billion. The financial crisis in 2008 dramatically reduced state revenues and curtailed the growth in state and local government support of colleges and universities. In 2009, Congress passed the American Recovery and Reinvestment Act (ARRA) which partially off-set state government cuts to higher education. In addition to state and local revenue, public institutions collected net tuition revenue of $56.3 billion in 2011, for a total of about $143.8 billion available to support general operating expenses. [26]

ARRA funds have been exhausted and tax revenues in many states continue to languish. When adjusted for inflation, projected state appropriations for higher education in fiscal year 2012 have declined to $72.5 billion, a cut of more than 15% from the 2008 peak. In per capita terms, the decline is even steeper when one takes into account the increase in student enrollment. Because of differences in migration and demographic trends, southern and western states have experienced larger enrollment increases, hence a greater reduction in per capita funding. Universities have responded by increasing class size, using more part-time professors and increasing tuition.

The share of total revenue for general operating expenses originating from net tuition revenue increased from 32.2 percent in 2008 to 39.0 percent in 2011. But even before the financial crisis of 2008, states were shifting a larger proportion of university operating costs to tuition paying students. Essentially, this occurred because the operating costs of universities were increasing faster than increases in taxpayer support. At the University of Virginia, state funding has dropped from 26.2% of the budget in 1990 to 5.6% in 2012, but the University's total budget over the same period grew from $678 million to $2.58 billion.[27] In recent decades, many state flagship schools have promoted themselves as a "public ivy" that pursues a strategy of growing endowments, increasing the number of non-resident undergraduates who pay a tuition premium, and focusing more on high prestige graduate, professional and research programs.

One reason colleges have such a difficult time controlling costs is because they engage in so much cross-subsidization. Football subsidizes gymnastics, commuter students subsidize residential students, general education students subsidize majors, executive programs subsidize graduate degrees and so on. In addition to cross-subsidies that complicate accurate cost estimates, universities frequently offer programs and majors that cannibalize revenue. On the same university campus, it is not uncommon to have free standing economics departments in social sciences, the college of business and the college of agriculture. Given the cross-subsidies and revenue cannibalization, most universities have no idea what constitutes the real marginal revenue or costs associated with a single activity. Further complicating the process are philanthropic donations that are often tied to a particular major or field of study. Forced to respond to reductions in government support, colleges often make spending cuts based on university or state politics rather than service to constituents, academics or economic criteria.

Colleges have been able to cross-subsidize because they are able to bundle their services. The right to bundle services financed by student activity fees has been supported by the Supreme Court. In 1996, three law students attending the University of Wisconsin-Madison sued in federal court challenging the constitutionality of the university's mandatory student fee system. They argued that it was unconstitutional for portions of their student fee to fund political or ideological activities with which they disagreed. [28] In the 1996 case of *Southworth v. Grebe* the U.S. district court granted summary judgment in favor of the three law students when it ruled that the fee system violated the students' free-speech rights by compelling them to fund speech with which they disagreed. In 2000, the U.S. Supreme Court unanimously overturned the ruling and provided a legal framework for a student fee structure that allows universities to bundle activities and charge fees even for off-campus events. [29] Service bundling combined with high "switching costs" has allowed universities to exert substantial market power over their customers.

Few of us would buy a car from someone who required that we submit evidence of our income and net worth so that the seller could price discriminate based on our personal finances, but this is exactly how universities set tuition. Mark G. Yudof, president of the University of California, states that families with incomes under $60,000 pay no fees. "The real crunch," he says, is helping families that make roughly $100,000. "The most at risk at this time really are going to be the middle class."[30] Depending on where one works and lives in California, a family of four or five living on $100,000 may not feel like they are "middle class." In 1991, several Ivy League universities, including Harvard, Princeton and Yale were accused by the Justice Department of operating a "collegiate cartel" in which they colluded to fix prices. The defendants all belonged to an organization of financial aid officers known as the Overlap group that met to set the aid that would be awarded to any applicant applying to schools within the cartel. Eight Ivy League schools signed a consent decree and, while not admitting wrongdoing, each promised "to award financial aid solely on the basis of family income and assets and would not offer financial aid based on "merit" including academic achievement, talent or diversity." [31]

Most economic experts in positions of power failed to recognize how easy credit along with a variety of other policies fueled the housing bubble; many people believe the same dynamic is at work in higher education. One study compared tuition at two-year for-profit colleges that were "aid-eligible" versus tuition at two-year schools where students were not eligible to receive federal grants. Tuition at for-profit schools that were aid-eligible, meaning students qualified for federal aid was 75% higher than at comparable non-aid-eligible for-profit schools where students do not receive federal aid. The average difference was about $3,390 a year or about the same amount students attending aid-eligible schools receive in federal grants. The results are consistent with aid-eligible schools raising tuition to maximize aid. [32]

Until recently, colleges and universities have been successful in using the media to portray the increasing share of tuition as a consequence of penurious state government rather than runaway college costs. Households have largely paid for escalating tuition by increased borrowing. By the end of 2011, The Consumer Financial Protection Bureau estimated that total student debt used to pay for college passed outstanding credit card debt and was in excess of $1 trillion. The Federal Reserve Bank of New York employs a different survey method and estimates it to be a slightly lower at $904 billion. The Fed estimates that from the fourth quarter of 2008 to the first quarter of 2012 the outstanding balance of student debt rose by a whopping 41.4%. [33] Over the same period total household debt, including mortgages, credit cards and auto loans, declined by 10% indicating a gradual "deleveraging" among other debt categories. The change reflects higher tuition as well as reductions in financing alternatives such as home equity loans. As of the first quarter of 2012, a little over 9% of total student debt was delinquent 90 or more days with the government estimated to guarantee 90% of the outstanding balance of all student loans or approximately $900 billion. Some analysts forecast that the delinquency rate could surge to 20% by the end of 2013.

If the increase in student debt over the last five years is projected forward, outstanding debt would double in less than ten years, a rate of increase that is clearly unsustainable. Other demands on state tax revenue, such as public pension liability and Medicaid will continue to compete for slow growing tax revenue suggesting that the salad days of the 1980s and 1990s in state funding for public universities are unlikely to return anytime soon. Loath to cut administrative staff, colleges and universities will respond by continuing to shift more of the burden to tuition paying students, increasing class size and replacing tenured faculty with part time instructors. On-line technology could significantly reduce delivery costs in some areas but would only provide tuition relief to households if universities unbundled services and passed the savings on. Many universities anticipate using growth in on-line programs to further subsidize campus activities, clearly a zero sum game plan that competes for a shrinking pool of high school graduates. Going forward, it is almost certain that economic constraints will curtail growth in federally guaranteed student loans along with federal grants. Elite universities will continue to push for more federal research funding while the top-tier of public universities will increasingly mimic private universities in their continued efforts to privatize research and grow college endowments.

GOVERNMENT FUNDED RESEARCH TO COLLEGES AND UNIVERSITIES

In his 1960 farewell address, President Dwight Eisenhower cautioned the American people against the special interest influence of the "Military-Industrial Complex." Eisenhower believed the large increase in public contracting after WWII posed a threat to the democratic process that could alter the public interest role of universities:

"The free university, historically the fountainhead of free ideas and scientific discovery, has experienced a revolution in the conduct of research. Partly because of the huge costs involved, a government contract becomes virtually a substitute for intellectual curiosity...The prospect of domination of the nation's scholars by Federal employment, project allocation, and the power of money is ever present." [33]

Eisenhower was an unlikely establishment critic but it was his status as a retired five star general, former president of Columbia University and conservative Republican president that renders his warning so instructive. What is the economic justification for the billions of research dollars that flow to higher education? How is it allocated and has it compromised the integrity of the system as President Eisenhower feared?

Kealey traces justification for the government funding of science to the ideas of Francis Bacon and his "linear model of scientific research." This is the same Francis Bacon, by the way, who appeared in Chapter 2 and is credited by some with writing the plays attributed to William Shakespeare. In *The Advancement of Learning*, Bacon maintained that "Amongst so many great foundations of colleges in Europe, I find strange that they are all dedicated to professions and none left free to arts and sciences at large...If any man thinks philosophy and universality to be idle studies he doth not consider that all professions are from thence served and supplied." [34] Bacon championed state funded construction of university laboratories, fellowships and government subsidized salaries for professors. He believed that government funded academic science would spur new technology and lead to the creation of new wealth that would be shared by the larger society and is summarized below.

Academic Science → Technology → Wealth

Few question that new knowledge generates innovations that lead to the creation of wealth. Critics question whether government subsidized science is a necessary condition for innovation. More precisely what is the public interest role of government sponsored research in academia? Bacon's linear model had a significant influence on science policy in Europe but Britain and the U.S. were slow in developing national policies subsidizing science.

Prior to 1940, U.S. government spending on science was $74 million with agricultural research comprising about 40% of the total. By 1945, government funded research had increased to $1.59 billion with almost all of the growth attributable to research spending on defense and nuclear energy. [35] The end of WWII raised the possibility that the consensus for government funded research would end and the research infrastructure would be dismantled. This did not happen for two reasons. The atomic bomb was characterized as ending WWII and preventing an Allied invasion of Japan that would have likely cost hundreds of thousands if not millions of lives. As a result of the Manhattan Project, science assumed greater status in the popular culture. Second, the Cold War simply replaced warring against Germany and Japan, ensuring that large government expenditures on defense related research would continue. National defense continues to consume the lion's share of government subsidized research but Mowery and Rosenberg report data showing large increases in government sponsored non-military Research and Development (R&D) throughout the post WWII era. [36]

Many economic experts continue to maintain that government should subsidize science because the payoff from basic research is deferred far into the future resulting in a low present value. Essentially, this argument maintains that basic research is a public good that private industry has little incentive to underwrite because they are unable to capture all of the returns, most of which accrue to society at large. Attempts to link government subsidized research with multifactor productivity growth in the real economy are less than convincing. Robert Gordon characterizes 1913–1972 as the "golden age" of productivity growth for the U.S. economy. He attributes the 1913–1972 increase to widespread adoption of electricity and electric motors, improved communications as a result of the telephone and greater labor efficiency as a consequence of innovations such as air conditioning. In 1972, U.S. productivity declined to its pre-1913 level and then surged from 1996–2003 before declining again and becoming negative in 2007. [37] The Bureau of Labor Statistics estimate of multifactor productivity for 2010 was the highest annual rate since the agency began reporting the statistic in 1988. The role that government sponsored scientific research played in the 1913-1972 "golden age" of productivity growth is necessarily limited since government science was essentially non-existent before 1940.

Kealey is a vocal critic of both Bacon's linear model and the notion that government must subsidize scientific research by awarding grants to universities. Based on data from the U.S., UK and other OECD countries, he argues that there is little evidence supporting a link between economic growth and government funded research. Switzerland and Japan provide the least government support for research among developed countries but have the highest rates of patents per capita while the former Soviet Union had the highest rate of government subsidized research but was one of the least innovative societies. [38]

Some scientists at major research universities are on a grant treadmill that requires them to continually pursue funding in order to keep laboratories operating and research assistants working. Government funded grants to universities are broken into "direct costs" and "indirect costs" the latter sometimes called "overhead." Direct costs are the funds that are actually spent on equipment, materials and labor costs that are directly related to the research project for which the grant is awarded. Indirect costs or overhead refers to the part of the grant that is allocated to compensate the university for using its premises, i.e., labs, offices, libraries, computer network and general utilities such as water, electricity and waste disposal. The indirect costs for federal grants are based on a negotiated agreement between the government and the university. Top research universities receive a rate for indirect costs that can be 60 percent or more of direct costs so that if the directs costs for the grant are $10 million, indirect costs would be $6 million for a total of $16 million. The university's "office of sponsored programs" audits spending, assists faculty in identifying grants and helps in the submission of application forms, but their major purpose is to make sure the university receives its cut of indirect costs.

The office of sponsored research may audit the direct cost expenditures by research faculty but they typically expend little effort tracking how indirect costs are spent by the university since by definition they can be used for a large variety of operating expenses as long as they appear to be supporting the grant. Some universities have been accused of applying the "overhead" definition too broadly. Stanford is an eminent research university that receives millions of dollars annually in federal research grants and in 1990 had an overhead rate of

78 percent, which was one of the highest in the nation. Suspicious of such a high rate, federal auditors found that federal grant dollars allocated to indirect costs had been used to pay for daily floral arrangements delivered to the president, maintenance of a university-owned yacht and improvements in the presidential residence that included cedar lined closets and an antique commode. [39]

One federal auditor estimated that from 1980 to 1990, Stanford may have bilked taxpayers out of $185 million in indirect costs, a charge the university vigorously denied after agreeing to refund $3.4 million to government coffers. After more than a half century of significant federal research grants to universities, no one really knows how much taxpayer money has fallen through the "overhead" cracks. In recent years, universities required to return research grant money following federal audits include: Florida International-$27 million, NYU-$15 million, Texas-$12 million, Thomas Jefferson University-$12 million, Yale-$5.6 million, Northwestern-$5.5 million, South Florida-$4 million, University of California-$3.9 million, among others. All of these schools denied doing anything wrong and some accused the federal government of employing unreasonably strict rules for overhead allocation calling them an "unfunded mandate." [40] The current system may encourage research universities receiving large federal grants to increase fixed facilities and administrative staff as a means to justify billing Uncle Sam for ever higher indirect costs.

Traditionally, patents are granted to inventors rather than employers. Inventors who are employed by a corporation, agency, institute or university are still entitled to patent their discoveries unless their employment is tied to the specific purpose from which the patent arose. A university professor who creates a patentable process or device in the course of his general research agenda would be entitled to claim the patent, and the university's entitled to retain what are called "shop rights" which is the right to use the patent in its labs or classrooms without paying patent royalties. As a condition of employment, most employers require employees to sign an agreement that transfers patent rights to the employer if the discovery arose during their period of employment.

Historically, universities were not particularly interested in patent rights and most professors were eager to publish a new discovery in a high quality journal as soon as possible. Many of the most dynamic industries, such as computers, biotechnology, software, medical devices, etc., originated from research developed in universities then moved quickly to the public domain. Indeed, the public good argument for taxpayer subsidized research is based on the asser-tion that the benefits would be quickly and freely disseminated to the public.

A series of laws known collectively as The Bayh-Dole Patent and Trademark Act of 1980 was vigorously promoted by university lobbyists. Essentially the law allows universities to claim property rights to technology created under publicly funded grant programs. Most universities now have patent policies in the faculty handbook giving the school the right to patent discoveries made by research faculty and require faculty to disclose to the administration any discoveries that might potentially merit patent application. Universities encourage patentable research by awarding as much as one third of any profits derived from the pat-ent to the faculty member or members responsible for the discovery while the university keeps the remainder. University lobbyists sold the Bayh-Dole Act to politicians on the premise that the schools would patent new discoveries and sell the licensing to private companies, thus accelerating the time between dis-covery and the commercial availability of resulting products. Initially, Senator Harley Kilgoure of West Virginia included a recovery clause in Bayh-Dole that would have allowed taxpayers to recoup federal grant money and "prevent a giveaway of the fruits of publicly-funded research."[41] West Virginia is a poor state with few universities receiving significant federal grants but aggressive lobbying by research universities in the more populace states that garner the lion's share of federal grant dollars was successful in eliminating the recovery provision from the draft of Bayh-Dole that was eventually passed.

Ginsberg points out that Bayh-Dole allowed research universities to become "triple dippers." First, universities benefit directly from the grant funds won by research faculty which are used to pay salaries, graduate student stipends and other costs that would otherwise be borne by the university. Second, they collect a large sum in the form of indirect costs on every dollar of the grant. Third, Bayh-Dole allows universities to patent and then profit from the sale of licenses or royalties from discoveries made in campus labs that were financed by taxpayers. In general, the faculty share of patent royalty is treated as tax-able income but the not-for profit university's share accumulates tax free. Universities moved quickly to exploit Bayh-Dole. Before the law, there were only twenty-five technology transfer offices on college campuses, by 2005, there were over 3,300 such offices with some schools having multiple offices to supervise different kinds of research.[42]

The largest share of university patents are in molecular biology that are charac-terized by the Patent and Trademark Office as "upstream patents." Upstream patents are patents on pre-product development research that seek to profit by licensing discoveries to companies that will use the knowledge to develop commercially viable products. The confluence of public and private resources resulting from Bayh-Dole may have expedited scientific research in some areas but the marriage is not without consequences. Research universities appear to be "delving more deeply" into the available pool of commercial inventions by increasing "the number of inventions licensed without a concurrent shift in the underlying distribution of inventions."[43] The marginal benefits may still exceed the costs but, as universities collaborate with private interest groups to extend their ownership of intellectual property further upstream, there is evidence of diminishing returns to university research. By locking up intel-lectual property rights on basic and pre-development science, universities and private research companies can impose "serious costs on scientific enter-prise."[44] Rather than expedite research transfer, campus technology transfer offices delay discoveries entering the public domain by discouraging faculty from publishing research or presenting it at conferences until they have filed all provisional patent applications.

Florida State University received nearly a half billion dollars in federal research grants to develop the anticancer drug Taxol that the university then licensed to Bristol-Myers Squib. Between 1994 and 1999, the federal government's Medicare program paid for $700 million in Taxol prescriptions and licensing fees paid to Florida State eventually totaled more than $400 million. Taxpayers essentially paid twice for Taxol: once for the research and once for the high priced drug that was created as a consequence of federally funded research.[45] Other research institutions that have developed patentable drugs from federal funded research grants have sold the licenses to pharmaceutical companies in foreign countries where production of the drugs create off-shore jobs subsi-dized by American taxpayers.

To the degree that federally funded academic research benefits taxpayers throughout the U.S., public research dollars should be allocated to those insti-tutions that maximize the "social return." Alternatively, if Bayh-Dole allows universities to capture licensing profits derived from public money, then, by definition, the social benefits are diminished and less widespread. Have the experts constructed a system of publicly funded academic research in which much of the benefit accrues to universities and private companies in the local economy?

A 2004 report by the RAND Corporation provides a detailed analysis of the distribution of research funds to higher education. During the late 1990s, federal research dollars to universities grew at a much higher rate than total federal R&D but the distribution is largely skewed in favor of medical research and a few top tier universities. From 1996 to 2002, over 55 percent of all federal R&D funds awarded to higher education went to universities and colleges in only nine states: California, Illinois, Maryland, Massachusetts, Michigan, New York, North Carolina, Pennsylvania and Texas.[46]

Approximately 45% of the total research dollars awarded to higher education in 2002 went to the nation's 126 medical schools. The top ten states in federal R&D are home to 42% of the medical schools.[47] Despite the conventional wisdom that greater spending on medical research is always preferred to less, numerous studies have questioned the benefit/cost of large dollar expenditures on life sciences. In his 1966 speech launching the Medicare Program, Lyndon Johnson complained that the large and growing budget for medical research had little influence on life expectancy. Kealey maintains that the *status quo* in academic research is so entrenched that powerful interests are successful in portraying anyone who questions the benefit/cost of federal R&D as a philistine. Of course, medical research is important but so is research addressing the causes of spiraling health care costs, climate change, homeland security, efficient energy use, water management and a host of other issues. The U.S. is home to over 8,000 colleges and universities. When federal R&D to medical schools is deducted from the total, the distribution of non-medical school research dollars is even more concentrated. About half of all universities and colleges in all states that award PhD degrees successfully obtained R&D funds; however, the lion's share of non-medical federal R&D goes to a few top tier PhD granting universities.

The fact that in 2002 universities in the state of Pennsylvania received 76 times the amount of federal R&D awarded universities in South Dakota despite having only 15 times the population, would not matter if publicly funded science remained in the public domain.[48] In theory, a resident of Rapid City would receive the same net benefit on the returns from federal R&D flows to Carnegie-Mellon as someone who lived in Pittsburgh. However, if universities are allowed to privatize the benefits derived from federally funded R&D then the assertion that the citizens of Rapid City benefits in equal measure to those who live in Pittsburgh becomes somewhat specious.

A 1990 report by the Lower Mississippi Development Commission chaired by Arkansas Governor Bill Clinton questioned the geographic distribution of federal research dollars to universities. The report noted that the 110 higher education institutions in the portions of nine states that make up the region together garnered only 59 percent of the federal R&D funds that went to Johns Hopkins University alone. The tenor of the report is that despite Johns Hopkins being an eminent research university, geographic proximity to government agencies can be an advantage.[49]

According to *Forbes*, the nation's richest counties have for the last few years been concentrated in the Washington, DC suburbs. Loudon County, Virginia near Washington, DC is the richest county in the nation with a median annual household income of $115,574. The latest data shows that four of the top 10 richest counties are in Washington's Virginia suburbs with a fifth, Howard County, Maryland, equidistant between Washington and Baltimore, also among the nation's 10 wealthiest. While other parts of the nation have struggled, high paid federal employees and a private sector that gorges on government contracting have grown fat and happy. George Mason University's Center for Regional Analysis estimates that federal spending makes up 40% of the region's economy that was boosted by $81 billion in federal contract spending in 2011.[50]

As with the nation's wealthiest counties, access to the government trough matters. Federal spending on R&D to universities has played a prominent role in the development of Boston's 128 Corridor, Silicone Valley/Northern California, the Research Triangle in North Carolina and others areas in Michigan, Pennsylvania and Northern Illinois, all of which are the envy of civic leaders in economically lagging regions. The geographic clustering of federal R&D may reflect research productivity of many outstanding universities but there is also evidence that they benefit from proximity. The RAND report found that the top ten states that received the most federal R&D in the form of contracts "were home to sizable Department of Defense, NASA, and/or Department of Energy facilities." How research dollars are conveyed to universities (grant versus contract) is important because it sets the legal ground rules. The RAND report goes on to say that their analysis "disproves the persistent stereotype that all federal R&D funds are conveyed to universities and colleges via peer-reviewed grants."[51]

Just as the customer model and the large increase in non-teaching university employees changed undergraduate campus culture, the Military-Industrial Complex in combination with Bayh-Dole has privatized much university research and has changed the culture of many research institutions. One manifestation of the cultural change is the labor exploitation of young, post-doctoral scientists who are increasingly foreign born immigrants.

The fate of low skilled workers continues to dominate the immigration debate but the future of highly educated foreign workers is an important issue for universities and other research institutions. Immigrants now comprise the majority of new PhD degrees in mathematics, engineering and the sciences. In 2011, 76% of the 1,500 patents awarded the top ten research universities had a foreign born scientist listed as an inventor. Approximately 54% of the listed inventors included foreign born students, staff or post-doctoral researchers who are not professors and confront difficulty in maintaining visas necessary to stay in America.[52] Getting your name on a patent does not always translate into royalty checks. Many of these post-doctorates work as itinerant academic laborers in temporary positions that pay low wages and provide few benefits. Government research subsidies have created a university work environment that requires young scientists to hop from short-term contract to short-term contract with little job security beyond two or three years, no severance pay or moving expenses and few benefits—conditions that would be unacceptable for high skilled workers in private industry.

An obvious corollary in higher education is the exploitation of minority athletes among BSC schools. One study found that if going to college is a full time job, most student athletes would do financially better if they spent the hours engaged in university sports instead working in a fast food restaurant. Big time college sports enjoys a symbiotic but ethically questionable relationship with professional NFL and NBA franchises in which universities serve as a low cost training ground for professional athletes.[53] Similarly, Kealey argues that private industry funnels money through research universities precisely because higher education will impose low-wage, sweat shop conditions that would be unacceptable in the for-profit sector. He asserts that universities are such bad employers that many young scientists would have enjoyed more fulfilling careers had there been no government subsidies to research universities.[54] Too often, the current system trains young scientists in the narrow specialty of their PhD advisor and the science surrounding the current government contract, specialties that can quickly disappear in the face of rapidly changing technologies.

It is little wonder that many bright American students avoid a career in science. Who wants to work as a low paid postdoc with all of the attendant uncertainty when the starting salary for a new MBA or law graduate from a good school is two to three times larger? Research universities understand the ethical dilemma created by the current system but they also want to maintain a *status quo* that has served them well.

PHILANTHROPY AND UNIVERSITY ENDOWMENTS

Many of America's greatest universities originated in the entrepreneurial vision of a handful of industrialists that made their fortunes in steel, oil, automobiles, tobacco and finance. Many a gothic spire was subsidized by the blood, sweat and in some cases the long-term health of workers who literally battled their bosses in the streets for the right to earn a living wage. Gilded Age and Robber Barron fortunes accumulated in the 19th and 20th centuries established the initial endowments of many elite universities, with some like Duke and Carnegie-Mellon assuming the names of their benefactors. Over time, the growth in the reputations of these illustrious institutions correlated closely with their ability to accumulate additional wealth.

The private, not-for-profit model has been so successful that many public universities have entertained the notion of changing to private status. Like private equity versus public corporations, public universities are legally more restricted and required to be more transparent than their private counterparts. Following charges that former Penn State employee Jerry Sandusky sexually abused more than a half dozen young boys, some on campus, Pennsylvania Governor Tom Corbett warned the university to open its records and cooperate with prosecutors or risk losing taxpayer funding. Two weeks after the Governor's ultimatum representatives of the Penn State board of trustees met with Cornell University trustees to discuss the advantages of adopting the Cornell model of being a private land grant university that receives annual funding from the state for certain narrow educational missions. Whether or not the move by the trustees was an attempt to call the bluff of the governor, many people felt that the leaders of a public university should have been more concerned with the fate of the victims in the sexual abuse case than protecting administrators or minimizing legal liability in civil suits.[55]

The "public ivy league," which was built largely by state taxpayers, already operates in a manner similar to private universities. These institutions cater to an international student clientele and while they like to frame the strategy as promoting "geographic diversity" in pursuit of the best and brightest, the large tuition premium levied on non-residents doesn't hurt. Over 35 percent of the University of Michigan's undergraduate enrollment is out of state students who pay approximately $40,000 in annual tuition compared to the $14,000 charged Michigan residents. With less than 7 percent of the budget provided by the state, Michigan may be further along in the public to private transformation than many flagship schools. Other state universities enjoying the pumped up tuition revenue that comes from large numbers of out of state students include the University of Virginia, University of Wisconsin-Madison, University of Massachusetts-Amherst and the University of Arizona. A 2011 survey found that a top goal of admissions directors is recruiting more students who can pay higher fees. Among all four-year institutions, the admissions strategy judged most important over the next two or three years was the recruitment of more out-of-state students who pay substantially more tuition.[56] Significant demand by out of state students and the corresponding ability to levy a large tuition premium is only one part of the process required to transform a public university into a *de facto* private institution; the essential element is growth in the university endowment. The largest university endowments are managed by world class asset managers. Like many other investors, university investments were hit hard by the 2008 financial crisis with some endowments experiencing losses of more than 25%. Yeshiva University, which saw its endowment decline by 28%, had over $100 million invested with Bernie Madoff. Most endowments are now on the mend but they have yet to regain the lofty values of 2007. With $27.5 billion in 2010, Harvard has by far the largest university endowment but it was still 20% below its 2007 peak of more than $34.6 billion. With a half dozen exceptions, private universities dominate the list of the 30 largest endowments shown in the Table at the end of the chapter but there is some disagreement over how endowment wealth should be measured. If measured by expense ratio then tiny Grinnell College is the richest with an endowment 15 times its annual budget while Harvard's endowment annual expense ratio is only 10. If endowment per student is the measure chosen, then Princeton has the largest endowment followed by Yale and Harvard.[57]

Before the financial crisis, much of the public focus on university endowments centered on rising tuition at the same time many universities were earning tax free, double digit investment returns. In 2007, it was estimated that the tax exemption on university endowment income alone cost the U.S. Treasury $18 billion in revenue.[58] The growing gap between the haves and have-nots in higher education, especially in combination with tuition increases and government tax subsidies, caught the attention of the Senate Finance Committee, which held hearings on the issue in 2006 and 2007. The apparent anomaly between rising endowments and tuition was also highlighted in the popular press. In the first three months of 2008, the *New York Times* published fifteen articles on endowments, increasing tuition or the growing wealth gap in higher education.

When required to testify before the Senate Finance Committee to explain the simultaneous rise in tuition and endowment returns, university presidents responded with a variety of explanations in an attempt to justify their institution's behavior. One prominent explanation was a theory known as "inter-generational equity." The intergenerational equity argument for endowment disbursements maintains that the endowment should provide the same level of support to both current and future students. Endowment managers assume that the university will endure in perpetuity and adopt a spending rate that ensures the endowment can support the same activities in fifty years as it does today. The problem with this argument is that under certain assumptions; including rapidly rising tuition costs, the economically rational strategy would be to spend more today rather than pay more for the same service in the future.[59] Research suggests that large endowments may contribute to the agency problem and that high expense ratios may actually cause tuition increases. As endowments increase, universities spend even more money on fund raising.[60]

The real shame surrounding the system of university philanthropy is the fact that so many small colleges and their students make do with so little. The rich schools continue to get richer while the inequality gap in American society grows and credentialism is reinforced. Ego and the so-called "edifice complex" may tilt philanthropists to bricks and mortar construction at high prestige schools. Wealthy people who went to wealthy universities may also be more inclined to donate to their alma mater while those who attended low status colleges may assume more personal credit for their success and donate else-where. Certainly, rich institutions devote more resources to raising money and are better at managing and spending than smaller institutions. A consultant working with high net worth donors commented to the *New York Times*: ''One of the great lines from our experience was when we were sitting with a donor who said, 'I know how to give $100 million to my Ivy League university, but I don't know how to give $100 million to help kids in the city.'' Recalled H. Peter Karoff, founder of the Philanthropic Initiative, a strategic planning and consulting firm, ''We told him he would have to hire 20 people to do that well, and he wrote his check to the Ivy League school. Many of these huge gifts are what I call default gifts.''[61]

Tax law requires private foundations to spend 5 percent of their net worth each year as a means to ensure that such organizations carry out their social obligations and not simply hoard wealth. Hearings before the Senate Finance Committee on rising tuition and university mega endowments culminated with Senator Charles Grassley of Iowa proposing that the same rule be applied to not-for-profit university endowments or, alternatively, he suggested that the government should tax endowment income.[62] Senator Grassley and the Finance Committee simply did not buy into the arguments made by university experts regarding justification for large tuition increases in the same years the schools were earning, tax free double digit returns. The universities mounted a concerted lobbying effort that included the use of influential friends and alumni working in the media to defeat the proposal.

Increasingly, the expert educrats at the U.S. Department of Education who are partly responsible for the lackluster system of K-12 public schools, are turning their attention to higher education. Because of grade inflation, grades no longer serve as an indicator of student learning so regulators through accreditation bodies are enforcing something called Student Learning Outcomes. The U.S. Department of Education is ramping up the bureaucracy in order "to reach the President's [Obama] goal of regaining global leadership in college graduation rates by 2020, the United States must increase the percentage of citizens hold-ing college degrees from the current level of just under 40% to 60%. That is a sizable increase."[63] A similar "commitment" by government housing experts to increase home ownership proved disastrous. When government education experts establish a goal of dramatically increasing the number of credentials awarded, it does not bode well for cost control or academic quality. Under the current system, the price of a college degree will continue to increase along with the debt burden on taxpayers and middle income households while quality among the less selective state universities continues to erode.

Like many complex, piecemeal systems constructed by the experts, the whole of higher education is different from the intended sum of its parts. Faculty did not intend to dismantle a rigorous general studies program that educated students in the common culture while preparing them for difficult majors in a variety of disciplines. Certainly, no one intended for the cost of a bachelor's degree at a public university to exceed the financial capacity of middle-class households requiring students and their parents to assume a mountain of debt much of which is guaranteed by taxpayers. Few philanthropists believed that the tax free returns on their bequests would be hoarded and used to pay exorbitant salaries to administrators and star professors while students struggled to meet ever accelerating tuition. Certainly, few people other than President Eisenhower anticipated the corrupting influence of federal grants that removed taxpayer funded research from the public to the private domain, discouraged Americans from entering STEM fields and exploited young immigrant scientists.

The plague of experts who preside over a broken higher education system continue to insist to students, taxpayers, donors and themselves that it is the best of all possible worlds.

30 Colleges and Universities with the Largest Endowments (2010)

Institution Name	2010 Endowment ($000)	2009 Endowment ($000)	% Change
Harvard U.	$27,557,404	$26,138,239	5.4%
Yale U.	16,652,000	16,327,000	2.0%
Princeton U.	14,391,450	12,614,313	14.1%
The U. of Texas System	14,052,220	12,163,049	15.5%
Stanford U.	13,851,115	12,619,094	9.8%
Massachusetts Institute of Technology	8,317,321	7,880,321	5.5%
U. of Michigan	6,564,144	6,000,827	9.4%
Columbia U.	6,516,512	5,892,798	10.6%
Northwestern U.	5,945,277	5,445,260	9.2%
The Texas A&M U. System & Foundations	5,738,289	5,083,754	12.9%
U. of Pennsylvania	5,668,937	5,170,539	9.6%
U. of Chicago	5,638,040	5,094,087	10.7%
U. of California	5,441,225	4,937,483	10.2%
U. of Notre Dame	5,234,841	4,795,303	9.2%
Duke U.	4,823,572	4,440,745	8.6%
Emory U.	4,694,260	4,328,436	8.5%
Washington U. in St. Louis	4,473,180	4,080,554	9.6%
Cornell U.	4,378,587	3,966,041	10.4%
U. of Virginia	3,906,823	3,577,266	9.2%
Rice U.	3,786,548	3,612,884	4.8%
Vanderbilt U.	3,044,000	2,867,541	6.2%
Dartmouth College	2,998,302	2,824,894	6.1%
U. of Southern California	2,947,978	2,671,426	10.4%
New York U.	2,370,000	2,094,000	13.2%
Johns Hopkins U.	2,219,925	1,976,899	12.3%
U. of Minnesota and Affiliated Foundations	2,195,740	2,085,550	5.3%
Brown U.	2,155,330	2,017,292	6.8%
U. of Pittsburgh	2,032,798	1,837,216	10.6%
U. of North Carolina at Chapel Hill and Foundations	1,979,222	1,905,081	3.9%
Ohio State U.	1,869,312	1,651,561	13.2%

Source: *Inside Higher Education*

CHAPTER 8

COMBATING THE PLAGUE OF EXPERTS

In his 1862 message to Congress, President Abraham Lincoln spoke of "disenthralling" ourselves of "the dogmas of the quiet past" in order to "think anew." Despite their record of failure, many people continue to be enthralled by the idea that elites are largely responsible for the forward march of human progress and that the most important knowledge in society emanates from the top-down. This book is a modest effort to "disenthrall" the reader of that notion.

Bottom-up systems such as markets and liberal democracy require a leap of faith. The idea of turning over decision making to an amorphous and uncontrollable mob of market makers and renegade voters is counterintuitive and a little frightening; like Plato, we are inclined to believe that in matters of great importance we should defer to the experts. This inclination is not confined to people who have experienced widespread civil unrest or economic deprivation. Even those who have enjoyed the fruits of capitalism and democracy will sometimes find themselves unsettled by the seemingly arbitrary and capricious functioning.

Charles De Gaulle famously remarked that "the graveyards are full of indispensable men." In a successful bottom-up system, everyone is dispensable. If Providence assigns a political leader to the graveyard, the democratic process fills the vacancy with seamless precision. If a company closes its doors, new ones spring up to take its customers. To those who lack the faith, bottom-up systems appear to be in a perpetual state of uncertain disequilibrium; a kind of barely contained anarchy prevails with no one in charge. Outcomes can be unpredictable with everyone seeming to be dissatisfied because no one gets everything they want. Little wonder that those accustomed to following the directions of authoritarian regimes have difficulty adjusting to the cacophony of freedom; it is a learned process. Change seems to be the only constant but it is the capacity to adapt and transform chaos into order that renders these systems so resilient.

Not everyone is comfortable with the chaos or sympathetic to the idea that the most complete knowledge in society is widely dispersed across the population rather than concentrated in the articulated reason of the enlightened few. Skepticism of expert advice is not a rejection of labor specialization or a defense of "self-sufficiency," a circumstance that is almost always synonymous with subsistence living. Nineteenth century homesteaders on the Great Plains were largely self-sufficient but they occupied houses made of dirt and lived a diminished life style even by the modest standards of the time. The millions of people who specialize in a multitude of jobs that enhance our lives are largely responsible for the economic abundance that the average American enjoys. Instead, this book is an argument against blind obedience to the opinion of those granted the authority to make important decisions on behalf of the rest of us. Some of these experts occupy political or governmental positions but many others reside in the private sector.

Like death and taxes, the plague of experts will always be with us but there are a number of mechanisms that can substantially reduce their influence and our misguided dependence on top-down knowledge. The following is a brief discussion of bottom-up mechanisms to counteract the plague. Many have been around since the beginning of mankind but have been weakened or compromised by the gradual encroachment of the top-down model.

FREE SPEECH
"Congress shall make no law respecting an establishment of religion, or prohibiting the free exercise thereof; or abridging the freedom of speech of the press; or the right of the people peaceably to assemble, and to petition the government for the redress of grievances." The First Amendment to the Constitution may represent the most radical and beautiful idea ever conceived by government. Given the entrenched power of church and state in most parts of the 18th century world, imagine the founders of a new country writing a law that

gives anyone the right to say whatever they please, no matter how ridiculous or despicable.

Free speech is the cornerstone of the liberal tradition. Because anyone can say anything at any time, no one is granted final say or personal authority. It casts the widest and deepest possible net in an effort to exploit the ideas of anyone who wishes to participate. Because no one is allowed to set the agenda on public discourse, everything is fair game.

Of course, there are trade-offs with such a system. Small minorities holding distasteful, even loathsome opinions will be allowed to express their views despite the visceral reaction of the opposing majority. Many people will push the boundaries of common decency in an effort to provoke a response that will cause us to compromise or curtail this most basic right. Every generation seems to be presented with a new free speech challenge and while some generations have wavered, none has succumbed to the temptation of censorship. The pantheon of pornographers, racists, red-baiters, "Piss Christ artists," flag burners and assorted provocateurs, including advocates for restrictions on "hate speech," have attempted and pretty much failed to evoke disgust or shame sufficient to restrict free expression.

The current threat to free speech originates not among skin heads or public disgust with failed artists desperate for attention, but a hoard of Islamic Fundamentalists hostile to the liberal tradition and steeped in a religious culture that does not distinguish knowledge from belief. Not only do they believe civil law should grant *final say* and *personal authority* to the prophet Muhammad and whatever Ayatollah is currently presiding, they are steadfast in their belief that everyone else, including infidels, should do the same. Long separated by geography, the Internet and modern technology brings these people to our metaphorical door step and makes it much easier for third party provocateurs to stir up trouble for trouble's sake.

In late summer of 2012, the American ambassador to Libya and thirty other people worldwide were killed as a consequence of riots that ostensibly began as a demonstration against an anti-Islamic video. Government spokesmen were quick to register their disgust with its content but no one seriously suggested that the right to make deplorable films should be curtailed. In the early 1980s, Ayatollah Khomeini issued a *fatwa* against Salman Rushdie for his book the *Satanic Verses;* this was a precursor of things to come. Rushdie was a British citizen but far too few experts in government, academia and the media came to his defense. With a nod to George Kennan, the best way to counter Islamic Fundamentalists is for world supporters of free speech to coordinate a concerted policy of "intellectual containment" that aggressively challenges every threat to free expression, no matter how small or seemingly insignificant. There will be more deaths and more outrage but the liberal tradition will prevail because the alternative is unacceptable.

A second and in some ways more insidious threat to free expression originates from a conflict between the liberal tradition of public inquiry and the changing economics of broadcast journalism. A critical function of a free press is to perform "peer review" or fact checking to assist the public in ferreting out the best ideas and most able leaders. Instead, Americans are increasingly tuning into "news media" that regurgitate their pre-conceived opinions and frames every issue in a partisan context down to our chicken sandwiches. Fact checking is an expensive, slow, unglamorous and often tedious process in contrast to the cheap and abundant "commentary" offered by a parade of experts who have honed their "opinions" to match the demographic and political profile of their audience.

There are a number of high quality blogs and internet forums that provide "open source" political opinion for those willing to take the time to look. As for network and cable news, maybe someday some of us will tune in to the opposition just to see if we are still capable of listening quietly to an opposing point of view without growing apoplectic. Or maybe we will decide to simply tune out. A third party point of view could break the partisan logjam but neither politicians nor self-sorting "journalists" appear to be willing to voluntarily surrender their duopoly, not even for the sake of liberal democracy.

MARKETS

The market system has been denounced, vilified and summarily dismissed by an army of critics who have proposed alternative delivery systems, most of which include an expanded role for top-down expert planners; yet, measured by standards of cost, efficiency and freedom, all of these alternative have failed miserably. Markets do such a great job of literally "delivering the goods" that it is a media event when they fail. More often than not, new stories framed as examples of a break-down in the system are actually markets doing the job that they do best. When prices go up or down and send the signal that goods or services have become relatively more or less valuable, they are actually per-forming their intended function. Businesses and people can adjust their plans accordingly. Artificial attempts by government to reverse or delay these price signals invariably aggravate problems of shortage or surplus.

If beef prices are high, it might be a good time for consumers to eat more chicken and farmers to raise more cows. If enough consumer and farmers respond in the predicted way, the price of beef will eventually decline and the price of chicken will rise. If Gulf shrimp are too high because of the BP oil disaster it might a good time to eat the farm raised variety, a substitution that is good for consumers and good for the natural population of shell fish in the Gulf.

Every day in America there are literally billions of market transactions con-summated; each transaction plays a role in setting the corresponding price of the good or service in question as well as the relative prices of substitutes and complements. Each price is a summary of information that is available not only to the transacting parties but to others who might be watching prices as a prelude to making a consumption or production decision. The price we pay for our Starbucks coffee this morning reflects weather patterns in the coffee growing region of Columbia just as the price of a lunch time coke at *Subway* incorporates drought conditions in the corn-belt.

The one example of consistent "market failure" is in the under production of public goods that have "positive" externalities like education and the over pro-duction of "bads" like pollution which create a negative externality. Examples of failure in the market for private goods are far more difficult to identify mostly because people "voluntarily" engage in private transactions. The notion that an individual consumer should subjugate their personal preferences to those identified by an expert is the definition of top-down elitism.

There are "markets in everything" as the authors of the economics blog *Marginal Revolution* constantly remind us but this doesn't prevent them from being perennially under attack. Americans have a love/hate relationship with the market system; they love it when it works in their favor and detest it when they have to pay more. The vast majority of people understand that when the allocation of goods and services is taken away from markets and turned over to top-down expert planners, it may benefit a few special interests, including the planners, but most of us lose.

VOTING

The benefits of liberal democracy have been discussed in Chapter 3 and espoused by some of the most eloquent writers in the English language. Rather than cover the same ground in far less erudite fashion, I will briefly review a few of the technical and administrative problems with our system of voting, perhaps the most powerful of all bottom-up processes.

In any given year, voter turnout in federal elections averages about 48%; in other words, we are using about one half of the collective brain to decide who will lead the country. For elitists, low voter turnout is not only acceptable but desirable since those who fail to vote are presumed to be less informed; a presumption that runs counter to the liberal tradition. "Spahn and Sain and pray for rain" was the mantra of the old Milwaukee Braves who boasted only two reliable starting pitchers in their line-up but a similar prayer is common among political strategists who often hope for inclement weather to suppress turnout and improve the chances of a polarizing candidate.

An important issue at the forefront of the voter debate is the effect new voter ID laws will have on turnout in states that enacted the laws. Defenders of the picture ID law claim that fraud is a pervasive problem and that it is relatively easy to steal elections because there is only a small chance of getting caught. Perpetrators can register illegal immigrants under false names, manipulate absentee ballot voting and orchestrate impostors to vote for deceased citizens who remain on voter rolls. Critics maintain that the problem does not end with the election but carries over to vote recounts when "misplaced" ballots are later "found," a circumstance that has occurred in more than one election. Absentee ballots that were originally rejected for good reason can later be reconsidered by people who are less than impartial judges in a process that can be very subjective.

Opponents of voter ID laws claim advocates are being disingenuous and that their real intention is to suppress voting by people who are more likely to vote for Democratic candidates. In Pennsylvania, the Majority Leader was caught on film bragging that the new voter ID law would suppress turnout and deliver Pennsylvania's electoral votes to Mitt Romney. Voter ID laws were passed in a number of states despite little evidence indicating voter impersonation is a pervasive form of election fraud. Out of 2,068 confirmed cases of fraud since 2000, only 10 cases or less than one half of one percent were "voter impersonation" fraud that would be prevented by picture ID. Most investigations of the issue suggest that the largest category of voter fraud is related to absentee ballots, which is estimated to amount to nearly one fourth of total fraud cases.

Advocates of liberal democracy believe greater voter participation is always preferable to less, assuming the votes are legitimate. If there are pervasive problems in voting, including fraud, bad ballot design, inaccurate machines, absentee balloting procedures, uncounted votes, etc., then these should be addressed. But if voter ID laws are a cynical effort by state legislatures to suppress voting as suggested by the Pennsylvania Speaker, then American democracy is confronting a far more serious threat than the occasional fraudulent vote.

IMMIGRATION

The U.S. economy has always had an insatiable appetite for temporary workers who live on the fringes of society. The ignoble institution of slavery originated in the pedestrian demand for seasonal workers in Southern agriculture and the highly romanticized American cowboy was an itinerant laborer of diverse ethnic origin who moved on when the cattle drive ended. Itinerant immigrant workers built the railroads, dams and highways of the West; they picked apples in Washington; and they followed the wheat harvest from Texas up the breadbasket of America into Canada. At the beginning of the 20th century, roadside shacks occupied by workers in Western logging camps were called "Skid Row" because logs were skidded down dirt streets to the mill. The phrase later became a pejorative to describe the neighborhoods of boardinghouses and cheap residential hotels where itinerant workers wintered.

The word "hobo," believed to be derived from the railroad expression "ho, boy," conjures a caricature of a ne'er-do-well tramp who steals apple pies cooling on kitchen window sills. Most hobos at the turn of the 20th century were itinerant immigrant laborers who used freight trains to travel from job-to-job in pre-automobile America. Joe Hill, the famous hobo union organizer who many thought was unjustly executed by the state of Utah in 1915, was a Swedish born immigrant named Joel Hägglund. The subculture was so pervasive that hobo comedians were a staple on the vaudeville theater circuit; Charlie Chaplin's Little Tramp was derived from the humor of the era. But life for itinerant immigrant laborers was far from a burlesque house comedy bit. In response to low wages and unsafe work conditions, thousands of migratory workers joined the International Workers of the World. In an effort to foment fear and resentment among the population, politicians and the media warned that a "Bolshevik Menace" was stalking the land but not everyone succumbed to the hysteria. Novelist John Steinbeck wondered "at what point did we come to fear the man with a hole in his shoe" and in his song *Deportee,* Woody Guthrie commemorated Mexican workers who were killed in a California plane crash and dismissed by the media as "just deportees."

Many U. S. citizens are still uncomfortable with immigration, fearful that immigrants will take jobs from American workers. The old saw that many of these immigrants do work that most Americans find distasteful is repeated because it is often true. Jobs in fruit and vegetable farming, meat processing and agriculture in general, tend to be seasonal and require periodic relocation; most Americans want permanent, non-seasonal employment in a fixed location so that they can buy a house and their kids can attend the same school. Even in industries like construction, immigrants often work in the less desirable jobs such as roofing, asphalting, concrete or landscaping. Some studies find evidence that immigrant workers depress wages in low skilled jobs while other research reveals no influence or a very small one. Americans may actually benefit in the long-run if "bubble" jobs are partly filled with immigrants. Home building has been in the doldrums for five years and will be a long time returning to pre-bubble employment levels, many construction workers would have been better off had they developed skills in less cyclical industries.

Immigration advocates often stress the disproportionately large number of immigrants responsible for patent applications and business start-ups. Immigrants make up an eighth of the American population but founded twenty-five percent of the nation's new engineering and technology firms. Perhaps more importantly, enclaves of immigrants or diaspora networks have played a crucial role in growing the collective brain. It is estimated that approximately 215 million people or about 3% of the world population lives outside their country of origin. More than 22 million Indians are scattered around the earth and there are more Chinese people living outside China than there are Frenchman living in France. There have always been small enclaves of ex-patriots living in surprising places but ease of travel and inexpensive international communications have expanded their size and significance to economic development.

Information technology allows engineers and researchers in different countries to bounce ideas off one another to the advantage of everyone involved.

216

Immigrants will frequently recognize a business opportunity and quickly communicate the idea to contacts in their home country that will assist in bringing the idea to fruition. Networks of immigrants who share the same language frequently have an advantage in the development of cross border trade, particularly when one nation is an emerging economy in which the rule of law may be weak and navigating the bureaucracy requires culture specific knowledge. This is one of the reasons why so much direct foreign investment in countries like China goes through immigrant diasporas living in another country.

Referred to as "sea turtles", over the last decade, some 500,000 Chinese people have studied abroad and then returned home. Many of these foreign educated Chinese are employed in influential jobs that provide advice to the government while others are moving into the upper ranks of the Communist Party. The Brookings Institution estimates that in 2012 about 15-17% of the Chinese Central Committee will be foreign educated, up from only 6% in 2002. The returning sea turtles have borne witness to the benefits of freedom and, while they are unlikely to transform China into a liberal democracy anytime soon, if they can just prevent it from regressing into one man rule like the former Soviet Union, the future world will be a better place.

Immigration can import youth and ideas to aging countries that will stimulate the collective brain. It can help grow the economy and restore solvency to old age pension programs. Like markets and democracy, the idea that immigration can benefit the residents of the destination country as well as the immigrant may seem counter-intuitive; all it takes is a little trust.

THE FAMILY

One of society's most important bottom-up building blocks is the family. When children are prevented from achieving their full potential, families suffer and so does society. More that 15 million children under age 18 live in households with incomes below the U.S. Census Bureau's poverty threshold or about 21 percent of all children in the United States. Poverty impacts children in a variety of ways, including living conditions, nutrition, school quality and access to healthcare. There are significant racial/ethnic disparities in poverty statistics for children. About 36 percent of Black children, 33 percent of Hispanic children and 12 percent of White children live in households below the poverty threshold. A common trait among households below the poverty line is that most are single parent households.

Approximately 41 percent of all births in the United States now occur outside of marriage, a dramatic increase from only 17 percent in 1980. While serving as the Assistant Secretary of Labor in 1965, Daniel Patrick Moynihan wrote a report titled *The Negro Family: The Case for National Action* that chronicled the decline in the number of African American households with both the mother and father living with their children. Moynihan argued that the trend was not entirely due to lack of economic opportunity but was partly attributable to social pathology of the African-American ghetto culture with roots in slavery and Jim Crowe. A number of critics attacked the report as patronizing, arguing that it stereotyped black Americans in its suggestion of below average academic performance and widespread social pathology. Some even characterized it as racist.

Nearly fifty years after the Moynihan Report, motherhood outside of marriage appears to vary as much by social class as it does by race. College educated women account for less than 10 percent of the births outside of marriage while the number is 60 percent for women with a high school diploma or less. Nearly one in two children, or about 44 percent of children living in households headed by a single female, are below the poverty line compared to 27 percent of children living in a male-headed household. In contrast, only 11 percent of children living in married-couple families live in poverty. Depending on the time period examined, economists estimate that from 20 to 40 percent of the observed increase in income inequality in recent years can be attributed to the increase in the number of children born outside marriage.

Common sense suggests that the income of a household with two working parents is going to provide more money to spend on their children than households with only one parent. Two parents, as opposed to one, have more time to monitor their children's activities and reinforce desirable behavior while discouraging the undesirable. One important measure of children's present and future well being is academic achievement. Black males who identified their fathers as their role model maintained significantly higher grades and exhibited less truancy than peers who identified a member of the extended family as a role model or lacked a role model. Absence of a paternal role model also has a negative influence on the behavior of black females. Children raised in two parent families have fewer behavioral problems and score higher on mathematics and reading tests than kids that are raised in one parent families. The difference in behavioral issues and math scores between the two family groups remains the same over time but the gap in reading scores widens as the children aged.

Until the trend in single parent households stabilizes or reverses, inequality in household income will continue to increase even in the presence of sharply higher economic growth. Both children and society will continue to incur a cost that is represented by unfulfilled potential.

CREDENTIALISM AND CREATIVE DESTRUCTION

Credential cartels take the form of professional associations, unions, licensing and status arrangements as discussed extensively in Chapter 2. Many credential requirements are motivated to exclude entry and protect incumbent jobs while discriminating against the young and those trying to enter the profession. As long as the job market was growing and the cost of the credential cartels was sufficiently constrained, this was not a major concern. However, both of these circumstances no longer apply. Unemployment rates among recent college graduates have been at an unusually high level for more than four years and show no sign of subsiding. The cost that credential cartels add to education, health care and a variety of other industries can no longer be ignored. States need to revisit the plethora of jobs that currently require licensing and remove the obvious cartels from their rosters. Alternative routes to teacher certification, long discussed, need to be seriously reconsidered and acted on. The same is true for the health care field.

Unnecessary credential requirements have been combined with a job placement system that has become increasingly mechanized. Employment software screens large numbers of applications searching for key words or phrases and then saves or junks applicant resumes based on the search results. Certainly, there are shortages of qualified applicants, especially in STEM fields, but increasing evidence suggests that software systems may be partly to blame. In a weak economy, one or two openings can elicit a plethora of electronic applications since many job seekers follow a "shotgun" approach and apply for anything and everything. Software makes it easier and cheaper to cull through applicant resumes and identify a pool of the most qualified.

But in a buyers' market, companies can increase the number of requirements in the screen so that virtually everyone is rejected. One manager for a human resource department anonymously applied for a job in his own company using the proprietary software and, despite knowing the job qualifications and all of the buzzwords that were supposed to overcome the screen, he was rejected. One critic tells of a fairly generic engineering job eliciting over 25,000 applications with no one passing the hurdle set by the screen. Some career counselors call this the "unicorn" effect: an employer looking for a mythical employee who doesn't exist. When screening software is combined with psychological tests and other requirements, the job application process can prove daunting.

Companies are likely passing over some applicants who would be highly productive employees but do not have a skill set that exactly matches the job qualifications. Perhaps with a little extended on- the-job training, applicants could be brought up to speed. Companies could also ask the vendors to tweak the software to make it more forgiving. One of the themes of this book is that despite their certitude, the experts are often wrong. Frequently, the best employee is going to be someone who is a little bit different from the idealized "unicorn" defined by the experts.

Credentialism and creative destruction are linked in that the former is often used to subvert the latter. Credentials can obstruct technological change and economic efficiency in order to protect the vested interest of incumbents. Experts claim to orchestrate "orderly" change and manage the anarchy that comes from bottom-up systems. The problem with expert managed change is that it is more prejudicial and inefficient than the alternative. The government engineered bankruptcy of GM discussed in Chapter 4 gave special consideration to UAW members over IBEW members at the Moraine, Ohio plant despite the latter staffing one of the most efficient auto plants in the nation. This kind of preferential "managed change" is the rule rather than the exception.

Chapter 2 raised the question of whether or not the so-called "meritocracy" has devolved into a credential cartel not unlike Mark Twain's river boat pilots association. The spiraling cost of higher education combined with a number of arbitrary admission policies at elite universities has contributed to this perception. The idea of someone working their way through a state university without incurring a mountain of debt is becoming an increasingly elusive goal that should be restored. Universities, especially elite universities, receiving any kind of federal benefits, including tax subsidies, federal research grants, subsidized student loans, etc., should be required to identify low cost online general education programs and then admit a significant number of the best, most highly qualified students into their undergraduate majors as junior transfer students. The transfer program would be based solely on a blind, merit based admission system. Rather than occupying the cellar of higher education, on-line instruction could go a long way toward breaking the credential cartel and introducing an element of creative destruction into the meritocracy. Like the GI Bill following WWII, it would likely alter the undergraduate culture of many universities for the better and could be used to appeal to a different kind of higher education philanthropist.

Creative destruction is disturbing. It imposes change at a time when it is most unwelcome. Joseph Shumpeter believed that in time, top-down experts would replace capitalism's rude and oafish capacity for abrupt change with a tamed version that would ultimately lead to a "stationary state." "Socialism of a very somber type would almost automatically come into being" as the risk taking and adventurous are essentially frozen out in favor of those who support past-perpetuating choices. He famously predicted that "capitalism would end, not with a bang but a whimper."

FOOTNOTES

PREFACE AND CHAPTER 1 FOOTNOTES

1. Leake, J. 2010. "Scientists say Dolphins Should Be Treated as Non-human Persons," *The Sunday Times*, January 3

2. Graham, P. 2007. Is it Worth Being Wise? http://paulgraham.com/wisdom.html. February.

3. Ibid.

4. Gawande, A. 2009. *The Checklist Manifesto*, Metropolitan Books, Henry Holt Company, New York, NY.

5. Rousseau, J.J. 1968. *The Social Contract*, p. 115.

6. Godwin, W.1969. *Enquiry Concerning Political Justice*, p. 206.

7. Ibid. p. 156.

8. Trotsky, L. 1925. *Literature and Revolution,* Published originally by the United Soviet Socialist Republic.

9. Shirir, William. 1960. *The Rise and Fall of the Third Reich*, Simon and Shuster, New York, NY. p.100.

10. Nietzsche, F. 1954. *Thus Spoke Zarathustra*, Translated by Walter Kaufmann, Random House, New York, p.3-5.

11. Smith, A.1976. *The Theory of Moral Sentiments*, Indianapolis Liberty Classic Part III, Chapter 3.

12. Burke, E. 1967. *Reflections on the Revolution in France*, p.55

13. Ibid. p. 76.

14. Hayek, F. 1979. *Law, Legislation and Liberty,* p.157

15. Mensa Constitution. 2007. *Mensa International.* November 29.

16. Beam, A. 2008. "After 49 Years, Charles Van Doren Talks," *The New York Times, Opinion,* July 21.

17. Phelan, James. 1964. "Have You Ever Been a Boo Hoo," *The Saturday Evening Post*, March 21. p. 16.

18. Kaufman, Alan 2009. *IQ Testing 101.* New York: Springer Publishing. pp. 151–153.

19. Herbert, B. 1994. "In America; Throwing a Curve," *The New York Times,* Opinion, October 26.

20. Herrnstein, Richard and Charles Murray. 1994. *The Bell Curve,* The Free Press, New York, NY. p. 105

21. Goldberger, Arthur and Charles Manski 1995. "Review Article: The Bell Curve" by Herrnstein and Murray, *Journal of Economic Literature,* XXXIII, 2, 762–777.

22. Turkheimer, E., A. Haley, M. Waldron, B. D'Onofrio and I. Gottesman. 2003. *Socioeconomic Status Modifies Heritability of IQ in Young Children,* Research Article, http://www.psychologytoday.com/files/u81/Turkheimer_et_al___2003_.pdf

23. Herrnstein, Richard and Charles Murray. 1994. *The Bell Curve,* The Free Press, New York, NY.

24. Brinch, C. and T. Galloway. 2012. "Schooling in Adolescence Raises IQ Scores," *Proceedings of the National Academy of Sciences,* 109 (2) 425–430.

25. Diener, C. and C. Dweck. 1978. "An Analysis of Learned Helplessness: Continuous Changes in Performance, Strategy, and Achievement Cognitions Following Failure," *Journal of Personality and Social Psychology,* 36, 451–462

26. Herrnstein, Richard and Charles Murray. 1994. *The Bell Curve,* The Free Press, New York, NY.

27. *The Economist*. 2012. "In Praise of Misfits," June 2

28. Logan J. and N. Courtney. 2012. (forthcoming) "Unusual Talent: a Study of Successful Leadership and Delegation in Entrepreneurs with Dyslexia," *Journal of inclusive practice in Further and Higher Education.*

29. March, J. 1991. "Exploration and Exploitation in Organizational Learning," *Organization Science*, 2 , 71–87, 79,86

30. Ridley, M. 2010. *The Rational Optimist: How Prosperity Evolved*, Harper Perennial. New York, NY.

31. Ridley, M. 2010. "Humans: Why They Triumphed," *The Wall Street Journal*, May 22, W1.

32. Woolley, Anita, Christopher Chabris, Alex Pentland, Nada Hashmi, Thomas Malone. 2010. "Evidence for a Collective Intelligence Factor in the Performance of Human Groups," *Science*, 330, 6004

33. Allen, Robert. 2008. "A Review of Gregory Clark's A Farewell to Alms: A Brief Economic History of the World," *Journal of Economic Literature*, 46, 4.

34. Neal, Larry. 1990. *The Rise of Financial Capitalism: International Capital Markets in the Age of Reason*, Cambridge: New York and Melbourne: Cambridge University Press.

35. Maddison, Angus. 2001. *The World Economy: A Millennial Perspective*, Paris OECD.

36. Kuran, Timor. 2011. *The Long Divergence*, Princeton University Press: Princeton, New Jersey

37. Acemoglu, D. and J. Robinson. 2012. *Why Nations Fail: The Origins of Power, Prosperity and Poverty*, Crown Publishers, A Division of Random House. Ch.3

38. Wrigley, EA. 2010. *Energy and the English Industrial Revolution*, Cambridge University Press

39. Bryce, R. 2012. "Renewable Energy Can't Run the Cloud," *The Wall Street Journal*, May 29. A11.

40. McKeown, Thomas. 1979. *The Role of Medicine: Dream, Mirage or Nemesis?* Oxford: Basil Blackwell. UK.

41. McKinlay, John and Sonja. 1977. The Questionable Contribution of Medical Measures to the Declining Mortality in the United States in the Twentieth Century. *Milbank Memorial Fund Quarterly, Health and Society*, 55, 3, p.414.

42. Easterly, William. 2006. *The White Man's Burden: Why the West's Efforts to Aid the Rest Have Done So Much Ill and So Little Good.* Penguin Press HC,

43. Sachs, Jeffrey. 2005. *The End of Poverty: Economic Possibilities for Our Time*, Penguin Books.

44. Collier, P. 2007. *The Bottom Billion: Why the Poorest Countries are Failing and What Can Be Done About It*, Oxford University Press.

45. Kremer, Michael. 1993. "The O-ring Theory of Development," *Quarterly Journal of Economics*, 208, 3. 551–575.

46. Eppig, Christopher, Corey Fincher and Randy Thornhill. 2010. Parasite Prevalence and the Worldwide Distribution of Cognitive Ability, *Proceedings of the Royal Society of Biological Sciences*, June 30.

47. Ibid.

CHAPTER 2 FOOTNOTES

1. Wilson, A. N. 2012. *Hitler*, Basic Books, New York, NY.

2. Ibid.

3. Rollyson, C. 2012. Exorcising the Demon-King: Was the Third Reich Inevitable or the Monstrous Product of a Single Man's Mind?" *The Wall Street Journal*, April -8.

4. Hochschild, A. 2003. *The Unquiet Ghost: Russians Remember Stalin* , Mariner Books, New York. p. 115.

5. Ibid. p. 118

6. Ibid. p. 119–120

7. Russell, B. 1998. Bertrand Russell: Autobiography, Routledge, London. p. 333.

8. Hochschild, A. 2003. *The Unquiet Ghost: Russians Remember Stalin* , p. 120.

9. Chesterton, C. K. 1908. *Orthodoxy,* John Lane Company 1908. Reprinted Ignatius Press, San Fransisco. p. 29

10. *The Economist*, 2012. "Why They Won't Calm Down," September 15. p. 46.

11. Shapiro, James. 2010. *Contested Will: Who Wrote Shakespeare?* Simon and Shuster, New York. p. 11

12. Ibid. p.12-13.

13. Ibid. 173-174

14. Ibid. 183-184

15. Teachout, Terry. 2010. Denying Shakespeare, *The Wall Street Journal*, April 23.

16. Posner, F. 1993. *Case Closed: Lee Harvey Oswald and the Assassination of JFK*," Random House, New York. p. 12-13.

17. Ibid. p. 24.

18. Ibid. p. 114.

19. Ibid. p. 107.

20. Ibid. preface,

21. Zweig, Jason and Mary Pilon. 2010. "*Is Your Advisor Pumping up His Credentials?*" *The Wall Street Journal*, October 16.

22. Twain, M. 1883. *Life on the Mississippi,* E-book Conversion. p. 52. http://mark-twain.classic-literature.co.uk/life-on-the-mississippi/ebook-page-52.asp

23. Hubbard, L. 1999. "Hair-brained Politics," *Salon*, September 13. http://www.salon.com/1999/09/13/hair/

25. Simon, S. 2011. "A License to Shampoo: Jobs Needing State Approval Rise," *The Wall Street Journal*, February 7.

25. Kleiner, M. and A. Krueger. 2008. *The Prevalence and Effects of Occupational Licensing*, National Bureau of Economic Research, Paper Number 14308, September.

26. Kling, Arnold. 2010. "What's Stalling the Next Economic Revolution," The American. The Journal of the American Enterprise Institute. September 9.

27. Hogan, D.B. 1980. *The Regulation of Psychotherapists Volume I. A Study in the Philosophy and Practice of Professional Regulation*, Ballinger, USA

28. Berg, Ivar. 1970. *Education and Jobs: The Great Training Robbery*, New York, Praeger, New York.

29. Brooks, David. 2000. *Bobos in Paradise: The New Upper Class and How They Got There*, Simon and Shuster, New York, NY. p. 14.

30. Ibid. p. 15

31. Ibid. p. 18

32. Baltzell, Digby. 1964. *The Protestant Establishment: Aristocracy and Class in America,*Random House, NY, NY

33 Brooks, David. 2000. *Bobos in Paradise: The New Upper Class and How They Got There*, Simon and Shuster, New York, NY. p. 19-20

34. Ibid. 28.

35. Lemann, Nicholas. 1999. *The Big Test: The Secret History of the American Meritocracy*, Farrar, Straus and Giroux, New York, NY. p. 42-52.

36. Ibid.

37. Brooks, David. 2000. *Bobos in Paradise: The New Upper Class and How They Got There*, Simon and Shuster, New York, NY. p. 25-26.

38. Ibid. p. 30

39. Halberstam, D. 1972. The Best and the Brightest, New York: Random House, p. 41.

40. The term "War Hawk" was first used around the war of 1812 to describe someone who advocates war. The first print citation of "chickenhawk," someone who advocates war but avoids service appeared in The New Republic during the 1980s.

41. MacPherson, Myra. 1984. *Long Time Passing: Vietnam and the Haunted Generation*, Doubleday, New York, NY

42. Regents of the University of California vs. Bakke, U.S. Supreme Court, 438, 265, June 28, 1978.

43. *Grutter vs. Bollinger*. 2003. 539, U.S., 306.

44. Moores, John. 2004. "College Capers," *Forbes*, March 29. http://www.forbes.com/forbes/2004/0329/040.html

45. Cho, S. 1994. "A Theory of Racial Mascotting," Presented at the First Annual Asian Pacific American Law Professors Conference, October 14.

46. Espenshade, T. J. and C. Y. Chung. 2005. "The Opportunity Cost of Admission Preferences at Elite Universities," *Social Science Quarterly*, 86, 2, 293–305.

47. Golden, Daniel. 2006. *The Price of Admission How America's Ruling Class Buys it Way Into Elite Universities and Who Gets Left Outside the Gates*, Three Rivers Press-A Division of Random House. New York, NY.

48. Ibid.

49. Meers, J. and H. Rosen. 2007. "Altruism and the Child-Cycle of Alumni Giving," *National Bureau of Economic Research*, W13152.

50. Liptak, A. 2008. "A Hereditary Perk the Founding Fathers Failed to Anticipate," *The New York Times*, January 15. http://www.nytimes.com/2008/01/15/us/15bar.html

51. Codevilla, A. 2010. "America's Ruling Class and the Perils of Revolution," *The American Spectator*, July-August

52. Moses, Jennifer. 2011. "The Escalating Arms Race for Top Colleges," *The Wall Street Journal*, February 5, C3.

53. Fallows, James. 1985. "The Case Against Credentialism," *The Atlantic*, December.

54. Evans, Terr. 2010. "Penn State Tops Recruiter Rankings," *The Wall Street Journal*, September 13.

55. Fallows, James. 1985. "The Case Against Credentialism," *The Atlantic*, December.

56. Deresiewicz, William. 2008. "The Disadvantages of an Elite Education," *American Scholar*, Summer.

57. *Century Foundation*, 2004. "Left Behind: Unequal Opportunity in Higher Education," p. 9

58. Fallows, James. 1985. "The Case Against Credentialism," *The Atlantic*, December.

59. Foster, R. and S. Kaplan. 2001.Survival and Performance in the Era of Disontinuity, Creative Destruction. Currency Book, DoubleDay. P. 7-12.

60. Banchero, S. 2012. "Top Schools Join Move to Offer Free Courses Online," *The Wall Street Journal*, July 18, A6

61. Codevilla, A. 2010. "America's Ruling Class and the Perils of Revolution," *The American Spectator*, July-August

62. Lawrence, J. 2006. "Congress Full of Fortunate Sons—and other Relatives," USA Today, August 8. http://www.usatoday.com/news/washington/2006-08-07-relatives-cover_x.htm

63. Stiglitz, J. 2012. *The Price of Inequality: How Today's Divided Society Endangers our Future*, Norton.

Chapter 3 Footnotes

1. Plato, 1961. *The Republic*, Translated by Paul Shorey in *Collected Dialogues*, ed. Edith Hamilton and Huntington Cairns, (Princeton University Press). (464e, 484b, 474c)

2. Ibid. 484b

3. Ibid. 474c

4. Rauch, J. 1993. *Kindly Inquisitors: The New Attacks on Free Thought*, University of Chicago Press: A Cato Institute Book, Chicago, Illinois. p46.

5. Dyson,F. 1988. *Infinite in all Directions*, Harper and Row. p.11.

6. Rauch, J. 1993. *Kindly Inquisitors: The New Attacks on Free Thought*, University of Chicago Press: A Cato Institute Book, Chicago, Illinois. p 48.

7. Ibid. 49.

8. Offit, P. 2011. "Junk Science Isn't a Victimless Crime," *The Wall Street Journal*, January 11.

9. Williams, M. 2011. "Jenny McCarthy's Autism Fight Grows More Misguided," *Salon*, January 6.

10. Ghosh, P. 2010. "Journal Stem Cell Work 'Blocked'," BBC News, February 2. http://news.bbc.co.uk/2/hi/8490291.stm

11. Jolis, A. 2012. "The Climate Kamikaze: The Hockey Stick and the Climate Wars," *The Wall Street Journal*, March 15, A13.

12. Happer, W. 2012. "Global Warming Models are Wrong Again," *The Wall Street Journal*, March 27.

13. Ibid.

14. Retraction Watch. http://retractionwatch.wordpress.com/

15. Thomson Reuters Web of Science-News and Ideas. http://thomsonreuters.com/products_services/science/science_products/a-z/web_of_science/

16. Stevens, H. 2012. "Cancer Research of Ten Years Useless: Fraudulent Studies," *Gaia Health*, August 14.

17. Naik, G. 2012. "Grade Inflation Creeps Into Science Journals," *The Wall Street Journal*, August 25, A2

18. Van Noorden, R. 2012. "Record Number of Journals Banned for Boosting Impact Factor with Self-Citations," *Nature*, June 29, http://blogs.nature.com/news/2012/06/

record-number-of-journals-banned-for-boosting-impact-factor-with-self-citations.html

19. Van Noorden, R. 2012. "Researchers Feel Pressure to Cite Superfluous Papers," *Nature*, Feb. http://www.nature.com/news/researchers-feel-pressure-to-cite-superfluous-papers-1.9968

20. Wilhite, A. and E. Fong. 2012. "Coercive Citation in Academic Publishing," *Science*, 333, 6068, 542-543

21. Rauch, J. 1993. *Kindly Inquisitors: The New Attacks on Free Thought*, University of Chicago Press: A Cato Institute Book, Chicago, Illinois. Chapter 4 and 5.

22. Scott, E. 2007. "Biological Design in Science Classrooms," Proceedings of the National Academy of Sciences, May 15.

23. Witt, J. 2005. "*Evolution News and Views: Dover Judge Regurgitates Mythological History of Intelligent Design*," Discovery Institute, December 20.

24. Discovery Institute. 2005. "*Dover Intelligent Design Decision Criticized as a Futile Attempt to Censor Science Education*," December 20.

25. *Kitzmiller vs. Dover Area School District* 04 cv 2688 (December 20, 2005). p. 22, 77.

26. Ibid. p. 66.

27. Rubin, P. 2010. "Environmentalism as Religion," *The Wall Street Journal*, April 22.

28. Ibid.

29. Sykes, C. 1995. *Dumbing Down Our Kids: Why American Children Feel Good About Themselves But Can't Read, Write Or Add*. St. Martin's Press: New York, NY.

30. Roth, K. 1994. "Second Thoughts About Interdisciplinary Studies," *American Educator*, Spring

31. Rubin, P. 1994. "The Assault on the First Amendment: Public Choice and Political Correctness," *Cato Journal*, 14(1), 23-35.

32. Will, G. 2012. Elizabeth Warren's Identity Politics," The Washington Post, May 23.

33. Morson, B. 2007. "CU Regents Fire Ward Churchill," *Rocky Mountain News*, July 25.

34. Flynn, K. 2005. "Confirmed, Ward Churchill is a Fraud," *Rocky Mountain News*, Front Page Magazine, June 10.

35. *Fat Studies: An Interdisciplinary Journal of Body Weight and Society*, Taylor Francis Group http://www.tandfonline.com/toc/ufts20/current

36. Bawer, B. 2012. *The Victim's Revolution*, Broadside Publishers.

37. Locke, J. 1690. *Essay Concerning Human Understanding*, London, Book 4, Ch 19, Sec. 11.

38. Ahmari, S, 2012. "The Grievance Brigades," *The Wall Street Journal*, September 6. A15

39. Locke, J. 1690. *Essay Concerning Human Understanding*, London, Book 4, Ch 20, Sec. 17.

40. Ibid. Ch16, Sec. 4.

41. Campbell, J. 2003. "The Stagnation of Congressional Elections," *Life After Reform When the Bipartisan Campaign Reform Act Meets Politics*, Edited by Michael Malbin. A Campaign Finance Institute Book, Rowman and Littlefield Publishers. P.150-151.

42. McCarty, N, K. Poole and H. Rosenthal. 2009. "Does Gerrymandering Cause Polarization," *American Journal of Political Science*, 53, 3, 666-680.

43. Carson, J., H. Crespin, C. Finocchiaro, D. Rohde. 2007. "Redistricting and Party Polarization in the U. S. House of Representatives," *American Politics Research*, Sage Publications, 36,6, 878-904.

44. Ibid. 878.

45. Buttonwood. 2012. "Democracies and Debt," *The Economist*, September 1. p. 71.

46. Ibid. 71.

47. Ibid. 71.

48. Eberstadt, N. 2012. "Are Entitlements Corrupting Us: American Character is at Stake," *The Wall Street Journal,* September 1. C1

49. De Rugy, V. 2012. "A Nation of Government Dependents," Mercatus Center-George Mason University, February 6. http://mercatus.org/publication/nation-government-dependents

50. Bluey, R. 2012. "Chart of the Week: Nearly Half of All Americans Don't Pay Income Tax," *Scribe-Heritage Investigates* http://blog.heritage.org/2012/02/19/chart-of-the-week-nearly-half-of-all-americans-dont-pay-income-taxes/

CHAPTER 4 FOOTNOTES

1. Kwoh, L. 2012. "You Call That Innovation," *The Wall Street Journal,* May 23, B1.

2. Adams, S. 2010. *Dilbert,* http://search.dilbert.com/comic/business%20jargon. January 9.

3. Leonard, A. 2009. "What's Good for General Motors….," *Salon,* May 29. http://www.salon.com/2009/05/29/good_for_general_motors/

4. Boaz, D.2008. *The Politics of Freedom: Taking on the Left, the Right and the Threats to Our Liberties,* The Cato Intitute, Washington DC. p.117.

5. Surowiecki, J. 2003. "Hong Kong Hooey," The Financial Page, *The New Yorker,* November 17.

6. Chapman, S. 1989. "Japan Bashers Try and Turn Trade War into a Race War," Chicago Tribune, July 23.

7. Wolverson, R. 2011. "China Dreams," *Time Magazine-US,*March 28. P1. http://www.time.com/time/magazine/article/0,9171,2059631,00.html

8. Time. 1969. "Japan's Struggle to Cope With Plenty," http://www.time.com/time/magazine/article/0,9171,901205,00.html

9. Tyson, L. 1992. *Who's Bashing Whom?: Trade Conflict in High Technology Industries.* Institute for International Economics: Washington DC

10. Katz, R. 2012. "What's Killing Japanese Electronics?" The Wall Street Journal, March 22, A10.

11. Weber, W. and M. Devaney. 2002. The Global Economy and Japanese Bank Performance, *Managerial Finance*, 24,12. 33-46.

12. Rauch, J. and J. Sackett. 1992. *The Outnation: A Search for the Soul of Japan*, Harvard Business School Press.

13. Devaney, M. 2007. "MBA Education, Business Ethics and the Case for Shareholder Value," *Journal of Academic Ethics*, 5,2,4.

14. Knight, R. 2010. "Capturing the Hearts and Minds of MBAs," *Financial Times*, October 3.

15. Byrne, J. 2011. "Harvard Adjusts MBA Program to Changing Times," CNN Money-A Service of CNN, Fortune & Money, January 24.

16. Mintzberg, H. 2004. *Managers, Not MBAs*, Berrett-Koehler Publishers, Inc.

17. Gladwell, M. 2005. *Blink: The Power of Thinking Without Thinking*, Little, Brown and Company, New York.

18. Friedman, M. 1970. 'The Social Responsibility Is To Increase Its Profits," *New York Times Magazine*, Sept. 13.

19. Roll, R. 1984. "Orange Juice and Weather," *American Economic Review*, 74, 5, 861-880.

20. *The Economist*, 2007. "The Business of Making Money: Private Equity's Strengths and it Increasingly Apparent Weaknesses," Briefing Public Versus Private Equity, July 7-13, 68-70.

21. Stromber, P., E. Hotchkiss and D. Smith. 2011. "Private Equity and the Resolution of Financial Distress," *Social Science Research Network*, April.

22. Acharya, V.V., M. Hahn and C. Kehoe. 2008. "Corporate Governance and Value Creation: Evidence from Private Equity," Draft Paper

23. Harford, J and A. Kolasinski. 2012. "Do Private Equity Sponsors Sacrifice Long-Term Value for Short-Term Profit? Evidence from a

Comprehensive Sample of Large Buyouts and Exit Outcomes," *Social Science Research Network*," January.

24. McCrum, D. 2012. "Private Equity Profits Called into Question, *Financial Times*, January 23.

25. Fleischer, V. 2008. "Two and Twenty: Taxing Partnership Profits in Private Equity Funds," *New York University Law Review*, 83,1. April.

26. Burrough, B. and J. Helyar. 1989. *Barbarians at the Gate: The Fall of RJR Nabisco*, Harper Row. New York, NY.

27. Hickel, J. 1983. "The Chrysler Bail-Out Bust," The Heritage Foundation, July 13. http://www.heritage.org/research/reports/1983/07/the-chrysler-bail-out-bust

28. Levin, D. 1989. "GM versus Ross Perot: Breaking Up is Hard to Do," *The New York Times Magazine*, March 26.

29. Ibid.

30. Isidore, C. 2006. "GM Kicked by Biggest Investor," *CNN-Money*, October 6.

http://money.cnn.com/2006/10/06/news/companies/gm_kerkorian/index.htm

31. Shepardson, D. 2012. "Treasury to Lose $25 Billion on Auto Bailout," *The Detroit New*, August 13. http://www.detroitnews.com/article/20120813/AUTO01/208130392

32. Terlep, S. 2012. "UAW Freezes Rival Out of Rebound," *The Wall Street Journal*, April 29.

33. Neuman, W., L. McKnight and R. Solomon. 1997. *The Gordian Knot: Political Gridlock on the Information Highway*, MIT Press.

34. Michaels, E., H. Handfield-Jones and B. Axelrod, 2001. *The War for Talent*, Harvard Business School Press, Boston.

35. Gladwell, M. 2009. "The Talent Myth," in *What the Dog Saw*, Little Brown and Company, Hachette Book Group, New York, NY. P. 359.

36. Ibid. p. 359

37. Weil, J. 2000. "Energy Traders Cite Gains, But Some Math Is Missing," *The Wall Street Journal*, September 20.

38. Gladwell, M. 2009. "Open Secret," in *What the Dog Saw*, Little Brown and Company, Hachette Book Group, New York, NY. P. 164.

39. Staff to the SEC on Governmental Affairs, 107th Cong., Financial Oversight of ENRON: The SEC & Private Sector Watchdogs 73, 115 (Comm. Print 2002), http://hsgac.senate.gov/100702watchdogsreport.pdf.

40. Gladwell, M. 2009. "The Talent Myth," in *What the Dog Saw*, Little Brown and Company, Hachette Book Group, New York, NY. P. 364.

41. Ibid. p.359

42. Devaney, M. 2007. "MBA Education, Business Ethics and the Case for Shareholder Value," *Journal of Academic Ethics*, 5,2,4.

43. Powers Commission. 2002. *Report of Investigation by the Special Investigative Committee of the Board of Directors of Enron Corporation*, February 1.

CHAPTER 5 FOOTNOTES

1. Janis, I. 1982. *Groupthink: Psychological Studies of Policy Decisions and Fiascoes*, Boston: Houghton Mifflin. P. 38.

2. Kaufmann, C. 2004. "Threat Inflation and the Failure of the Marketplace of Ideas: The Selling of the Iraq War," *International Security*, The MIT Press,29, 1, pp. 5-48

3. Corrigan, G. 2003. *Mud, Blood and Poppycock: Britain and the First World War*, Cassell, London. p. 28.

4. Tuchman, B. 1962. *The Guns of August*, The Macmillan Company, New York. p.10.

5. Bernhardi, F. 1911. *Germany and the Next War*, J.G. Cotta, Stuttgart and Berlin, Translated by Allen Powles.

6. Tuchman, B. 1962. *The Guns of August*, The Macmillan Company, New York. p.17.

7. Ibid. 79.

8. Ferguson, N. 1999. *The Pity of War*, Basic Books. p.64

9. Tuchman, B. 1962. *The Guns of August*, The Macmillan Company, New York. p.112.

10. Corrigan, G. 2003. *Mud, Blood and Poppycock: Britain and the First World War*, Cassell, London. p. 55.

11. Hochschild, A. 2011. *To End All Wars: A Story of Loyalty and Rebellion 1914-1918*, Houghton-Mifflin-Harcourt, Boston and New York. XIV.

12. Keynes, J.M. 1920. *The Economic Consequences of the Peace*, Harcourt, Brace and Howe. New York. p.238

13. Ibid. p. 236.

14. Corrigan, G. 2003. *Mud, Blood and Poppycock: Britain and the First World War*, Cassell, London. p. 405.

15. World War I Executions-History Learning Site. http://www.historylearningsite.co.uk/world_war_one_executions.htm

16. Hochschild, A. 2011. *To End All Wars: A Story of Loyalty and Rebellion 1914-1918*, Houghton-Mifflin-Harcourt, Boston and New York. XII.

17. Ibid. XII.

18. Tuchman, B. 1962. *The Guns of August*, The Macmillan Company, New York.p. 22.

19. Kipling, R. 1895. *The Young British Soldier*, http://www.readbookonline.net/readOnLine/2711/

20. Yeats, W.B. 1919. *The Second Coming*, The Literature Network, http://www.online-literature.com/donne/780/

21. Walker, M. 2012. "Book Attacking Euro Riles German Politicians," *The Wall Street Journal*, May 22. A4.

22. Ibid.

23. Nixon, S. 2012. "The Theory on Italy and Germany's Endgame for the Euro," *The Wall Street Journal*, July 13, C10.

24. *Telegram, George Kennan to George Marshall February 22, 1946. Harry S. Truman Administration File, Elsey Papers.* Truman Library. Also appeared in Kennan, G. or X. 1947. "The Sources of Soviet Conduct," *Foreign Affairs*, July.

25. Karnow, S. 1983. *Vietnam: A History*, The Viking Press, New York, p.366.

26. Drury, S. 2003. "Saving America: Leo Strauss and the Neoconservatives," Evatt Foundation. http://evatt.org.au/papers/saving-america.html

27. Kristol, W. and R. Kagan. 1996. "Toward a Neo-Reaganite Foreign Policy," *Foreign Affairs*, 75,4, 18-32.

28. Project for a New American Century. 2000. "Rebuilding America's Defenses," September. p.14.

29. Hersh, S. 2003. "Selective Intelligence," *The New Yorker*, May 12.

30. Plato, 1961. *The Republic*, Translated by Paul Shorey in *Collected Dialogues*, ed. Edith Hamilton and Huntington Cairns, (Princeton University Press). (459c)

31. Schumpeter, J. 1954. *History of Economic Analysis* (New York: Oxford University Press), p.43.

32. Sowell, T. 1987. *A Conflict of Visions*, William Morrow and Company Inc. New York, NY. P. 58-59.

33. Page, S. 2003. "Prewar Predictions Coming Back to Bite," *USA Today*, April 1. http://www.usatoday.com/educate/war28-article.htm

34. Blustein, P. 2005. "Wolfowitz Strives to Quell Criticism," *The Washington Post*, March 21, A1.

35. Griffis, M. 2012. *Casualties in Iraq*, http://antiwar.com/casualties/

36. Tonsor, S. 2005. "Why I Too am Not a Neo-conservative," *Equality, Decadence and Modernity: The Collected Essays of Stephen Tonsor*, ISI Books, Wilmington, Delaware, p.308.

37. Gee, K. 2012. "Tax Liens Trigger More Foreclosures," *The Wall Street Journal*, July 14, A2.

38. Rao, J.2012. "The Other Foreclosure Crisis: Property Tax Lien Sales," National Consumer Law Center, p. 8. http://www.nclc.org/images/pdf/foreclosure_mortgage/tax_issues/tax-lien-sales-report.pdf

39. Mill, J.S. 1848. *Principles of Political Economy*, London: John W. Parker. P. 142.

40. Berg, J.J. Dickhaut, and K. McCabe. 1995. "Trust Reciprocity, and Social History," *Games and Economic Behavior*, 10, p.122-42

41. Parikh, C. 2010. "Who Wants to be a Millionaire?" Capital Ideas On-line. http://www.go2cio.com/articles/index.php?id=3603

42. North, D. 1990. *Institutions, Institutional Change and Economic Performance*, Cambridge: Cambridge University Press. P. 54.

43. Zak, P. and S. Knack. 2001. "Trust and Growth," *The Economic Journal*, 111, April, p. 296.

44. Aghion, P., Y. Algan, P. Cahuc and A. Shleifer. 2009. "Regulation and Distrust," National Bureau of Economic Research. July 3. p. 41. http://discovery.ucl.ac.uk/17763/1/17763.pdf

45. Bloomberg.com. 2009. "Madoff Tipster Cites SEC Ineptitude." February, 4. http://www.bloomberg.com/apps/news?pid=newsarchive&sid=a_UBDG13Gld0

46. Devaney, M. 2010. "Greed Without Trust: Financial Crisis and the Breakdown in Spontaneous Order," *Advances in Psychology Research*, Editor, A. M Columbus, Volume 68, First Quarter, Nova Science Publishers.

47. Chernow, R. 2004. *Alexander Hamilton*, The Penguin Press, New York, New York. p.299

48. *The Economist*. 2012. "Too Big not to Fail," February 18-24th. p.22.

49 Ibid. p.22.

50. Ibid.. p.22.

51. Stewart, J. 2011. "Volcker Rule, Once Simple, Now Boggles," *New York Times*, October 21.

52. Devaney, M. 2008. "The Ethanol Boondoggle (Revisited)," *Southeast Missourian*, May 13.

53. *The Economist*, Measuring The Impact of Regulation: The Rule of More, February 18. p. 77.

54. *The Economist*. 2012. "Of Sunstein and Sunsets," February 18-24th. p.28.

55. Organization for Economic Cooperation and Development (OECD). 1999. Regulatory Reform in the United States, Enhancing Market Openness Through Regulatory Reform. P. 38

56. Bovard, J. 1995. "Archer Daniels Midland: A Case Study in Corporate Welfare," Cato Institute, September, 26, Policy Analysis, No. 241. p.1.

57. *The Economist*. 2012. "Of Sunstein and Sunsets," February 18-24th. p.30

58. Ibid

CHAPTER 6 FOOTNOTES

1. Isaacson, W. 2007. *Einstein: His Life and Universe*, Simon and Shuster, New York, NY. p. 77.

2. Ibid. p. 78.

3. Ibid. p. 93

4. Ibid. p. 78.

5. Ibid. p. 78.

6. American Economic Association. http://www.aeaweb.org/honors_awards/clark_medal.php

7. Kocher, M and M. Sutter. 2001. "The Institutional Concentration of Authors in Top Journals of Economics During the Last Two Decades," *The Economic Journal*, June, 111. 405-421

8. Hodgson, G. and H. Rothman, 1999. "Editors and Authors of Economics Journals: A Case of Institutional Oligopoly?" *The Economic Journal*, 109, February. 165-186.

9. Auerbach, R. 2008. *Deception and Abuse at the Fed*, University of Texas Press. p. 142.

10. Acemoglu, D. and J. Robinson. 2012. *Why Nations Fail: The Origins of Power, Prosperity and Poverty*, Crown Publishers, A Division of Random House. p. 128.

11. Summers, Lawrence 1998. Lawrence H. Summers Testimony, July 30, http://www.treasury.gov/press/releases/rr2616.htm

12. Isaacson, W. 2007. *Einstein: His Life and Universe*, Simon and Shuster, New York, NY. p. 496.

13. Clauretie, T. and G. Sirmans. 2006. *Real Estate Finance*, Thomson Southwestern, Fifth Edition.p. 44.

14. Ibid. p. 44.

15. Ibid. p.45.

16. Rutenberg, J. and J. Zeleny, 2011. "Gingrich on Defensive Over Freddie Mac Fees," The New York Times, Novermber 16. http://thecaucus.blogs.nytimes.com/2011/11/16/freddie-mac-reportedly-paid-gingrich-at-least-1-6-million/

17. Poterba, J. and T. Sinai. 2008. Tax Expenditures for Owner Occupied Housing: The Deduction for Property Taxes and Mortgage Interest and the Exclusion of Imputed Rental Income. Unpublished Manuscript.

18. Devaney, M. and W. Rayburn. 1993. "Neighborhood Racial Transition and Housing Returns: A Portfolio Approach," *Journal of Real Estate Research*. Vol. 8, No. 2, pp. 1-14.

19. Pinto, E. "Acorn and the Housing Bubble," *The Wall Street Journal*, November 12.

20. Wallison, P. 2010. "Government Housing Policy and the Financial Crisis," *Cato Journal*, 30,2, 397-406.

21. Steele, B. 2008. *Ontological Security in International Relations: Self Identity and the IR Security*, Routledge, New York, p.187.

22. Greenspan, A. 2004. Remarks by Chairman Alan Greenspan: The Mortgage Market and Consumer Debt, October 19. At America's Community Bankers Annual Convention, Washington DC, http://www.federalreserve.gov/boarddocs/speeches/2004/20041019/default.htm

23. Krugman, P. 2009. "How Did Economists Get it So Wrong?" *The New York Times*, September 2.

24. Fisher, R. and H. Rosenblum. 2012. "How Huge Banks Threaten the Economy," *The Wall Street Journal,* April 4.

25. Farrell, M. 2012. "JP Morgan Trading Loss: $5.8 billion," CNNMoney, July 13. http://money.cnn.com/2012/07/13/investing/jpmorgan-earnings/index.htm

26. Shenn, J. 2007. "Structured Vehicles are Subprime Oasis of Calm, Moody's Says," *Bloomberg*, July 23. http://www.bloomberg.com/apps/news?pid=newsarchive&sid=a5GuxhHxihhE&refer=bond

27. Scott, K. and J. Taylor. 2009. "Why Toxic Assets are So Hard to Clean Up," *The Wall Street Journal*, July 20.

28. Taleb, N. 2007. *The Black Swan: The Impact of the Highly Improbable*, Random House, New York, NY.

29. MacKenzie, D.. F. Muniesa and L. Siu. 2007. *Do Economists Make Markets?* Princeton University Press.

CHAPTER 7 FOOTNOTES

1. Arum, R. and J. Roksa. 2011. *Academically Adrift: Limited Learning on College Campuses*, The University of Chicago Press.

2. Babcock, P. and M. Marks. 2010. The Falling Time Cost of College: Evidence from Half a Century of Time Use Data, *National Bureau of Economic Research Working Paper*, 15954. April.

3. Ginsberg, B. 2011. *The Fall of the Faculty: The Rise of the All-Administrative University and Why it Matters*, Oxford University Press. p.25

4. Glazer, E. and M. Korn. 2012. "Colleges Must Learn to Make the Sale: Universities Hire Marketing Chiefs to Prove They're Worth the Money; Critics Call it More Bloat," *The Wall Street Journal*, August 16. B10

5. Margolin, J. and T. Sherman. 2006. "How UMDNJ Became a Patronage Pit," *Newark Star Ledger*, April 4, p. 1.

6. WSFA 12. 2008. "Former Two Year Chancellor Roy Johnson Says He's Guilty," March 11, http://www.wsfa.com/Global/story. asp?S=7771338&nav=menu33_2_1

7. Lewin, T. 2011. "Private College Presidents Getting Higher Salaries," Education, *New York Times*, December 4.

8. Devaney, M. and W. Weber. 2003. "Abandoning the Public Good: How Universities Have Privatized Higher Education," *Journal of Academic Ethics*. 1: 175-179

9. Labaree, D. 1997. *How to Succeed in School Without Really Learning: The Credentials Race in American Education*, New Haven, Yale University Press. p. 32.

10. Devaney, M. 2005. "Grade Inflation Is a Bigger Problem at Less Selective Universities," *Southeast Missourian*, January 18.

11. Nemko, M 2008. "America's Most Overrated Product: The Bachelor's Degree," *Chronicle of Higher Education*, 54:34, B17-18

12. Vaznis, J. 2008. "Hub Grads Come Up Short in College: Most From Class of 2000 Have Failed to Earn Degrees," *Boston Globe*, November 17.

13. Martorell, Paco, and Isaac McFarlin, Jr. (Forthcoming). "Help or Hindrance? The effects of College Remediation on Academic and Labor Market Outcomes," *The Review of Economics and Statistics*

14. Sowell, T. 1993. *Inside American Education: The Decline, The Deception, The Dogmas*, The Free Press, A Division of Macmillan, Inc. New York. p. 24

15. Johnson, V. 2003. *Grade Inflation: A Crisis in Higher Education*, New York, Springer-Verlag.

16. Ibid.

17. Callahan, D. 2004. *The Cheating Culture: Why More Americans are Doing Wrong to Get Ahead*, Harcourt, NY.

18. National Association of Scholars. 1996. *The Dissolution of General Education: 1914-1993: A Report from the National Association of Scholars*. Princeton, NJ.

19. American Council of Trustees and Alumni. 2004. *The Hollow Core: Failure of the General Education Curriculum*, April. Washington DC.

20. American Council of Trustees and Alumni. 2000. *Losing America's Memory: Historical Illiteracy in the 21st Century*, February. Washington DC

21. Taylor, S. and K. Johnson. 2007. *Until Proven Innocent*, New York: St. Martin's Press.

22. Wilson, R. 2009. "Notoriety Yields to Tragedy in Iowa Sexual-Harassment Cases: After 2 Suicides, Colleagues Question University's Role," *Chronicle of Higher Education*, February 20, A1.

23. Windschuttle, K. 1996. *The Killing of History: How a Discipline is Being Murdered by Literary Critics and Social Theorists*, Quality Books Inc. Sydney, Australia.

24. Bloom, A. 1987. *The Closing of the American Mind*, Simon and Schuster, New York, NY.

25 Kimball, R. 1991. *Tenured Radicals: How Politics Has Corrupted Our Higher Education*, Harper and Row, New York, NY

26. State Higher Education Finance FY 2011. http://www.sheeo.org/finance/shef/SHEF_FY11.pdf

27. Nicas, J. and C. Mcwhirter. 2012. "Universities Feel the Heat Amid Cuts," WSJ Online. June 14. http://online.wsj.com/article/SB10001424052702303734204577466470850370002.html

28. *Southworth v. Grebe*. 1996. U.S. District Court for the Western District of Wisconsin, November 29.

29. U.S. Supreme Court. 2000. Board of Regents Univ. Wisc. v. Southworth, 529 U.S. 217. http://www.oyez.org/cases/1990-1999/1999/1999_98_1189/

30. Fain, P. 2009. "At Public Universities: Less for More," *New York Times*, October 26.

31. Ostrow, R. and L. Gordon. 1991. "8 Ivy League Schools Sign Collusion Ban," *Los Angeles Times*, May 23.

32. Cellini, R. and C. Goldin. 2012. "Does Federal Student Aid Raise Tuition? New Evidence on For Profit Colleges," *National Bureau of Economic Research*, 17827.

33. Eisehnower, D. 1961. Military-industrial Complex Speech. In *Public Papers of the President*, 1035-1040.

34. Bacon, F. 1859. *The Advancement of Learning*, The Works of Francis Bacon, Lord Chancellor of England, Parry and McMillan Book 2. p.185.

35. Devaney, M. 2005. "Government Subsidized Academic Research: Economic and Ethical Conflicts," *Journal of Academic Ethics*, 2, 273-285.

36. Mowery, D. and N. Rosenberg. 1989. *Technology and the Pursuit of Economic Growth*, Cambridge, MA.

37. Gordon, R. 2000. "Does the New Economy Measure up to the Great Inventions of the Past?" *Journal of Economic Perspectives*, 14, 4, 49-74.

38. Kealey, T. 1996. *The Economic Laws of Scientific Research*, New York, NY. St. Martins Press.

39. Depalma, A. 1991. "Stanford to Alter Its Accounting of Overhead on Research Grants," *New York Times*, July 23, A9.

40. Brainard, J. 2005. "Have Federal Constraints on Reimbursing Overhead Gone Too Far?" *Chronicle of Higher Education*, August 5.

41. Bouchard, R. 2007. "Balancing Public and Private Interests in the Commercialization of Publicly Funded Medical Research: Is there a Role for Compulsory Government Royalty Fees?" *Boston University Journal of Science and Technology and Technology Law*, 13, Summer, p. 173.

42. De Larena, L. 2007. "The Price of Progress: Are Universities Adding to the Cost," *Houston Law Review*, 43, Spring, 1412.

43. Thursby, J. and M. Thursby. 2002. "Who is Selling the Ivory Tower? Sources of Growth in University Licensing," *Management Science*, 48,1. 90-104.

44. Eisenberg, R. and R. Nelson. 2002. "Public vs. Proprietary Science: A Fruitful Tension?" *Daedalus*, Spring.

45. De Larena, L. 2007. "The Price of Progress: Are Universities Adding to the Cost," *Houston Law Review*, 43, Spring, 1426.

46. Fossum, D., L. Painter, E. Eiseman, E. Ettedgui, and D. Adamson. 2004. *Vital Assets: Federal Investment in Research and Development at the Nation's Colleges and Universities*, RAND Science and Technology. P. 12

47. Ibid. p. 12-13.

48. Ibid. Appendix D. Pennsylvania and South Dakota.

49. Lower Mississippi Delta Development Commission. 1990. *The Delta Initiatives*, May 14.

50. Vardi, N. 2012. "America's Richest Counties," *Forbes*, April 24. http://www.forbes.com/sites/nathanvardi/2012/04/24/americas-richest-counties/

51. *Vital Assets: Federal Investment in Research and Development at the Nation's Colleges and Universities*, p. 25.

52. Hoover, K. 2012. "Foreign Inventors Dominate Patents Awarded to Top Research Universities," *The Business Journal*, June 26.

53. Noll, D. 1991. "The Economics of Intercollegiate Sports." In *Rethinking College Athletics*, J. and D. James, eds. Temple University Press, 1991.

54. Kealey, T. 1996. *The Economic Laws of Scientific Research*, New York, NY. St. Martins Press.

55. Ganim, S. and J. Murphy. 2012. "Penn State's 'informal' Discussion About Possibly Going Private Meets With Mixed Reactions," *The Patriot News*, March 14.

56. Jaschik, S. 2011. "Clashes of Money and Values: A Survey of Admissions Directors," *Inside Higher Ed*, September 21.

57. Waldeck, S. 2009. "The Coming Showdown Over University Endowments: Enlisting the Donors," *Fordham Law Review*, 77,4.

58. Gravelle, J. 2007. Senate Finance Committee, Senior Specialist in Economic Policy, http://finance.senate.gov/press/Gpress/2008/prg01 1408b.pdf.

59. Hansmann, H. 1990. *Why Do Universities Have Endowments?*, 19 J. LEGAL STUD. 3, 14, 17-18.

60. Core, J., W. Guay and R. Verdi. 2006. "Agency Problems of Excess Endowment Holdings in Not-for-Profit Firms," *Journal of Accounting and Economics*,41,3, 307-333..

61. Strom, S. 2007. "How Long Should Gifts Just Grow?" *New York Times*, November 12.

62. Tamar, L. 2008. "College Presidents Defend Rising Tuition, But Lawmakers Sound Skeptical," New York Times Online, September, 9. http://www.nytimes.com/2008/09/09education/09college.html

63. U.S. Department of Education. 2010. *Productivity: Improving Learning Outcomes While Managing Costs*, http://www.ed.gov/technology/ draft-netp-2010/productivity

BIBLIOGRAPHY

Acemoglu, D. and J. Robinson. 2012. *Why Nations Fail: The Origins of Power, Prosperity and Poverty*, Crown Publishers, A Division of Random House.

Acharya, V.V., M. Hahn and C. Kehoe. 2008. "Corporate Governance and Value Creation: Evidence from Private Equity," Draft Paper.

Adams, S. 2010. *Dilbert*, http://search.dilbert.com/comic/business%20jargon. January 9.

Aghion, P., Y. Algan, P. Cahuc and A. Shleifer. 2008. "Regulation and Distrust," National Bureau of Economic Research. July 3.

Ahmari, S, 2012. "The Grievance Brigades," *The Wall Street Journal*, September 6. A15.

AIER. 2003. American Institute for Economic Research. *Hayek, Dewey and Embodied Cognition*. Summer Conference.

Allen, Robert. 2008. "A Review of Gregory Clark's A Farewell to Alms: A Brief Economic History of the World," *Journal of Economic Literature*, 46, 4.

American Council of Trustees and Alumni. 2000. *Losing America's Memory: Historical Illiteracy in the 21st Century*, February. Washington DC.

American Council of Trustees and Alumni. 2004. *The Hollow Core: Failure of the General Education Curriculum*, April. Washington DC.

Arum, Richard and Jopisa Roksa. 2011. *Academically Adrift: Limited Learning on College Campuses*, University of Chicago Press, Chicago, IL.

Auerbach, R. 2008. *Deception and Abuse at the Fed*, University of Texas Press.

Babcock, P. and M. Marks. 2010. "The Falling Time Cost of College: Evidence from Half a Century of Time Use Data," *National Bureau of Economic Research Working Paper*, 15954. April.

Baltzell, Digby. 1964. *The Protestant Establishment: Aristocracy and Class in America*, Random House, NY, NY

Banchero, S. 2012. "Top Schools Join Move to Offer Free Courses Online," *The Wall Street Journal*, July 18, A6

Bawer, B. 2012. *The Victim's Revolution*, Broadside, NY.

Beam, A. 2008. "After 49 Years, Charles Van Doren Talks," *The New York Times, Opinion*, July 21

Berg, Ivar. 1970. *Education and Jobs: The Great Training Robbery*, New York, Praeger, New York.

Berg, J.J. Dickhaut, and K. McCabe. 1995. "Trust Reciprocity, and Social History, " *Games and Economic Behavior*, 10, 122-42.

Bernhardi, F. 1911. *Germany and the Next War*, J.G. Cotta, Stuttgart and Berlin, Translated by Allen Powles.

Bickel, A. 1986. *The Least Dangerous Branch: The Supreme Court at the Bar of Politics*," Yale University Presss.

Bloom, A. 1987. *The Closing of the American Mind*, Simon and Schuster, New York, NY.

Bloomberg.com. 2009. "Madoff Tipster Cites SEC Ineptitude." February, 4. http://www.bloomberg.com/apps/news?pid=newsarchive&sid=a_UBDG13Gld0

Blustein, P. 2005. "Wolfowitz Strives to Quell Criticism," *The Washington Post*, March 21, A1.

Bovard, J. 1995. "Archer Daniels Midland: A Case Study in Corporate Welfare," Cato Institute, September, 26, Policy Analysis, No. 241.

Bouchard, R. 2007. "Balancing Public and Private Interests in the Commercialization of Publicly Funded Medical Research: Is there a Role for

Compulsory Government Royalty Fees?" *Boston University Journal of Science and Technology Law*, 13 Summer, 173.

Brainard, J. 2005. "Have Federal Constraints on Reimbursing Overhead Gone Too Far?" *Chronicle of Higher Education*, August 5. 1

Brinch, C. and T. Galloway. 2012. "Schooling in Adolescence Raises IQ Scores," *Proceedings of the National Academy of Sciences*, 109 (2) 425-430.

Brooks, David. 2000. *Bobos in Paradise: The New Upper Class and How They Got There*, Simon and Shuster, New York, NY.

Bryce, R. 2012. "Renewable Energy Can't Run the Cloud," *The Wall Street Journal*, May 29. A11.

Bryner, S. 2011. "From Hired Guns to Hired Hands: Reverse Resolvers in the 111th and 112th Congresses, Center for Responsive Politics," July 12. http://www.opensecrets.org/news/Hired%20Guns%20to%20Hired%20Hands.pdf

Burke, E. 1967. *Reflections on the Revolution in France*, London: J. M. Dent and Sons.

Burke, E. 1967. *The Correspondence of Edmund Burke*, Chicago; University of Chicago Press, Volume 1.

Burrough, B. and J. Helyar. 1989. *Barbarians at the Gate: The Fall of RJR Nabisco*, Harper Row. New York, NY.

Buttonwood. 2012. "Democracies and Debt," *The Economist*, September 1. p. 71.

Byrne, J. 1991. "The Best B-Schools: Big Changes Since 1988 Have Made a Lot of Graduates Happier," *Business Week*, October 28. 102-107.

Byrne, J. 2011. "Harvard Adjusts MBA Program to Changing Times," CNN Money-A Service of CNN, Fortune & Money, January 24.

Callahan, D. 2004. *The Cheating Culture: Why More Americans are Doing Wrong to Get Ahead*, Harcourt, NY.

Campbell, J. 2003. "The Stagnation of Congressional Elections," *Life After Reform When the Bipartisan Campaign Reform Act Meets Politics*, Edited by Michael Malbin. A Campaign Finance Institute Book, Rowman and Littlefield Publishers. P.150-151.

Carson, J., H. Crespin, C. Finocchiaro, D. Rohde. 2007. "Redistricting and Party Polarization in the U. S. House of Representatives," *American Politics Research*, Sage Publications, 36,6, 878-904.

Center for Responsive Government. 2012. Revolving Door: Former Members, Open Secrets.Org. http://www.opensecrets.org/revolving/top.php?display=Z

Cellini, R. and C. Goldin. 2012. "Does Federal Student Aid Raise Tuition? New Evidence on For Profit Colleges," *National Bureau of Economic Research*, 17827.

Chernow, R. 2004. *Alexander Hamilton*, The Penguin Press, New York, New York. p.299

Clark, Gregory. 2007. *A Farewell to Alms*. Princeton New Jersey, Princeton University Press.

Clauretie, T. and G. Sirmans. 2006. *Real Estate Finance*, Thomson Southwestern, Fifth Edition.

Codevilla, A. 2010. "America's Ruling Class and the Perils of Revolution," *The American Spectator*, July-August.

Collier, P. 2007. *The Bottom Billion: Why the Poorest Countries are Failing and What Can Be Done About It*, Oxford University Press.

Commodity Futures Trading Commission (May 7, 1998). http://www.cftc.gov/opa/press98/opa4142-98.htm

Core, J., W. Guay and R. Verdi. 2006. "Agency Problems of Excess Endowment Holdings in Not-for-Profit Firms," *Journal of Accounting and Economics*,41,3, 307-333..

Corrigan, G. 2003. *Mud, Blood and Poppycock: Britain and the First World War*, Cassell, London. p. 55.

Deane, Phyllis and Herbert Cole. 1979. *British Economic Growth, 1688-1959: Trends and Structure*, Second Edition. Cambridge: Cambride University Press.

De Larena, L. 2007. "The Price of Progress: Are Universities Adding to the Cost," *Houston Law Review*, 43, Spring, 1412.

Depalma, A. 1991. "Stanford to Alter Its Accounting of Overhead on Research Grants," *New York Times*, July 23, A9.

Deresiewicz, William. 2008. "The Disadvantages of an Elite Education," *American Scholar*, Summer.

De Rugy, V. 2012. "A Nation of Government Dependents," Mercatus Center-George Mason University, February 6. http://mercatus.org/publication/nation-government-dependents

Devaney, M. 2007. "MBA Education, Business Ethics and the Case for Shareholder Value," *Journal of Academic Ethics*, 5,2,4.

Devaney, M. and W. Rayburn. 1993. "Neighborhood Racial Transition and Housing Returns: A Portfolio Approach," *Journal of Real Estate Research*. Vol. 8, No. 2, pp. 1-14.

Devaney, Mike. 1995. "Make Affirmative Assimilation the Goal," *St. Louis Post-Dispatch*, May 16.

Devaney, M. 2005. "Government Subsidized Academic Research: Economic and Ethical Conflicts," *Journal of Academic Ethics*, 2, 273-285.

Devaney, M. 2010. "Greed Without Trust: Financial Crisis and the Breakdown in Spontaneous Order," *Advances in Psychology Research*, Editor, A. M Columbus, Volume 68, First Quarter, Nova Science Publishers.

Devaney, M. 2006. "Ethanol Boondoggle," *Southeast Missourian*, September 20.

Devaney, M. 2008. "The Ethanol Boondoggle (Revisited)," *Southeast Missourian*, May 13.

Devaney, M. 2008. "Corn Ethanol and Alternative Energy-and the Cost of Taxpayer Subsides," *Southeast Missourian*, September 11.

Diener, C. and C. Dweck. 1978. "An Analysis of Learned Helplessness: Continuous Changes in Performance, Strategy, and Achievement Cognitions Following Failure," *Journal of Personality and Social Psychology*, 36, 451-462.

Discovery Institute. 2005. "*Dover Intelligent Design Decision Criticized as a Futile Attempt to Censor Science Education*," December 20.

Drucker, P. 1989. *The New Realities*, New York: Harper and Row.

253

Drury, S. 1998. *Leo Strauss and the American Right*, St. Martin's Press, New York, NY.

Drury, S. 2003. "Saving America: Leo Strauss and the Neoconservatives," Evatt Foundation.

Dyson,F. 1988. *Infinite in all Directions*, Harper and Row. p.11.

Easterly, William. 2006. *The White Man's Burden: Why the West's Efforts to Aid the Rest Have Done So Much Ill and So Little Good*. Penguin Press HC.

Eberstadt, N. 2012. "Are Entitlements Corrupting Us: American Character is at Stake," *The Wall Street Journal*, September 1. C1

Eisenberg, R. and R. Nelson. 2002. "Public vs. Proprietary Science: A Fruitful Tension?" *Daedalus*, Spring.

Eisehnower, D. 1961. Military-industrial Complex Speech. In *Public Papers of the President*, 1035-1040

Eppig, Christopher, Corey Fincher and Randy Thornhill. 2010. Parasite Prevalence and the Worldwide Distribution of Cognitive Ability, *Proceedings of the Royal Society of Biological Sciences*, June 30.

Espenshade, T. J. and C. Y. Chung. 2005. "The Opportunity Cost of Admission Preferences at Elite Universities," *Social Science Quarterly*, 86, 2, 293-305.

Evans-Pritchard, A. 2010. "The Death of Paper Money," *Daily Telegraph*, July 25.

Evans, Terr. 2010. "Penn State Tops Recruiter Rankings," *The Wall Street Journal*, September 13.

Ewers, J. 2005. "Is the MBA Obsolete?" *U.S. News and World Report*, April 11. 50-53.

Fain, P. 2009. "At Public Universities: Less for More," *New York Times*, October 26.

Fallows, James. 1985. "The Case Against Credentialism," *The Atlantic*, December.

Fat Studies: An Interdisciplinary Journal of Body Weight and Society, Taylor Francis Grouphttp://www.tandfonline.com/toc/ufts20/current

Ferguson, N. 1999. *The Pity of War*, Basic Books, London.

Fisher, R. and H. Rosenblum. 2012. "How Huge Banks Threaten the Economy," *The Wall Street Journal*, April 4.

Fleischer, V. 2008. "Two and Twenty: Taxing Partnership Profits in Private Equity Funds," *New York University Law Review*, 83,1. April.

Flynn, K. 2005. "Confirmed, Ward Churchill is a Fraud," *Rocky Mountain News* via *Front Page Magazine*. 10 June

Freeman, R.E. 1984. *Strategic Management: A Stakeholder Approach*, Pitman Series in Business and Public Policy.

Freeman, R.E., A. Wicks and B. Parmar. 2004. "Stakeholder Theory and the Corporate Objective Revisited," *Organizational Science*, 15, 3, 364-369.

Friedman, M. 1970. 'The Social Responsibility Is To Increase Its Profits," *New York Times Magazine*, Sept. 13.

Fukuyama, F.2006. *America at the Crossroads: Democracy, Power, and the Neoconservative Legacy*, New Haven: Yale University Press.

Galston, W. 2012. "Are Entitlements Corrupting Us: They're Part of the Civic Compact, *The Wall Street Journal*, September 1. C1.

Ganim, S. and J. Murphy. 2012. "Penn State's 'informal' Discussion About Possibly Going Private Meets With Mixed Reactions," *The Patriot News*, March 14.

Gawande, Atul. 2009. *The Checklist Manifesto*, Metropolitan Books, Henry Holt Company, New York, NY.

Gee, K. 2012. "Tax Liens Trigger More Foreclosures," *The Wall Street Journal*, July 14, A2.

Ghosh, P. 2010. "Journal Stem Cell Work 'Blocked'," BBC News, February 2. http://news.bbc.co.uk/2/hi/8490291.stm

Ghoshal, S. 2005. "Bad Management Theories Are Destroying Good Management Practices," *Academy of Management Learning and Education*. 4,1. 75-92..

Ginsberg, B. 2011. *The Fall of the Faculty: The Rise of the All-Administrative University and Why it Matters*, Oxford University Press.

Gladwell, M. 2005. *Blink: The Power of Thinking Without Thinking*, Little, Brown and Company, New York.

Gladwell, M. 2009. "The Talent Myth," in *What the Dog Saw*, Little Brown and Company, Hachette Book Group, New York, NY.

Glazer, E. and M. Korn. 2012. "Colleges Must Learn to Make the Sale: Universities Hire Marketing Chiefs to Prove They're Worth the Money; Critics Call it More Bloat," *The Wall Street Journal*, August 16.B10.

Godwin, W.1969. *Enquiry Concerning Political Justice*, Toronto: University of Toronto Press, Volume 1.

Goldberger, Arthur and Charles Manski 1995. "Review Article: The Bell Curve" by Herrnstein and Murray, *Journal of Economic Literature*, XXXIII, 2, 762-777.

Golden, Daniel. 2006. *The Price of Admission How America's Ruling Class Buys it Way Into Elite Universities and Who Gets Left Outside the Gates,* Three Rivers Press-A Division of Random House. New York, NY.

Gordon, R. 2000. "Does the New Economy Measure up to the Great Inventions of the Past?" *Journal of Economic Perspectives*, 14, 4, 49-74.

Gordon, J. 2012. "A Short (Sometimes Profitable) History of Private Equity," *The Wall Street Journal*, January 17.

Gordon, R. and J. Howell. 1959. *Higher Education for Business*, New York: Columbia University Press.

Graham, Paul. 2007. Is it Worth Being Wise? http://paulgraham.com/wisdom.html. February.

Griffis, M. 2012. *Casualties in Iraq*, http://antiwar.com/casualties/

Happer, W. 2012. "Global Warming Models are Wrong Again," *The Wall Street Journal*, March 27.

Harford, J and A. Kolasinski. 2012. "Do Private Equity Sponsors Sacrifice Long-Term Value for Short-Term Profit? Evidence from a Comprehensive

Sample of Large Buyouts and Exit Outcomes," *Social Science Research Network*," January.

Harrison, J. and R. E. Freeman. 1999. "Stakeholders, Social Responsibility and Performance: Empirical Evidence and Theoretical Perspectives," *The Academy of Management Journal*, 42, 5, 479-485.

Hayek, F. 1979. *Law, Legislation and Liberty*, Chicago: University of Chicago Press, Volume 3. p.157

Hayek, F. 1945. "The Use of Knowledge in Society," *American Economic Review*, XXXV, 4, 519-530.

Hayek, F. 1974. *The Pretense of Knowledge*. Acceptance Speech for The Sveriges Riksbank Prize in Economic Science in Memory of Alfred Nobel, December 11, 1974,

Herbert, B. 1994. "In America; Throwing a Curve," *The New York Times*, Opinion, October 26.

Herrnstein, Richard. 1971. "IQ," *Atlantic Monthly*, September, 228, pp. 43-64.

Herrnstein, Richard and Charles Murray. 1994. *The Bell Curve*, The Free Press, New York, NY.

Hersh, S. 2003. "Selective Intelligence," *The New Yorker*, May 12.

Hochschild, A. 2011. *To End All Wars: A Story of Loyalty and Rebellion 1914-1918*, Houghton-Mifflin-Harcourt, Boston and New York. xii, xiv, 83.

Hodgson, G. and H. Rothman, 1999. "Editors and Authors of Economics Journals: A Case of Institutional Oligopoly?" *The Economic Journal*, 109, February. 165-186.

Hogan, D.B. 1980. *The Regulation of Psychotherapists Volume I. A Study in the Philosophy and Practice of Professional Regulation*, Ballinger, USA

Hoover, K. 2012. "Foreign Inventors Dominate Patents Awarded to Top Research Universities," *The Business Journal*, June 26.

Hwang, Suein and Rachel Emma Silverman. 2002. "McKinsey's Close Relationship With Enron Raises Question of Consultancy's Liability," *The Wall Street Journal*, January 17, 2002;

Isaacson, W. 2007. *Einstein: His Life and Universe*, Simon and Shuster, New York, NY

Jampol, J. 1998. "New Visions for Executive Education," *Time,* March 30.

Janis, I. 1982. *Groupthink: Psychological Studies of Policy Decisions and Fiascoes*, Boston: Houghton Mifflin

Jaschik, S. 2011. "Clashes of Money and Values: A Survey of Admissions Directors," *Inside Higher Ed*, September 21.

Jensen, Arthur. 1969. How Much Can We Boost IQ and Scholastic Achievement," *Harvard Educational Review*, Winter, 39, 1.

Johnson, V. 2003. *Grade Inflation: A Crisis in Higher Education*, New York, Springer-Verlag.

Jolis, A. 2012. "The Climate Kamikaze," *The Wall Street Journal*, March 15, A13.

Karnow, S. 1983. *Vietnam: A History*, The Viking Press, New York,

Katz, R. 2012. "How Japan Blew its Lead in Electronics?" *The Wall Street Journal*, March 22, A10.

Kaufmann, C. 2004. "Threat Inflation and the Failure of the Marketplace of Ideas: The Selling of the Iraq War," *International Security*, The MIT Press, 29, 1, 2004, pp. 5-48

Kaufman, Alan 2009. *IQ Testing 101*. New York: Springer Publishing. pp. 151–153.

Kealey, T. 1996. *The Economic Laws of Scientific Research*, New York, NY. St. Martins Press.

Kennan, G. or X. 1947. "The Sources of Soviet Conduct," *Foreign Affairs*, July.

Keynes, J.M. 1920. *The Economic Consequences of the Peace*, Harcourt, Brace and Howe. New York.

Kimball, R. 1991. *Tenured Radicals: How Politics Has Corrupted Our Higher Education*, Harper and Row, New York, NY.

Kipling, R. 1895. *The Young British Soldier*, http://www.readbookonline.net/readOnLine/2711/

Kitzmiller vs. Dover Area School District 04 cv 2688 (December 20, 2005). p. 22, 77, 66.

Kleiner, Morris and Alan Krueger. 2008. *The Prevalence and Effects of Occupational Licensing*, National Bureau of Economic Research, Paper Number 14308, September.

Kling, Arnold. 2010. "What's Stalling the Next Economic Revolution," The American. The Journal of the American Enterprise Institute. September 9.

Knight, R. 2010. "Capturing the Hearts and Minds of MBAs," *Financial Times*, October 3.

Kocher, M and M. Sutter. 2001 "The Institutional Concentration of Authors in Top Journals of Economics During the Last Two Decades," *The Economic Journal*, June, 111. 405-421

Kremer, Michael. 1993. "The O-ring Theory of Development," *Quarterly Journal of Economics*, 208, 3. 551-575.

Kristol, W. and R. Kagan. 1996. "Toward a Neo-Reaganite Foreign Policy," *Foreign Affairs*, 75,4, 18-32.

Kristol, W. and R. Kagan.. 2000. *Present Dangers: Crisis and Opportunity in American Foreign and Defense Policy*, 12.

Kuran, Timor. 2011. *The Long Divergence*, Princeton University Press: Princeton, New Jersey.

Kwoh, L. 2012. "You Call That Innovation," *The Wall Street Journal*, May 23, B1.

Labaree, D. 1997. *How to Succeed in School Without Really Learning: The Credentials Race in American Education*, New Haven, Yale University Press.

Leaf, C. 2005. "The Law of Unintended Consequences," *Fortune*, September 9, 250.

Leake, Jonathon. 2010. "Scientists say Dolphins Should Be Treated as Non-human Persons," *The Sunday Times*, January 3.

Lederman, D. 2011. "Back to (Semi-) Normal," *Inside Higher Education,* January 27.

Lemann, Nicholas. 1999. *The Big Test: The Secret History of the American Meritocracy*, Farrar, Straus and Giroux, New York, NY.

Lemley, M. 2005. "Patenting Nanotechnology," *Stanford Law Review*, 58, November, 613ff.

Lewin, T. "Private College Presidents Getting Higher Salaries," Education, *New York Times*, December 4

Locke, J. 1690. *Essay Concerning Human Understanding*, London, .

Locke, J. 1690. Second Treatise of Government (10thedition). http://www.gutenberg.org/files/7370/7370-h/7370-h.htm.

Loehkin, John. 2005. Resemblance in Personality and Attitudes between Parents and Their Children: Genetic and Environmental Contributions," In *Unequal Chances: Family Background and Economic Success*, ed. Samuel Bowles, Herbert Gintis and Melissa

Osborne Groves, 192-207. New York, Russell Sage Foundation: Princeton and Oxford: Princeton University Press.

Logan J. and N. Courtney. 2012. (forthcoming) "Unusual Talent: a Study of Successful Leadership and Delegation in Entrepreneurs with Dyslexia," *Journal of inclusive practice in Further and Higher Education.*

MacKenzie, D.. F. Muniesa and L. Siu. 2007. *Do Economists Make Markets?* Princeton University Press, July 2.

MacPherson, Myra. 1984. *Long Time Passing: Vietnam and the Haunted Generation*, Doubleday, New York, NY.

Maddison, Angus. 2001. *The World Economy: A Millennial Perspective*, Paris OECD.

Mann, M. 2012. *The Hockey Stick and the Climate Wars*, Columbia University Press.

March, J. 1991. "Exploration and Exploitation in Organizational Learning," *Organization Science*, 2 , 71-87, 79,86

Margolin, J. and T. Sherman. 2006. "How UMDNJ Became a Patronage Pit," *Newark Star Ledger*, April 4, 1.

Market Openness Through Regulatory Reform. 2012. OECD. http://www.oecd.org/regreform/2756360.pdf

Martorell, Paco, and Isaac McFarlin, Jr. Forthcoming. "Help or Hindrance? The effects of College Remediation on Academic and Labor Market Outcomes," *The Review of Economics and Statistics.*

McCarty, N, K. Poole and H. Rosenthal. 2009. "Does Gerrymandering Cause Polarization," *American Journal of Political Science*, 53, 3, 666-680.

McCrum, D. 2012. "Private Equity Profits Called into Question, *Financial Times*, January 23.

McGrath, A. 1998. *Historical Theology, An Introduction to the History of Christian Thought.* Oxford: Blackwell Publishers. p.214-5

McKeown, Thomas. 1979. *The Role of Medicine: Dream, Mirage or Nemesis?* Oxford: Basil Blackwell. UK.

McKinlay, John and Sonja. 1977. The Questionable Contribution of Medical Measures to the Declining Mortality in the United States in the Twentieth Century. *Milbank Memorial Fund Quarterly, Health and Society*, 55, 3, p.414.

Meers, J. and H. Rosen. 2007. "Altruism and the Child-Cycle of Alumni Giving," *National Bureau of Economic Research*, W13152.

Mensa Constitution. 2007. *Mensa International.* November 29.

Merry, R. 2012. *Where They Stand: The American Presidents in the Eyes of Voters and Historians*, Simon & Shuster.

Michaels, E., H. Handfield-Jones and B. Axelrod, 2001. *The War for Talent*, Harvard Business School Press, Boston.

Mintzberg, H. 2004. *Managers, Not MBAs*, Berrett-Koehler Publishers, Inc.

Mill, J.S. 1848. *Principles of Political Economy*, London: John W. Parker.

Moores, John. 2004. "College Capers," *Forbes*, March 29.

Morson, B. 2007. "CU Regents Fire Ward Churchill,. *Rocky Mountain News*, July 25.

Moses, Jennifer. 2011. "The Escalating Arms Race for Top Colleges," *The Wall Street Journal*, February 5, C3.

Mowery, D. and N. Rosenberg. 1989. *Technology and the Pursuit of Economic Growth*, Cambridge, MA.

Murray, Charles. 1984. "*Losing Ground: American Social Policy 1950-1980.*" New York: Basic Books.

Naik, G. 2012. "Grade Inflation Creeps Into Science Journals," *The Wall Street Journal*, August 25, A2

Nasar, S. 1998. *A Beautiful Mind: The Life of Mathematical Genius and Nobel Laureate John Nash*, Simon and Shuster. New York,NY.

National Association of Scholars. 1996. *The Dissolution of General Education: 1914-1993: A Report from the National Association of Scholars*. Princeton, NJ.

Neal, Larry. 1990. *The Rise of Financial Capitalism: International Capital Markets in the Age of Reason*, Cambridge: New York and Melbourne: Cambridge University Press.

Nemko, M 2008. "America's Most Overrated Product: The Bachelor's Degree," *Chronicle of Higher Education*, 54:34, B17-18

Neuman, W., L. McKnight and R. Solomon. 1997. *The Gordian Knot: Political Gridlock on the Information Highway*, MIT Press.

Nixon, S. 2012. "The Theory on Italy and Germany's Endgame for the Euro," *The Wall Street Journal*, July 13, C10.

North, D. 1990. *Institutions, Institutional Change and Economic Performance*, Cambridge: Cambridge University Press.

Offit, P. 2011. "Junk Science Isn't a Victimless Crime," *The Wall Street Journal*,

Organization for Economic Cooperation and Development (OECD). 1999. Regulatory Reform in the United States, Enhancing.

Ostrow, R. and L. Gordon. 1991. "8 Ivy League Schools Sign Collusion Ban," *Los Angeles Times*, May 23.

Page, S. and L. Hung. 2001. "Problem Solving by Heterogeneous Agents," *Journal of Economic Theory*, 97, 123-163.

Page, S. 2003. "Prewar Predictions Coming Back to Bite," *USA Today*, April 1. http://www.usatoday.com/educate/war28-article.htm

Parikh, C. 2010. "Who Wants to be a Millionaire?" Capital Ideas On-line. http://www.go2cio.com/articles/index.php?id=3603

Pfeiffer, J. and Fong. 2002. "The End of Business Schools? Less Success Than Meets the Eye," *Academy of Management Learning and Education*. 1,1. 78-89.

Pfiffner, J. 2004. "Did President Bush Mislead the Country in His Arguments for War with Iraq?" *Presidential Studies Quarterly*, 34, 1. 25-32.

Pierson, F. 1959. *The Education of American Businessmen: A Study of University-College Programs in Business Administration*. New York: McGraw-Hill.

Phelan, James. 1964. "Have You Ever Been a Boo Hoo," *The Saturday Evening Post*, March 21.

Pinto, E. 2008. "Sizing Total Federal Government and Federal Agency Contributions to Subprime and Alt-A Loans in the U.S. First Mortgage Market as of 6:30:08." and Before the Committee on Oversight and Government Reform United States House of Representatives December 9.

Plato, 1961. *The Republic*, Translated by Paul Shorey in *Collected Dialogues*, ed. Edith Hamilton and Huntington Cairns, (Princeton University Press). 459c.

Pomeranz, Kenneth. 2000. *The Great Divergence: China, Europe and the Making of the Modern World Economy*, Princeton New Jersey, Princeton University Press.

Poskanzer, S. 2002. *Higher Education Law*, Johns Hopkins University, Baltimore, p.43.

Posner, Gerald. 1993. *Case Closed: Lee Harvey Oswald and the Assassination of JFK*, Random House, New York.

Powers Commission. 2002. *Report of Investigation by the Special Investigative Committee of the Board of Directors of Enron Corporation*, February 1.

Project for a New American Century. 2000. "Rebuilding America's Defenses," September. p.14.

Proterba, J. and T. Sinai. 2008. Tax Expenditures for Owner Occupied Housing: The Deduction for Property Taxes and Mortgage Interest and the Exclusion of Imputed Rental Income. Unpublished Manuscript.

Rauch, J. and J. Sackett. 1992. *The Outnation: A Search for the Soul of Japan*, Harvard Business School Press.

Rauch, J. 1993. *Kindly Inquisitors: The New Attacks on Free Thought*, University of Chicago Press: A Cato Institute Book, Chicago, Illinois. p. 126-127 .

Rhoades, G. 2007. "The Study of American Professions," in *Sociology of Higher Education: Contributions and Their Contexts*, edited by Patricia Gumport, 113-146. Baltimore: Johns Hopkins University

Ridley, M. 2010. *The Rational Optimist: How Prosperity Evolved*, Harper Perennial. New Yok, NY.

Ridley, M. 2010. "Humans: Why They Triumphed," *The Wall Street Journal*, May 22, W1.

Roll, R. 1984. "Orange Juice and Weather," *American Economic Review*, 74, 5, 861-880.

Rollyson, C. 2012. Exorcising the Demon-King: Was the Third Reich Inevitable or the Monstrous Product of a Single Man's Mind?" *The Wall Street Journal*, April -8.

Roth, K. 1994. "Second Thoughts About Interdisciplinary Studies," *American Educator*, Spring 1994.

Rousseau, J.J. 1968. *The Social Contract*, New York Penguin Books, p. 115

Rubin, P. 1994. "The Assault on the First Amendment: Public Choice and Political Correctness", *Cato Journal*, 14(1), 23-35.

Rubin, P. 2010. "Environmentalism as Religion," *The Wall Street Journal*, April 22.

Sachs, Jeffrey. 2005. *The End of Poverty: Economic Possibilities for Our Time*, Penguin Books.

Schmitt, B. 1930. *The Coming of War 1914*, University of Chicago Library.

Schneider, M. 2006. "Endowments Can Become Too Much of a Good Thing," *Chronicle of Higher Education*, June 2, B 18.

Scott, K. and J. Taylor. 2009. "Why Toxic Assets are So Hard to Clean Up," *The Wall Street Journal*, July 20.

Scott, E. 2007. Biological Design in Science Classrooms," Proceeding of the National Academy of Sciences, May 15.

Segal, N. 2012. *Born Together — Reared Apart*," Harvard University Press.

Sen, A. 2010. *Development as Freedom*, Knopf Publishers.

Shapiro, James. 2010. *Contested Will: Who Wrote Shakespeare?* Simon and Shuster, New York.

Sherwell, B. 2011. "War of words over global warming as Nobel laureate resigns in protest," *Daily Telegraph*, September 25.

Shirir, William. 1960. *The Rise and Fall of the Third Reich*, Simon and Shuster, New York, NY. p.100.

Schumpeter, J. 1954. *History of Economic Analysis* (New York: Oxford University Press), p.43.

Smith, A.1976. *The Theory of Moral Sentiments*, Indianapolis Liberty Classic

Smith, A. 1937. *An Inquiry into the Nature and Causes of the Wealth of Nations*, New York Modern Library.

Smith, A. 1766. "Lecture on the Influence of Commerce on Manners," Reprinted in D. B. Klein ed. *Reputation: Studies in the Voluntary Elicitation of Good Conduct*, University of Michigan 1997.

Sowell, T. 1987. *A Conflict of Visions*, William Morrow and Company Inc. New York, NY.

Sowell, T. 1993. *Inside American Education: The Decline, The Deception, The Dogmas*, The Free Press, A Division of Macmillan, Inc. New York. p. 24

State Higher Education Finance. 2012. A Project of the Staff of State Higher Education Officers.

Stevens, H. 2012. "Cancer Research of Ten Years Useless: Fraudulent Studies," *Gaia Health*, August 14.

Stewart, J. 2011. "Volcker Rule, Once Simple, Now Boggles," *New York Times*, October 21.

Stigler, G. 1971. "The Theory of Economic Regulation," *The Bell Journal of Law, Economics and Management Science*, 2, 1, 243-263.

Stiglitz, J. 2012. *The Price of Inequality: How Today's Divided Society Endangers our Future*, Norton.

Strom, S. 2007. "How Long Should Gifts Just Grow?" *New York Times*, November 12.

Stromber, P., E. Hotchkiss and D. Smith. 2011. "Private Equity and the Resolution of Financial Distress," *Social Science Research Network*, April.

Summers, Lawrence 1998. Lawrence H. Summers Testimony, July 30, http://www.treasury.gov/press/releases/rr2616.htm

Sykes, C. 1995. *Dumbing Down Our Kids: Why American Children Feel Good About Themselves But Can't Read, Write Or Add.* St. Martin's Press: New York, NY

Tamar, L. 2008. "College Presidents Defend Rising Tuition, But Lawmakers Sound Skeptical," New York Times Online, September, 9. http://www.nytimes.com/2008/09/09education/09college.html

Teachout, Terry. 2010. "Too Complicated for Words: Are Our Brains Big Enough to Untangle Modern Art?" *The Wall Street Journal*, W14, June 26.

Teachout, Terry. 2010. Denying Shakespeare, *The Wall Street Journal*,

The Economist. 2012. "In Praise of Misfits," June 2.

The Economist, 2005. "Free Degrees to Fly: Already a Big Business, is Higher Education Poised for a Take-off?" February 26, 67-70.

The Economist, 2007. "The Business of Making Money: Private Equity's Strengths and it Increasingly Apparent Weaknesses," Briefing Public Versus Private Equity, July 7-13, 68-70.

The Economist. 2012. "Of Sunstein and Sunsets," February 18-24th. p.30

The Economist. 2012. "Too Big not to Fail," February 18-24th. p.22

The Economist, Measuring The Impact of Regulation: The Rule of More, February 18.

Thurow, L. 1992. *Head to Head: The Coming Economic Battle Among Japan, Europe, and America.* New York: Morrow.

Thursby, J. and M. Thursby. 2002. "Who is Selling the Ivory Tower? Sources of Growth in University Licensing," *Management Science,* 48,1. 90-104.

Tonsor, S. 2005. "Why I Too am Not a Neo-conservative," *Equality, Decadence and Modernity: The Collected Essays of Stephen Tonsor,* ISI Books, Wilmington, Delaware, p.308

Trotsky, L. 1925. *Literature and Revolution,* Published originally by the United Soviet Socialist Republic.

Tuchman, B. 1962. *The Guns of August,* The Macmillan Company, New York. p.22.

Turkheimer, E., A. Haley, M. Waldron, B. D'Onofrio and I. Gottesman. 2003. *Socioeconomic Status Modifies Heritability of IQ in Young Children,* Research Article, http://www.psychologytoday.com/files/u81/Turkheimer_et_al_ _ _2003_.pdf

Twain, Mark. 1883. *Life on the Mississippi.* James R. Osgood and Company, Boston-MA

Tyson, L. 1992. *Who's Bashing Whom?: Trade Conflict in High Technology Industries.* Institute for International Economics: Washington DC

U.S. Department of Education. 2010. *Productivity: Improving Learning Outcomes While Managing Costs,* http://www.ed.gov/technology/draft-netp-2010/productivity

Van Noorden, R. 2012. "Record Number of Journals Banned for Boosting Impact Factor with Self-Citations," *Nature,* June 29, http://blogs.nature.com/news/2012/06/record-number-of-journals-banned-for-boosting-impact-factor-with-self-citations.html

Van Noorden, R. 2012. "Researchers Feel Pressure to Cite Superfluous Papers," *Nature,* Feb.http://www.nature.com/news/researchers-feel-pressure-to-cite-superfluous-papers-1.9968

Vardi, N. 2012. "America's Richest Counties," *Forbes,* April 24.

Vaznis, J. 2008. "Hub Grads Come Up Short in College: Most From Class of 2000 Have Failed to Earn Degrees," *Boston Globe,* November 17.

Waldeck, S. 2009. "The Coming Showdown Over University Endowments: Enlisting the Donors," *Fordham Law Review*, 77,4.

Walker, M. 2012. "Book Attacking Euro Riles German Politicians," *The Wall Street Journal*, May 22. A4.

Wallison, P. 2010. "Government Housing Policy and the Financial Crisis," *Cato Journal*, 30,2, 397–406.

Weber, W. and M. Devaney. 2002. "The Global Economy and Japanese Bank Performance," *Managerial Finance*, 24,12. 33–46.

Wessel, David and Chip Cummins. 2011. "Arab World Built Colleges, but Not Jobs," *The Wall Street Journal*, February 5, A11.

Wilhite, A. and E. Fong. 2012. "Coercive Citation in Academic Publishing," *Science*, 333, 6068, 542-543.

Will, G. 2012. "Elizabneth Warren's Identity Politics," The Washington Post, May 23.

Williams, M. 2011. "Jenny McCarthy's Autism Fight Grows More Misguided," *Salon*, January 6.

Wilson, R. 2009. "Notoriety Yields to Tragedy in Iowa Sexual-Harassment Cases: After 2 Suicides, Colleagues Question University's Role," *Chronicle of Higher Education*, February 20, A1.

Wilson, A. N. 2012. *Hitler*, Basic Books, New York, NY.

Wilson, C. 2011. "The Most Gerrymandered Congressional Districts," *Slate*, December 13.http://www.slate.com/slideshows/news_and_politics/the-most-gerrymandered-congressional-districts.html#slide_14

Windschuttle, K. 1996. *The Killing of History: How a Discipline is Being Murdered by Literary Critics and Social Theorists*, Quality Books Inc. Sydney, Australia.

Witt, J. 2005. *"Evolution News and Views: Dover Judge Regurgitates Mythological History of Intelligent Design"*

Woolley, Anita, Christopher Chabris, Alex Pentland, Nada Hashmi, Thomas Malone. 2010. "Evidence for a Collective Intelligence Factor in the Performance of Human Groups," *Science*, 330, 6004.

World War I Executions-History Learning Site. http://www.historylearn-ingsite.co.uk/world_war_one_executions.htm

Wrigley, EA. 2010. *Energy and the English Industrial Revolution,* Cambridge University Press.

WSFA 12. 2008. "Former Two Year Chancellor Roy Johnson Says He's Guilty," March 11, http://www.wsfa.com/Global/story.asp?S=7771338&nav=menu33_2_1

Zak, P. and S. Knack. 2001. "Trust and Growth," *The Economic Journal,* 111, April, 295-321.

Zuckert, C. and M. Zuckert. 2006. *The Truth About Leo Strauss.* University of Chicago Press, Chicago and London.

Zweig, Jason and Mary Pilon. 2010. "*Is Your Advisor Pumping up His Credentials?*" *The Wall Street Journal,* October 16.

www.ingramcontent.com/pod-product-compliance
Lightning Source LLC
Chambersburg PA
CBHW060747100426
42813CB00032B/3425/J